The M
REVOLUTION
in SIXTEENTH-
CENTURY
EUROPE

The MILITARY REVOLUTION in SIXTEENTH-CENTURY EUROPE

DAVID ELTIS

I.B. Tauris Publishers
LONDON • NEW YORK

First published in paperback in 1998 by
I.B.Tauris & Co. Ltd
Victoria House, Bloomsbury Square
WC1B 4DZ

175 Fifth Avenue
New York, NY 10010

In the United States of America
and in Canada distributed by
St Martin's Press
175 Fifth Avenue
New York, NY 10010

A full CIP record for this book is available from the British Library

A full CIP record for this book is available from the Library of Congress

ISBN 1 86064 352 3

Library of Congress catalog card number available

Set in Monotype Bembo by Ewan Smith, London

Printed and bound in the United States of America

CONTENTS

ACKNOWLEDGEMENTS

I would like to thank Dr Gerald Harriss, Dr Maurice Keen, Dr C.S.L. Davies and especially Dr Penry Williams for their criticism and guidance in the many stages of my research into late medieval and early modern military history, and Dr Lester Crook of I.B.Tauris for his generous assistance in making this book possible in the form in which it lies before you today.

CHAPTER I
INTRODUCTION

This book introduces the military revolution of the sixteenth century, draws the distinction between it and earlier attempts to define a military revolution in the early modern period, and shows how the revolution affected England and other countries in practice. In doing so it introduces the reader to an invaluable source for the study of these developments: military theory. Sixteenth-century theory and practice were more interdependent than might at first be realised. It is only through the theory that we gain a really clear insight into the rationale behind the changes in the art of war during the century. Equally, previous attempts to understand the military writings of the period have suffered from a failure to relate them to overall military developments.

This was particularly true of English military theorists, for, as we shall see, many of the most important writings owe their existence to the need to propagate military change and bring continental military developments to the attention of a native English audience. England's military change during the century was but one dimension of a wider European modernisation, which English military theorists belatedly sought to communicate.

My interest in English military theory in the sixteenth century began when by chance I came across Maurice Cockle's *A Bibliography of English Military Books up to 1642 and of Contemporary Foreign Works* (London, 1900). At that time I was embarked on a study of medieval military theory. The wealth of sixteenth-century material in Cockle's work astounded me, used as I was to the paucity of late medieval literature on war. In England, translations and reworkings of Vegetius's *De Re Militari*, 1,000 years old by the later Middle Ages, were the chief resource of the student of late medieval strategic and tactical thought. Soon, the few dozen works identified by Cockle were multiplied by further research, and in particular the discovery of Henry J. Webb's splendid *Elizabethan Military Science: The Books and the Practice* (London, 1965). My attention shifted, at first partially and then completely, to the richer fields of the sixteenth century and brought me in the process to consider wider issues of military change.

Writing in 1937, Sir Charles Oman considered the sixteenth century the least interesting period in English military history.[1] The reason for Oman's opinion is clear enough. The Tudor years were largely years of peace.[2] There was no episode to grip the historical imagination in the same way as the Hundred Years' War and the English Civil Wars in the surrounding centuries. Barely four years later, G.A. Hayes-McCoy argued that the sixteenth century was the time when the outmoded laws of chivalry were at last discarded, the art of fortification was developed and modern military theory and modern military organisation were born.[3]

Whether the sixteenth century saw the death of chivalry as Hayes-McCoy argued is debatable.[4] For the Earl of Essex and many others in the late sixteenth century the honourable single combat was still very much alive.[5] Tournaments were as much a sixteenth-century preoccupation as a medieval one.[6] The splendid pageantry of Leicester in the Netherlands in the 1580s and of Philip II in England in the 1550s merely continued a tradition stretching back beyond Henry VIII's splendid affairs in the earlier decades of the century.[7] That there were other far-reaching changes in equipment, organisation, military theory and siege warfare during the sixteenth century can be more easily proven. It is the central argument of this book that the sixteenth century was a period of massive change in all aspects of war; these are carefully detailed in Chapters 3–4.

The idea that the early modern period saw a military revolution, affecting a variety of aspects of the conduct of war, is not new. We have already seen G.A. Hayes-McCoy's instinct in 1940–1 that major change was afoot during the century. In Italy, Piero Pieri showed clear signs of awareness of a major break in European military history in the sixteenth century in his *Il Rinascimento e la crisi militare italiana* (Turin, 1952). In 1958, J.R. Hale found the period 1519–59 a decisive break point.[8] Other historians have sensed a difference between the late fifteenth and early sixteenth century and the medieval warfare of preceding centuries.[9] However, it was on none of these writers that subsequent debate settled, but on a brief work by a specialist in Swedish history, Professor Michael Roberts. His Belfast Inaugural Lecture of 1956, *The Military Revolution* (1956), entranced and bewildered an entire generation. After first attacking part of it,[10] Professor Geoffrey Parker has since given Professor

Roberts's thesis the supreme compliment of adapting it for presentation, in modified form, in his own more complicated thesis, *The military revolution. Military innovation and the rise of the West 1500–1800* (Cambridge, 1988). Other writers have continued to keep their distance, showing parts of Roberts's analysis to be untenable.[11]

Previous work on military theory has not stressed its relevance to military change, but has rather concentrated on almost every other aspect. This has been particularly true of the treatment of sixteenth-century English military writers by historians. But for the bow and musket controversy, which has received considerable scholarly attention,[12] mainstream aspects of military development and their reflection in the military theory published in England have not been systematically examined. Henry J. Webb, to whom we owe our fullest account of military literature in the century so far, has concentrated on medical, scientific, philosophical and classical questions at the expense of a closer examination of military change.[13] C.G. Cruickshank, who briefly surveyed English military theory in the sixteenth century in 1966[14] and 1969[15] did look at it from a more strictly military point of view, but found it wanting, as did Cyril Falls in 1950[16] and Thomas M. Spaulding two years earlier.[17] All of these writers, with the exception of Webb, concentrated on a relatively narrow selection of authors, and this in part contributed to their failure to perceive important developments within the literature. None of them consulted the contemporary foreign literature as a point of departure or used Max Jähns's splendidly detailed survey of European military theory published in three volumes in the late nineteenth century.[18] Thus previous writers on war in the sixteenth century have tended to neglect military theory as a source, while those historians who have written on England's military theorists have failed to grasp its true potential. This book does not examine English military theory as such, but uses it as a tool to explain sixteenth-century developments. The reader curious to know more about the writers of England's military revolution can turn to any of the above works or take up the present author's 1991 Oxford D.Phil. thesis, 'English Military Theory and the Military Revolution of the Sixteenth Century', which examines them in detail.

Before launching straight into the debate on the military revolution, it would perhaps be wise to make a few general observations. Though this study is based in particular on a careful use of sixteenth-century military writers, it is neither purely a book on military theory nor just a book on military change, but a study of both, where each illuminates the other. It has a special focus on England's development, but, as will be seen, England was backward in adopting the military advances of others in the sixteenth century. A word should also be said on the matter of dates. Why begin in about 1500 or end around 1600? The ending point is simpler to explain. Between 1585 and 1604 England was engaged in continuous struggle with Spain. Hostilities came to a complete end in 1604, when James I made peace. For the next twenty years England engaged in no military activity at all, until Mansfeld's expedition of 1624 and Buckingham's failed attempts on France and Spain in the mid-1620s. England was not engaged in continuous military activity again until the Civil Wars. For England, 1604 marks an effective stopping point, by which time the country had absorbed much of what the military revolution had to offer. For Europe, 1600 is a more arbitrary stopping point, particularly as several powers had proceeded far faster than England in adopting superior military practices.

Many of those acquainted with the military revolution debate may now wonder how it is possible to cease an examination of major change in the art of war before Gustavus Adolphus and the Thirty Years' War. To answer that and to see the rationale for starting this analysis of military change in around 1500, the reader is recommended to read Chapters 2–4, which elucidate both these and a host of other matters vital to an understanding of the military revolution of the sixteenth century.

Notes

1. C.W.C. Oman, *A History of the Art of War in the Sixteenth Century* (London, 1937), p. 368.

2. C.G. Cruickshank, *Army Royal. Henry VIII's invasion of France, 1513* (Oxford, 1969), p. 190. See also Chapter 4 below.

3. G.A. Hayes-McCoy, 'Strategy and tactics in Irish warfare 1593–1601', *Irish Historical Studies*, II (1940–1), pp. 257–9.

4. Maurice Keen, *Chivalry* (New Haven and London, 1984), p. 238. For a more detailed analysis see A.B. Ferguson, *The Indian Summer of English Chivalry* (Durham, North Carolina, 1960).

5. Anthony Esler, *The aspiring mind of the Elizabethan younger generation* (Durham, North Carolina, 1966), pp. 96–7. *True Newes from one of Sir Fraunces Veres Companie Concerning Delftes Isle* ..., STC 24652 (London, 1591), sigs. A3–A3v.

6. For an overview: Alan Young, *Tudor and Jacobean Tournaments* (London, 1987). For another perspective: Jan Dop, *Eliza's Knights: Soldiers, Poets and Puritans in the Netherlands 1572–1586* (Amsterdam, 1981).

7. Anthony Esler, *The aspiring mind of the Elizabethan younger generation* (Durham, North Carolina, 1966), p. 90. R.C. Strong and J.A. van Dorsten, *Leiciester's Triumph* (London, 1964). R.C. McCoy, 'From the Tower to the tiltyard: Robert Dudley's return to glory', *Historical Journal*, XXVII (1984), pp. 429–35. J.J. Scarisbrick, *Henry VIII* (London, 1968), pp. 14, 18 and 77–9.

8. J.R. Hale, 'Armies, navies and the art of war' in G.R. Elton (ed.), *New Cambridge Modern History*, II (Cambridge, 1958), p. 481.

9. Otto Hintze, Geoffrey Parker and W.F. Cook come to mind. W.F. Cook provides a good general introduction to Hintze and Parker in his *The Hundred Years' War for Morocco. Gunpowder and the Military Revolution in the Early Modern World* (Oxford, 1994), pp. 10–11.

10. Geoffrey Parker, 'The "Military Revolution" 1560–1660 – a myth?', *Journal of Modern History*, XXVI (1976), reprinted in Parker, *Spain and the Netherlands 1559–1659* (London, 1979), pp. 86–103.

11. D.A. Parrott, 'Strategy and Tactics in the Thirty Years' War: "The Military Revolution"', *Militärgeschichtliche Mitteilungen*, XVIII (1985). John A. Lynn, 'Tactical Evolution in the French Army', *French Historical Studies*, XIV (1985).

12. See the introductions to two modern editions of works by sixteenth-century military authors: J.X. Evans (ed.), *The Works of Sir Roger Williams* (Oxford, 1972) and J.R. Hale (ed.), Sir John Smythe, *Certain Discourses Military* (Ithaca: New York, 1964).

13. Henry J. Webb's principal contribution is *Elizabethan Military Science. The Books and the Practice* (London, 1965). He has also written numerous articles for which see the bibliography.

14. C.G. Cruickshank, *Elizabeth's Army* (2nd edn, Oxford, 1966), pp. 189–99.

15. Cruickshank, *Army Royal*, pp. 105–12.

16. C. Falls, *Elizabeth's Irish Wars* (London, 1950), pp. 42–5.

17. Thomas M. Spaulding, 'Elizabethan Military Books' in J.G. MacManaway (ed.), *Joseph Quincy Adams Memorial Studies* (Washington, 1948), pp. 495–507.

18. The volume which chiefly concerns us is Max Jähns, *Geschichte der Kriegs-wissenschaften vornehmlich in Deutschland. Erste Abteilung. Altertum, Mittelalter, XV. und XVI. Jahrhundert* (Munich and Leipzig, 1889).

CHAPTER 2

THE MILITARY REVOLUTION
AND THE HISTORIANS

In 1956, Michael Roberts used his inaugural lecture at Queen's University Belfast to expound an early modern 'military revolution'.[1] Two years later he restated his argument in the second volume of his biography of Gustavus Adolphus with a few minor alterations.[2] The 'military revolution of the sixteenth century' which forms the centrepiece of the present study exists quite independently of Professor Roberts's 'military revolution', to which it bears no relation. This can not be said of Professor Geoffrey Parker's military revolution thesis of 1988,[3] which is a reformulation of Professor Roberts's argument with major corrections of emphasis and much new material. His fundamental sympathy towards Professor Roberts's original thesis was already apparent in an article of 1976, 'The "Military Revolution" 1560–1660 – a myth?'[4] which, though critical of many aspects of Roberts's thesis, ended by wishing it many more years of success.

Other writers have been more wholehearted in their criticism.[5] However, none of them has made any attempt to replace it, contenting themselves with the refutation of small sections of Roberts's complex argument or adopting some of his ideas while rejecting others. This chapter will go further and propose an alternative vision to the thesis of Professor Roberts and indeed that of Professor Parker, who has reworked the former after his own fashion in his more recent work on the same subject. It is natural to start this inquiry with Michael Roberts's complicated thesis, which has dominated all subsequent debate on military change in early modern Europe.[6] After summarising Professor Roberts's argument and the main criticisms it has received at the hands of earlier critics, a brief résumé of the differences between it and Geoffrey Parker's subsequent 'military revolution' thesis will prepare the reader for the detailed criticism of first Professor Roberts's thesis and then Professor Parker's that will

follow. Only then will we be free to venture to establish an alternative vision of military development, already hinted at in the work
of many earlier scholars, and especially G.A. Hayes-McCoy, Piero
Pieri, Sir John Hale[7] and Wilhelm Erben, which gives the sixteenth
century the attention it deserves as a period of unprecedented
military change.

Before engaging the theories of Roberts and Parker more closely,
it would be well to note the sudden explosion of works on the
'military revolution', which has occurred in the last few years after
decades of neglect. In 1991 Jeremy Black launched his *A Military
Revolution? Military change and European Society 1550–1800*, which
stakes a claim for the period 1660–1760 as the real period of
revolutionary change, at the same time as sniping at some aspects of
Parker's theory of military change.[8] Brian Downing has developed
an approach – in some respects similar to my own and in others to
Parker and Roberts – in a book which is really more devoted to
political than military developments.[9] Finally, W.F. Cook has
developed some separate ideas on the 'military revolution' of the
sixteenth century in his study of military activity in Morocco.[10] All
three of these books have added to the excitement of the field for
the scholar. However, as they have tended to adopt positions close
to those of Parker and Roberts it is simpler first to deal thoroughly
with the latter two historians and then, by way of afterword, handle
any specific problems raised by these more recent works, which
sometimes adopt positions similar to those advanced in my 1991
thesis[11] and this book.

Professor Roberts's argument may be summarised as follows. Bows
could generate more firepower than the firearms that succeeded
them in the inventories of Europe's armies: 'on the battlefield
firearms long represented a big step backward'. In fact, 'by a curious
paradox, the coming of the hand-gun brought a steep decline in
firepower: the superiority of the longbow in speed, accuracy and
mobility was so marked that even in the late seventeenth-century
military writers were pleading for its reintroduction'.[12] The firearms
employed by infantry and cavalry alike by the mid-sixteenth century
marked no advance, but were rather a retrogade step, which involved
a decline in military training. Roberts is crystal clear on this point.
'The soldier of the middle ages ... had been highly trained over a
prolonged period.' Training subsequently declined:

> The mercenary in the middle of a pike-square needed little training and less skill ... So too with the musketeer ... The training of a bowman ... would be wasted on so imperfect an instrument as an arquebus or a wheel-lock pistol ... One reason why firearms drove out the bow and lance was precisely this, that they economised on training.[13]

The adoption of firearms by the cavalry rendered it worthless as an offensive force.[14] In fact, the widespread use of firearms by both infantry and cavalry signalled the end of the decisive battle. There simply was not enough offensive power left to achieve it. 'Contemporary theorists, rationalising their own impotence, extolled the superior science of the war of manoeuvre and condemned battle as the last resort of the inept or unfortunate commander.' However, this does at best imperfect justice to Lazarus von Schwendi, one of the two contemporary theorists Roberts cited, who positively criticised a commander who was insufficiently daring to hazard a battle when the circumstances required it.[15]

As a result of this apparently sorry state of affairs Roberts concluded that: 'Strategic thinking withered away; war eternalised itself.'[16] Then suddenly,

> Upon this ancien régime there now fell a major revolution. The first of the revolutionaries was Eric IV of Sweden in the 'sixties [1560s]; but his experiment passed unnoticed, and it was not until after 1590 that the revolution can really be said to have got under way.[17]

In what did this, Professor Roberts's 'revolution', consist? In two stages, between 1590 and 1609 and from 1617 to 1632, Maurice of Orange and Gustavus Adolphus supposedly revolutionised the conduct of war by reintroducing the decisive pitched battle. The relative importance of Maurice, his relations and Gustavus is redefined in Roberts's subsequent biography of the latter. However, in both accounts Roberts sees his 'revolution' as incomplete until the successful implementation of Gustavus's reforms.[18] They achieved this by dint of tactical reforms involving the use of differently constituted formations[19] and the end of the long neglect of training. Maurice and his cousins 'attempted to return to Roman models in regard to ... discipline and drill'.[20] Under Maurice 'drill for the first time in modern history became the pre-condition for military success'.[21] Even more surprising is Roberts's statement that for Londoño [in Roberts's conception a theorist of the pre-revolutionary *ancien régime*] 'drill and exercises were designed primarily to promote physical fitness ... for Maurice they were the fundamental postulates of tactics'.[22] In fact Londoño well realised the need for training.[23]

After Maurice's initial achievement Gustavus went further, creating 'a discipline and drill which were superior even to the Dutch'.[24] His more aggressive cavalry tactics were based on the sword rather than the *caracole*[25] and the introduction of mobile field artillery,[26] which together with the use of infantry volley fire[27] found a way out of the blind alley of sixteenth-century military development, restoring the offensive in war and at last making the decisive battle a reality.

Two years later Professor Roberts became aware that the cavalry of the pre-revolutionary *ancien régime* was not so feeble after all, but he clung to his initial conception.[28] His collected essays, published in 1967, continued to maintain that in the sixteenth century 'cavalry became a debilitated arm, fit only to snap its pistols at other horses as debilitated as themselves'.[29] Only with Gustavus did cavalry escape this debility and again help to allow decisive battles to be won, or so Roberts continued to argue.

With the decisive battle and the first use of scorched-earth policies and supply magazines[30] came a new envigorated conception of strategy.[31] Now war was fought over vast spaces by multiple, co-ordinated armies, using maps – a previously unheard of novelty.[32]

Gustavus's strategic 'revolution' spawned many developments. 'The most important of them was a marked increase in the scope of warfare, reflected in a corresponding increase in the normal size of the armies of the major powers.'[33] Hand in hand with the new larger armies went standardisation of weapons,[34] the introduction of uniforms,[35] the creation of standing armies[36] with a fixed hierarchy of ranks,[37] military academies[38] and more burdensome financial levies to pay for it all. In fact, behind

> all the great insurrectionary movements of the age – the Thirty Years' War, the English rebellion, the Fronde, the revolts in the Spanish realms – there lay as one major element in the situation (though of course not the only one) the crown's need for money; and that need was usually produced by military commitments whose dimensions were in part the result of the military revolution.[39]

As can readily be seen, Professor Roberts's thesis is so wide ranging as positively to discourage criticism. Specialists who have noticed the occasional flaw on his massive canvas have been awed by its scale and impressed by its sweeping conclusions. The criticisms that they have made have focused on a few points. First, Professor Geoffrey Parker and Dr David Parrott argued that the new small and shallow tactical units of Professor Roberts's revolution were quite capable of being beaten by the supposedly inferior, large, square formations of the 'old' kind, as at Nördlingen (1634).[40] Second, it has been shown that Roberts is wrong in thinking that the tactical use of field artillery was a novelty. As John A. Lynn has pointed out, the French army had made heavy use of it in the sixteenth century.[41] And finally, it has been argued that his criticisms did less than justice to the sixteenth-century Spanish army of Flanders, which as Professor Parker has shown, was capable of very great tactical flexibility.[42] However, these blows have not sufficed to dismiss the 'military revolution' thesis. Professor Parker, far from regarding the 'military revolution' as dead and buried, wished it many years of further life at the end of his often critical article of 1976 and proceeded to embody parts of it in his later book.

Parker's thesis of 1988 sought to explain the European military edge over extra-European peoples with reference to a 'military revolution' that had taken place in Europe in the three centuries from 1500 to 1800, but most particularly in the 180 years from 1530.[43] Unlike Roberts, he laid particular stress on the importance of developments in north European siege warfare after 1530.[44] But in so doing he rested his argument on the spread of the purpose-built, angle-bastioned fortification,[45] the *trace italienne*, which readers of his earlier work will recognise as a key part of his explanation of the military survival of the northern rebel provinces in the Netherlands. Also new was Parker's idea that this period saw the triumph of firepower[46] over 'shock' – the demise of the *arme blanche* and close-quarter combat. He also contributed a host of insights into the nature of war in early modern Europe which, though rarely closely connected with his underlying argument, have immeasurably enriched our understanding of the period. Nor is it my wish to dispute them. However, mixed in with Professor Parker's fresh emphases and new insights, are a number of assumptions shared with Professor Roberts. The increase in army sizes, the growing cost of war, with concomitant social strain and the growth of miltary literature and the demise of heavy cavalry, singled out by Professor Roberts as key factors in his theory of 1956, are all still there in Professor Parker's argument of 1988.[47] So too is the idea that the chief advantage of firearms was that they economised on training.[48] It is a difficult task indeed to separate out old and new in a work that so skilfully blends them together. A masterpiece of scholarship, Geoffrey Parker's thesis has, unlike Michael Roberts's, so far escaped significant challenge. The time has now come to question both. Of the two, Michael Roberts's has proved by far the most influential, and it makes sense to begin the process of clearing the ground for my own theory with a critical examination of some of the problems inherent in the Professor's initial study of 1956, *The Military Revolution*. In so doing, rather than restricting the discussion to an arid list of the difficulties in Roberts's approach, I will take the opportunity to set the scene for the subsequent exposition of the military revolution of the sixteenth century by pursuing some of the issues raised at length, in particular those which have major implications for an understanding of the period.

Professor Roberts argued, as we have seen, that the firepower of European armies declined in the course of the sixteenth century as a result of the replacement of the longbow by firearms. In fact it increased. First, the longbow had only marginal significance in continental armies. In the later Middle Ages small contingents of English bowmen fought in European battles in which England was uninvolved[49] and, for a time, in the later fifteenth century the French experimented with their own.[50] The crossbow was the preferred European missile-weapon before the arquebus eclipsed it. Relying on Genoese crossbowmen at Crecy (1346), the French were themselves well furnished with the weapon well into the sixteenth century.[51] The German states cultivated it with equal, if not greater, vigour, forming guilds to practise the crossbow.[52] Typically, in 1431, the German crusading infantry sent to face the Hussites were to be equipped with the crossbow and firearms. The Hussites chose the same weapons.[53] Thus both types of bow, not just the relatively unpopular English weapon, need to be considered. Even the Scots, despite their repeated exposure to the English longbow, did not use it exclusively. By the early sixteenth century they were using a mixture of crossbows and firearms as well as the longbow.[54]

The weakness of the crossbow and even more of the longbow lay in their inability to perforate plate armour. The penetration of the windlass-drawn crossbow was better than that of the longbow and early crossbow. The windlass drawn crossbow had a pull in the order of 1,200 lb, compared with the meagre 50 lb of a longbow. The danger to a well-armoured man was thus far greater in the case of the former.[55]

For a longbow arrow to stand any chance of penetrating plate armour it would have to strike at close range at a ninety-degree angle. Most late medieval plate armour was so elaborately sloped, fluted and curved as to make such a hit near impossible.[56] From the 1360s plate armour began to force out chain mail – then the best in common use.

The first medieval battle to show the superiority of plate over bows was Cocherel in 1364.[57] Arrows and crossbow bolts could penetrate chain mail, causing heavy casualties, which would have been greater still but for the use of large shields and heavy helmets as accessories by those who could afford them. Bows of the kind used by the Turks in the early fifteenth century were inferior to the longbow. Yet, in the opinion of a French contemporary traveller, light chain mail could be penetrated by them. How much easier therefore for the superior longbow and crossbow. 'A turkish arrow would perhaps pierce a light coat of mail, but would be turned aside by plate armour however thin.'[58]

Heavy chain mail was another matter. In August 1192, Richard I rode along the length of Saladin's army, receiving so many arrow hits from their light bows that he resembled a porcupine – yet his exploit left him none the worse for wear. For all the protection his expensive chain-mail armour gave him against Moslem bows, Richard found it inadequate seven years later at Chalus when it failed to prevent the penetration of a crossbow bolt. The resulting wound cost him his life.[59]

Plate was so effective that the use of shields diminished; it was sufficient of itself.[60] Both helm and shield began to fall out of use in the second half of the fourteenth century, when suits of plate armour or *harnois blanc* rendered them superfluous. Another consequence of the adoption of plate armour was the replacement of the sword by the axe, as in the Germanic knightly inventory. The axe and the halberd were better equipped to penetrate plate than were the spear and the sword. By the mid-sixteenth century a plate corslet had emerged as the standard armour of the pikeman, and like the morion or open helmet he wore was proof against crossbow and longbow alike.

Blaise de Monluc found that his pikemen came to no harm when they closed on a body of English archers at Boulogne in October 1544, writing that 'their arrows did no harm at all'.[61] William Harrison commented in the late sixteenth century that the 'Frenchmen and the rutters [pistol-armed cavalry]' derided 'our new archery in respect of their corslets'.[62] The Biscayan captain Martin de Eguiluz was quite confident in the ability of a plate corslet to keep out arrows.[63] Infantry armour in the later Middle Ages was frequently unable to do so, as excavations at the site of the Battle of Wisby have revealed. The English archers of the fourteenth century were often well protected, as were Flemish infantry in the same period. As a result both fought well, even against French men-at-arms. Yet Monstrelet considered the English archers at Agincourt poorly protected and by the mid-fifteenth century the French infantry were, in theory, better armoured.[64]

The man-at-arms had far fuller coverage with plate, and was immune to all but the most unlucky strikes by the second half of the fourteenth century. It was exactly this state of affairs that accounts for the outrage of contemporaries when firearms at last turned the scales on the man-at-arms. Before then, a gentleman could expect to be immune to the bolts and arrows of his social inferiors.[65] Unlike firearms, bows could not perforate plate armour at close range. Sir Roger Williams put the point quite succinctly in 1590. At most, 10 per cent of a cavalry squadron had armour sufficient to keep out a musket ball at 200 yards.[66] None of them would have anything to fear from arrow fire.[67] Writing in the 1540s, Fourquevaux considered that the longbow and the crossbow were effective only against unarmoured targets.[68] Half a century later, Sir John Smythe considered that medieval bows could penetrate the armour then in use, even if by the sixteenth century armour proved superior.[69] This was a perfectly fair point considering the transformation of armour in the course of the later Middle Ages. It is interesting to find a broad consensus among sixteenth-century writers of all persuasions that contemporary armour was equal to any bow. Not only Williams, Fourquevaux and Smythe, but also Barwick, Barret, Digges and Elizabeth I's mid-century arms supplier, Sir Thomas Gresham, agreed that this was the case.[70] The armoured gentleman had nothing to fear from a commoner with a crossbow or longbow.

The arquebus – and later the musket – changed all that. Able to penetrate even the best plate armour, they dramatically increased the firepower of the infantryman. A Spanish writer observed in 1590 that none of the soldiers he talked to had any faith in the ability of the plate corslet to stop an arquebus bullet. Even the target, a heavy, reinforced plate shield used in assaults, was proof only against arquebus shot and not against musket bullets. Monluc experienced at first hand the penetration of the arquebus at Forcha di Penne in 1528, when he was wounded several times.[71] Even the

heavily armoured men-at-arms began to find excuses to avoid attacking infantry armed with firearms, as in Piedmont in 1543.[72] They
tried their best to negate the effects of the arquebus and later the
musket by improving their armour. Some adventurous souls added
an outer sheet of metal or 'placard' over their breastplates as 'an
advancement of the proofe'.[73] Sir John Smythe, a romantic sixteenth-
century supporter of the longbow, was forced to concede that
muskets disgorged 'bullets of which no armours wearable can resist'.[74]
The musket's penetration of all armour in common use was generally
accepted by contemporaries.[75] The only exception to this acknowle-
dgement of the superior penetration of firearms was the view of Sir
John Smythe and one seventeenth-century theorist that the arquebus
was helpless against armour.[76] Whatever the penetration of an
arquebus, that of a pistol was likely to be less – yet the French
general Tavannes was of the opinion that the pistol was lethal even
against an armoured opponent.[77] In the absence of similarly clear
judgements by other writers it is impossible to make an overall
summary of opinion on the penetration of the arquebus. However,
it is clear from accounts of actions in the Italian wars that it posed
a danger to the man-at-arms as well.

Yet these terrifying weapons had their drawbacks. Some of them,
such as slow reloading and limited accuracy, could be mitigated by
training. The most pessimistic estimate I have seen for the time
needed to load, aim and fire a musket is a quarter of an hour. A
well-trained man could fire far more frequently until his barrel
overheated through repeated discharges.[78]

Practised soldiers had no difficulty in scoring hits. The Turks
established a position overlooking Fort St Elmo during the siege of
Malta in 1565. 'In it,' as an eyewitness narrated, 'they placed their
best arquebusiers, and no sooner did a man show himself than he
was shot down'.[79] Without training, as Blaise de Vigenère found,
arquebusiers tended to look away rather than aim their pieces out of
sheer terror 'turning their faces away in fear and astonishment.'[80]
Other defects, such as the uselessness of these match-ignited weapons
in a downpour, could not easily be removed with practice, but wet
weather posed difficulties for crossbowmen too, as at Crecy.[81] Theorists recommended that the arquebusier or musketeer try to protect
his match and touch-hole from the rain by holding it under his
armpit. If water reached the powder in his piece the soldier needed
a special implement to clear the barrel and another to clean it
before it was possible to reload with dry powder.[82] Sir John Smythe,

who held the most pessimistic view of firearms of all the sixteenth-century English military theorists, had this to say:

> The harquebus and musket also, being discharged but 7 or 8 shots in haste, do grow hot and then do work small effect but danger to the soldiers that do occupy them. If the powder, also, with the which they are charged be not well corned and with sufficient quantity of saltpeter, and kept very dry, it fireth the pieces and carrieth the bullets point and blank but a little way and many times they go not off at all. The match also, if it be not of very good substance, well wrought, and very well twisted, and kept very dry, it taketh no fire ...[83]

Smythe went on to point out that, even if all these problems were solved, the gun could still misfire if the touchpowder were moist.[84] The Italian Jacopo di Porcia, writing in the 1520s, took it as read that a commander would try to fight in the rain if his opponent had an advantage in firearms.[85] Training,[86] patience[87] and sensible precautions[88] could overcome the worst of these problems. However, as Smythe was well aware, in action there were too many things for a frightened man to get wrong. In his view the first volley, carefully loaded out of harm's way, had more effect than the next four put together.[89] Firearms also suffered from a slower rate of fire. According to Anders Lassen's report of 1941, a skilled archer could loose one arrow every four seconds.[90] In the view of Richard Mason in 1798, a bowman required five to ten seconds, depending on his skill.[91] At the end of the seventeenth century one musket shot a minute was considered good.[92] An unskilled musketeer might take ten minutes between shots, or sixty times the length of time taken by Mason's inexpert archer.[93] But it was the greatly improved penetration of these 'weapons of fire' that proved decisive. At close range in defence of a trench or breach they greatly exceeded bows of all kinds in the damage they wrought. At the siege of Thionville in 1558, Monluc found the French attack halted by a few arquebuses in a casemate. All who approached were pierced and killed; only when the position was turned could the advance resume.[94]

Firearms had a further massive advantage, the psychological effect of their discharge. Machiavelli, whose work on the art of war appeared in English guise in 1560–2,[95] considered that a band of peasants would be more frightened by the discharge of a single arquebus than the approach of twenty armed men.[96] It was common currency among the advocates of continental methods that the terror of an exchange of musketry sufficed to make one side break and run, obviating the need for a prolonged hand-to-hand battle. Near mid-century, Thomas Audley insisted: 'you must in no wise lake [lack] shotte sufficient for many tymes it hath bene that battells have bene gotten by shotte onlie wthout pushe or stroke stricken.'[97] In Audley's time 'shot' was understood to mean either archers or men with firearms, or both. It would be quite wrong to assume that Audley meant one or the other. However, many later writers repeated his contention, making it quite clear that it was the use of gunpowder rather than the bowstring that made the impact.[98] Robert Barret explicitly stated that 'a vollie of musket or hargebuze goeth with more terrour, fury, and execution, then doth your vollie of arrowes'.[99] In his late-century view, 'it is rarley seene ... that men come often to hand-blowes, as in old time they did: For now in this age the shot so employeth and busieth the field (being well backed with a resolute stand of pikes) that the most valiantest and skilfullest therein do commonly import the victorie ... before men come to many hand-blowes.'[100] This was exactly what happened at Kinsale (1601), when a little musketry gave Mountjoy the day.[101]

Battles went out of favour in the course of the sixteenth century not because of the inefficacy of firearms, as Professor Roberts has argued, but precisely because of their efficacy; their deadly effectiveness at close range. The battles of the early sixteenth century demonstrated this beyond a shadow of doubt. As armies copied the winning tactics used at Cerignola (1503), Bicocca (1522) and Pavia (1525) and vastly increased the number of men with firearms on their strength, commanders increasingly avoided battle rather than risk defeat. The idea of avoiding battle because it was by its very nature a risky enterprise long antedates the sixteenth century. Vegetius argued in the fourth century that: 'It is much better to overcome the enemy by famine, surprise or terror, than by general actions, wherein fortune has often a greater share than valour.' Many medieval and early modern writers were influenced by his views or came to the same conclusion independently. In the sixteenth century, however, it was not this general prudence but fear of the effect of firearms deployed defensively that prompted the avoidance of battle.[102]

Firearms together with cannon had greatly increased the power of the defence, both on the battlefield and within a fortified position. At Cerignola (1503), the Spanish infantry took up a position in a vineyard behind a ditch. Their arquebus and artillery fire started a French rout. The Spanish cavalry charged and pursued the French for 3 miles. Fabrizio Colonna commented that the ditch gave the

Spaniards their victory. More correctly, the ditch and their arquebusiers together gave them victory.[103] The Swiss attack at Bicocca
(1522) was broken by a defensive ditch held by arquebusiers with
artillery support. A pike charge disposed of the shaken Swiss and
clinched the victory.[104] Pavia (1525) was by contrast a highly
complicated engagement. However, the aspect of it that impressed
contemporaries was the victory over both the Swiss pikemen and
the French *gendarmerie* by the Spanish arquebusiers. A Spaniard felt
that the skirmishing tactics used were a 'way of fighting so new and
unaccustomed and totally amazing, cruel and miserable'. For all
that, they were soon commmonplace in Europe as news of their
efficacy spread.[105]

The fashion for entrenching the ground on which a commander
intended to offer battle lessened the difference between the two
main forms of war, siege and battle. Whether assaulting a breach or
storming a trench where the enemy was offering battle in the open
country, the commander faced the same problem. How was he to
dislodge entrenched arquebusiers and musketeers supported by
cannon without losing an unacceptable fraction of his assaulting
force? The answer was frequently to avoid attacking and wait in the
hope that the enemy withdrew, surrendered or melted away for lack
of pay or supplies. A typical example of a sixteenth-century 'battle
that never was' was Jalons in 1544. The two armies observed each
other and exchanged small-arms fire, but did not engage.[106] A force
that came off worst in terms of provisions and firewood during a
winter campaign of attrition of this kind could lose more men than
during a conventional campaign of bloody field engagements. When
Charles V pulled out on 1 January 1553 after an abortive campaign
for the three bishoprics of Metz, Toul and Verdun, his army was a
shadow of its former self. The retreating men 'suffered greatly from
cold and hunger and the routes were soon covered with unfortunates
scarcely able to move, whom one saw fall from exhaustion along
the hedgerows, never to move again'. When the French occupied
Charles's former camp before Metz they found 'the tents torn on all
sides, tombs freshly covered over and the dying who called out with
great cries'. The French troops, better lodged and provisioned, had
not suffered the same calamity.[107] A successful commander could
defeat his opponent without ever bringing him to battle by watching
his army melt away through desertion, ill-pay, cold and malnutrition.

Cold and hunger were effective weapons of war, as contemporaries well realised. In 1590 a Spanish writer concisely summed

up the realities of war in the sixteenth century, commenting that: 'in wars often more slaughter is caused by a shortage of provisions for the troops and the travail which results for this reason from thirst and hunger than in encounters or from the blows of the enemy'. The experienced Spanish commander, Londoño, reached an identical conclusion, as would any acute observer of war in the period. Modern historians have much to learn from Hans Delbrück's sympathetic treatment of this early modern approach to strategy in the teeth of the post-Napoleonic obsession with the decisive battle and a strategy built around it.[108]

When engagements did occur, they were either chance meetings between armies, as at Ceresole (1544), or surprises in which one commander was caught in the open before he had a chance to dig a prepared position to receive the onslaught of the other. That Ceresole happened even then owed to a change of spirit by Francis I, who rescinded his orders that no battles were to be fought in favour of a more liberal policy shortly before the battle. Francis I's reluctance to risk a decisive battle was the understandable consequence of his experience at Pavia in 1525. He not merely lost the battle and the peace settlement, but was himself captured and humiliated.[109] At Dreux in 1562, the Huguenots neglected to reconnoitre and found themselves so close to the Catholic army that they had no alternative but to fight.[110] In 1569, Coligny was caught moving from one field entrenchment to another and was forced to fight the battle of Moncontour without the benefit of a dug-in defence. Jarnac, in the same year, likewise saw the Huguenots surprised and defeated. Gembloux (1578) was fought and lost by the army of the States, when they were surprised *en marche*. At Turnhout (1597), it was the Spaniards' turn to be caught on the march. St Quentin (1557) was lost when the French army, unprepared for battle, was surprised in motion. Gravelines (1558) was lost by a French commander who let his force be surprised in the midst of a river crossing.[111] Deliberate attacks on prepared positions had gone out of fashion in the years after Pavia. There were exceptions, but they were few compared to the profusion of engagements of this type in the first quarter of the century. Arques (1589) in France and Heiligerlee (1568) in the Netherlands are classic examples of the unwisdom of such attacks on arquebusiers and muskets in field entrenchments. At Jemmingen (1568), Louis of Nassau was foolish enough to come out of his entrenched position in a premature counter-attack and was defeated.[112]

The use of firearms and artillery in field entrenchments was responsible for the slackening in the pace of war and the neglect of the pitched battle in the course of the sixteenth century. It was not the inefficacy of firearms, as Professor Roberts postulated, but their very effectiveness that brought this about.

Besides claiming that firearms were inefficacious in the sixteenth century, Professor Roberts also argued that they made training simpler and more economical. Roberts held that the bow was a weapon superior to the sixteenth-century firearm, just as the lance was more effective than a brace of pistols in a cavalry action.

In fact, sixteenth-century arquebusiers, musketeers and pikemen required considerable training to operate with effect, as did pistol-armed cavalrymen. Even those contemporaries who were sceptical of the superiority of firearms over the bow believed that firearms needed experienced owners if they were to be used to advantage.[113] None of them argued that the new weapons economised on training. The advocates of firearms promoted training in their usage with great zeal. Humphrey Barwick, who had been trained in musketry in French service in the 1550s, wished to see the English militia instructed in the new weapons forty-five days a year. It was the firearms that needed most attention: 'the armed pikes and halberds, launces and speares are better to be made perfect in six daies then the fiery weapons are in 60 daies'.[114] Yet the pike also had its demands to make. It was a long, cumbersome weapon, which could scarcely be used *en masse* without training. The Swiss pike was 18 feet long; other pikes in common use were only a few feet shorter.[115] As Lelio Brancaccio put it in 1610, the pike is 'more of an impediment than an advantage to those who do not know how to use it well (on account of its length)'.[116] The complexity of sixteenth-century tactical formations compounded the training problem. It took a long time and considerable practice to construct a pike-square out of several companies of troops. Men who had not trained together took even longer to form up as the Swiss found when they tried to order twenty-seven different contingents in a single square before the battle of Morat (Murten) in 1476.[117]

As the sixteenth century wore on the need for training was recognised across Europe. In England, a select militia was established at great cost in 1572–3 to see that at least part of the militia was trained in the use of pike and firearms. Successive Tudor governments built up considerable stocks of the new weapons before Elizabeth took the step of training men in their use. In May 1557, a Venetian observer noted with disapproval the absence of training in England. The troops that the court and nobles could raise and arm (*c.* 20,000–25,000 men) were, 'although armed', so deprived of training that 'there would be few among them who would know how to move under arms, and to handle the pike, harquebuse or other sort of weapon, it not being the custom in thatt kingdom for the inhabitants to perform any sort of exercise'.[118]

Elizabeth's Irish enemies copied her in this, as she in turn had copied the practice in France and Spain.[119] The French made an early start in the 1480s by inviting the Swiss to train their infantry at Pont-de-l'Arche.[120] The operation was discontinued after a few years, but training was soon resumed under the impetus of the Spanish successes with infantry in Italy.[121] It was not necessary to wait, as Professor Roberts has argued, until the reforms of Maurice of Orange and Gustavus to see training and discipline enforced. As will be seen, a large part of the military theory written in the sixteenth century was directed towards training. Works appeared in many European languages explaining training procedures, offering mathematical aids and other devices to help bring troops into exact formation and providing background information to make the purpose of the exercises clear. In England, Spain and Italy the vast bulk of such works appeared in the second half of the century. In France the genre never became popular, though the nation benefited from a rich literature of military memoirs generated by years of conflict.[122] The much-vaunted development of military academies in the early seventeenth century was merely a continuation of the work of the theorists and field commanders of the sixteenth century. Nor was the military school without precedent at this time: from the mid-sixteenth century artillery schools were common in Spain.[123]

When dealing with cavalry, Professor Roberts does not stop at accusing it of abandoning training by exchanging the lance for firearms. After 1560 it is supposed to have lost all offensive force due to the adoption of firearms and the tactic of the caracole. However, sixteenth-century cavalry was extremely varied both in armament, tactics and employment, and before proceeding further with an examination of Professor Roberts's claims, there would be no harm in a brief overview of the main types, starting with the man-at-arms.

The Biscayan captain Martin de Eguiluz considered men-at-arms to be more effective in battle than any other type of cavalry when he wrote in 1595.[124] The Spanish were notoriously short of men-at-arms, but retained lancers into the seventeenth century. The lance was discontinued in Spanish service by an edict of Philip III. In their equipment the Spanish lancers differed little from men-at-arms: 'These launciers are called light horsemen, notwithstanding they are aswel mounted as the men at arms, saving the barbd for their greves and maces: the most carrie one pistol but al carrie ... a good broad sword.'[125]

From 1529, mounted arquebusiers were attached to the French *gendarmerie*. The Spanish attached 100 'hargulatiers' (mounted arque-busiers) to every 500 lancers. Only a fraction of the former had good cuirasses. Most had a pistol in addition to their arquebus and all had an open helmet. The usual role of the hargulatier was reconnaissance and the seizure of strategic points in advance of an army.[126]

The appearance of the wheel-lock cavalry pistol has been variously dated between 1515 and 1534. Lindsay Boynton dates English cavalry pistols to after 1550. However, he refers to them as 'petronels', a word which in the early seventeenth century denoted a carbine. The pistoleers were very close to the men-at-arms in both the elaboration of their armour and their social status: 'and these men ought to be of the best degree, because the meanest in one of these Troopes [of pistoleers], is ever by his place a Gentleman and so esteemed'.[127] Other types, such as demi-lances (English cavalrymen), stradiots (light horsemen) and dragoons (the mounted arquebusier as adapted by the Dutch), completed the colourful range of sixteenth-century cavalry.

To return to Professor Roberts's argument, the cavalry lost all significance on the battlefield until Gustavus emancipated it by restoring the charge to its repertoire and ending the pernicious caracole. The caracole involved the discharge of pistols by ranks, a proceeding that Roberts has criticised for its ineffectiveness and for the sacrifice of impact and training involved.

In fact the use of pistols did involve a measure of training. By the mid-sixteenth century the French man-at-arms acquired a pistol as well as his other weapons. Yet, as François de la Noue observed, it did him little good without the careful understanding that his pistol-armed opponents brought to theirs: 'untill they have learned more steadfastly to keepe order and to be more carefull of their weapons, they will never worke the like effects with the pistoll, as the Reistres'.[128] The reason why sixteenth-century cavalrymen looked to the pistol was simple: the lance lacked penetration. The plate

armour of a sixteenth-century man-at-arms was more easily penetrated by a pistol bullet than by a lance thrust. 'The arms of our
ancestors', commented Gaspard de Saulx-Tavannes on events he had
witnessed in 1554, 'were the lance, the axe, the mace and the sword.
Of these the last remains with us. The rest are considered of little
value partly for being probing weapons, which neither pierce nor
penetrate easily and partly because the invention of pistols has proved
better.'[129] François de la Noue regarded it as a miracle if any man
were slain by a lance.[130]

Such was the psychological effect of the pistol that it was common
for one side to break after the second pistol was fired.[131] (Pistoleers
carried a brace of pistols.) Pistoleers notched up victories over
conventionally armed men-at-arms at St Quentin (1557), Dreux
(1562), Ivry (1590) and Turnhout (1597), despite the alleged inefficacy of their weapons and their assumed lack of training.[132]
Lancers were simply inferior. As Blaise de Monluc pointed out:
'with these arms [pistols] one can fight better *en masse* than with
lances, because if you do not fight in line the lancers get into more
difficulty and fighting in line is not as safe as in massed formation.'[133]

In Sir Roger Williams's view most pistols were badly loaded or
fired at too long a range.[134] In this he followed François de la Noue,
who felt that the sole reason why the *reiters* made better use of their
pistols than the men-at-arms, who had also taken to using pistols in
the late sixteenth century,[135] lay in the former's greater care and
undrstanding of these complicated weapons.[136] If the arquebus and
musket were best used at very close ranges of under 60 yards, the
pistol was not to be fired at more than 3 yards range in La Noue's
opinion: scarcely a recommendation. Yet La Noue was very satisfied
with the pistol and regarded its psychological effect in combat and
the excellent penetration as outweighing the disadvantages in its
use. Decades of experience stood him in good stead to make his
judgement.

The caracole so despised by Roberts was the cavalry's equivalent
of the skirmishing tactics used to such great effect by the Spanish
arquebusiers at Pavia (1525). Each rank of the cavalry formation
would approach the enemy in turn, discharging their pistols before
peeling away to allow the next rank to approach and do the same.
The main problem with this tactic was that it gave the impression
of flight. François de la Noue, an experienced Huguenot field
commander, felt that the caracole endangered the men carrying it
out 'for their turnes and returnes have beene taken for a flight:

whereupon they have beene so hotly pursued that they have taken their carrier out right'.[137] In fact, the caracole was far from being the only tactic used by cavalrymen on the field of battle in the sixteenth and early seventeenth centuries. Pistol-armed cavalrymen were perfectly capable of charging home in the manner that Professor Roberts imagined Gustavus to have reintroduced after half a century of neglect.[138]

In part, Professor Roberts is of course correct. Cavalry did decline in value as a battlefield weapon in the period he examined, though contemporaries were by no means united in that assessment.[139] But this was owing to the perfection of pike and firearms tactics by the infantry across Europe in the course of the sixteenth century and not to any marked decline in the quality of cavalry, whether men-at-arms, lancers, mounted arquebusiers, pistoleers or others.

This perfection of infantry tactics against cavalry is a point Roberts did not consider. Men armed with firearms alone would be run down by cavalrymen in the open field whether they formed up tightly to protect themselves or not. At Riberac (1568), a tight square of arquebusiers was simply ridden down.[140] Once supported by a pike-square, such shot could defy the cavalry to the last minute.

The techniques involved are elucidated well in Sir Charles Oman's comments on an illustration to an English manuscript (no. 129) preserved in All Souls' College library, Oxford.[141] Firearms within the pike-square itself could take the cavalry under fire at point-blank range as they struggled to make an opening in the serried ranks of pikes. At Ceresole (1544), both sides placed men armed with firearms inside pike-squares. The tactic had a certain novelty, but soon it was commonplace.[142] Such shot were equally effective against horse and foot. Cavalry halted by a pike-square made a target of such size that even the most inaccurate weapons could not fail to work to deadly effect. Arquebusiers 'shooting within twentie paces iust in the face of the horse, in my opinion will mayme the whole first ranke of the squadron'.[143] Natural obstacles could have the same effect as the pike-square in damming up the cavalry, but they could only be used defensively. A pike-square could advance even in the face of cavalry taking its arquebusiers and musketeers with it.

Piero Pieri found precisely this offensive use of infantry to be the key difference between the battles of the high and later Middle Ages and those fought by armies that had come under the influence of the Swiss successes of the late fifteenth and early sixteenth centuries, and adopted their methods. He reached this distinction only by counting battles such as Agincourt (1415), where infantrymen (archers) had attacked after an initially defensive posture, as 'counter-offensive', as opposed to 'offensive' battles in which the infantry (pikemen) attacked from the outset without first awaiting the enemy's assault in a prepared position.[144]

In these circumstances it was not surprising that the cavalry began to play a less dominant role on the battlefields of Europe and lost many nobles to the despised infantry, which had grown in prestige so startlingly in the early sixteenth century. It was suddenly an honour to trail a pike. The English men-at-arms had a long tradition of dismounting to steady their infantry. Their Burgundian counterparts copied them in this, but the French could not be persusaded to do so. General Köhler ascribed their reluctance to social prejudice. Whatever the inhibiting force, it was overcome in the early sixteenth century by the amazing spectacle of infantry holding its own and even advancing against the mounted arm. Henceforth, the cream of the French nobility, the chevalier Bayard among them, was prepared to serve with the infantry, greatly increasing its resilience.[145] Yet the cavalry of the sixteenth and early seventeenth centuries none the less notched up some notable successes, and several battles, including the 'Battle of the Spurs' (1513), Moncontour (1569), Mook (1574), Gembloux (1578), Courtras (1587), Ivry (1590), Turnhout (1597) and Nieuport (1600) were decided by the use of cavalry.[146] It was far from being the 'neutered arm' of Professor Roberts's conception. In the century before Gustavus cavalry not only charged home, but frequently carried the day as well. If it no longer played quite the dominant role it had adopted in the past this was owing not to any decay in the arm itself, but to the efficacy of firearms and the new infantry tactics that allowed them to face cavalry while supported by a stand of pikes or a terrain advantage.

If Gustavus did little new for the mounted arm, can the same be said of his use of mobile field artillery and the Maurician infantry reforms, which allegedly transformed the nature of war in the early seventeenth century? The use of mobile field guns in battle was certainly not new. The French armies enjoyed the use of tactically mobile, horse-drawn guns of a variety of calibres for well over a century before Gustavus's victories in Germany. Francis I deployed over seventy artillery pieces at Marignano in 1515. At Pavia, the French artillery was no less mobile and terrifyingly effective.[147]

The gun-carriages necessary for mobility on the field of battle were already available in the fifteenth century and before.[148] The key question was, however, not the provision of suitable carriages but having enough horses to allow for rapid movement.[149] The use of artillery in conjunction with infantry was visible in theoretical works long before Gustavus made his impact.[150] The use of cannon hidden within a body of infantry was a common ploy in German theoretical writings of the fifteenth and sixteenth centuries. Even the volley fire which Gustavus is supposed to have introduced to a bewildered Europe was not so new. Skirmishing tactics in the sixteenth century regularly involved one group of men firing a volley while another moved to take their place. Repeatedly, vollies were used and with great effect.[151] The sixteenth-century theorists also used the volley in their writings.[152] The small 550-man units which emerged from the Maurician reforms were to some extent new. Some sixteenth-century regiments were of this size, others not. Standardisation was far from universal, even in the mid-seventeenth century.[153]

However, other historians have questioned the significance of these 550-man units. Why, if they marked a breakthrough in tactics, were shallow formations of this kind decisively defeated by the tercios Roberts so derided at Nördlingen (1634)?[154] Why did they fail to become universal in seventeenth-century Europe if they were so efficacious?[155] Jeremy Black has argued that flexible formations were, on the contrary, universal, as were certain tactics.[156]

Finally there is the question of the restoration of Roman models and discipline, which Professor Roberts saw as the consequence of the Maurician reforms. Any sixteenth-century theorist would have been amazed to be told that he paid no attention to Roman models and that his contemporaries had not established a classical discipline. What Maurice and his circle did achieve was to make the focal point of interest in the classical world Aelian's work on tactics rather than Vegetius's summary of Roman military wisdom, which had guided military thinkers for centuries.[157] Sixteenth-century editions of Vegetius and of Machiavelli's *Dell'arte della guerra*, which leans heavily on Vegetius, combined to make the late-Roman author highly accessible to the reading public well before Aelian. Aelian was available in a much reprinted late fifteenth-century edition: *Veteres de re militari scriptores, scilicet Vegetii, Aeliani, Frontini et Modesti opera* (Rome, 1487), but it began to circulate heavily in vernacular translations only in the seventeenth century.

Justus Lipsius, the classical scholar whose work informed the Maurician reforms, certainly presented a picture of Roman practice that surpassed any previous attempts at portrayal in his *Justi Lipsii de militia Romana libri quinque* ... (Antwerp, 1596). In token of their admiration for this work, contemporaries had bought over 6,000 copies by 1630.[158] But the essence of the Roman achievement had long since been public knowledge, and all Lipsius could hope to do was present a definitive rather than an essentially new picture of Roman military practices. Imitation of classical models was a sixteenth-century pastime that drove two French kings to create 'legions'[159] and spurred contemporary theorists into advocacy on behalf of the most inappropriate formations simply because they had the sanction of antiquity. Machiavelli, in justification for his slavish imitation of Greek and Roman models, explained to his readers that 'the ancients did everything better and more sensibly than us'.[160] Even as hard-headed a soldier as Londoño takes time in this work to explain the weapons, armour and organisation of the Romans, and comments simply that it is advisable to follow the Romans in all matters relating to discipline.[161] What Maurice did for tactics, much as Lipsius had done for historical scholarship, was to refine what had gone before with the aid of a strong critical sense. He was not a revolutionary innovator but a gifted tinkerer.

After dealing with the foundations of Professor Roberts's 'military revolution' it remains to review a number of important points he made before concluding his argument. In particular, he considered it a novel characteristic of the 'military revolution' for resources to be systematically destroyed to deny them to the enemy. In fact war by fire has had a long and sad history, dating from long before the seventeenth century. The English used such tactics repeatedly in the Hundred Years' War. In 1339, Geoffrey le Scrope took a French cardinal to the top of a lofty tower near Cambrai. The whole countryside was lit for miles with the fires still burning from Edward III's work. 'Your eminence,' said Scrope, 'does it not seem that the silken thread that girdles France is broken?' The cardinal is said to have been so overcome that he fainted.[162] A century later the English still valued the same techniques as a means to bring the enemy to his knees.[163] In the sixteenth century, Francis I operated a vigorous scorched-earth policy against the army with which Charles V attempted to invade southern France in 1536.[164] Equally questionable is the supposition that before the great wars of the seventeenth century no use was made of fixed magazines. The French made use of them in the Hundred Years' War. False too is the assumption that war was never conducted over vast spaces before the Thirty Years'

War. Henry IV's campaigns during the French Wars of Religion were conducted over hundreds of miles from Normandy to the south of France. Francis I confronted the hostile coalition of 1544 with armies ranged from the Channel coast to the north of Italy and coordinated their strategy, moving troops from one front to the other as it suited him. After the victory won by the duke of Enghien at Ceresole (April 1544) in Italy, Francis I made the most fateful of these moves in his career, withdrawing so many of Enghien's troops north of the Alps as to negate all that had been won by the battle.[165] Equally surprising is the idea that maps were unavailable for commanders to plan their campaigns in the era before the 'military revolution'. References to their use abound in European military theory as far back as the fifteenth century. Robert de Balsac, in his late medieval treatise, recommended the prince to 'have a picture made,' or draw up plans of the country he hoped to conquer.[166] The Spanish sixteenth-century theorists Londoño and Alaba Y Viamont both suggested maps be used. Londoño preferred the one selected to be printed and distributed to subordinates.[167] Furthermore, the use of armour in no way prevented the use of uniforms in the period before the 'military revolution'. It was a simple matter to place a cloth surcoat over a coat of mail or the surface of plate armour bearing the cross of St George or whatever design the wearer favoured. There are many references to bodies of troops wearing uniforms in the Middle Ages, though of course the practice was not particularly common.[168] To make an unfavourable judgement on the military capacity of pre-seventeenth-century armies on the basis of these arguments in Roberts's text would be quite wrong.

Professor Roberts's argument that the normal size of European armies increased massively in the seventeenth century is also not as obviously true as might first be thought. It rests chiefly, though not solely, on the extraordinary paper expansion of the French army in Louis XIV's wars long after Gustavus. The size of the French regular army grew from 30,000 in the War of Devolution (1667–8) to 440,00 in the War of the League of Augsburg (1688–97).[169] Effective field armies in the eighteenth century were not so much larger than those of the sixteenth century before the 'military revolution'. Armies of 20,000–120,000 were the rule in the European conflicts of the eighteenth century.[170] Charles VIII disposed of over 50,000 men for his invasion of Italy in 1494. Francis I had over 40,000 men at Pavia (1525). Charles V marched on Landreçies in 1543 with over 50,000 men. The Spanish–English army of 1557 was 45,000 strong. Medieval

European armies were sometimes as large.[171] Professor Parker is less cautious than Lot in his estimates of sixteenth-century army sizes. In his view, Charles V commanded 150,000 at Metz (1552).[172] These larger armies certainly required more money to maintain them and this, in turn, created political friction for the regimes of the late seventeenth and eighteenth centuries. But one should be aware that the sixteenth century saw repeated state bankruptcies as a result of the cost of war. Political tension caused by the difficulties inherent in maintaining large field armies for protracted periods of time was not restricted solely to the period after Gustavus; it had a much longer history.

It is also worth pointing out, as Max Jähns noticed in his survey of the post-sixteenth-century European military theorists, that, whatever the possibilities for expansion in the overall strengths of the armed forces of the European powers in a period of rising wealth and population, the size of force their commanders could control in the field was limited. In the seventeenth century, Montecuccoli would not entertain the idea of armies larger than 30,000. Turenne considered an army of 50,000 'inconvenient both for commander and commanded'. Later still, St Cyr felt no man was equal to the task of commanding an army of 100,000. Yet, with the arrival of the wars of the French Revolution and Napoleon, armies of five times the size that Turenne had considered unmanageable were used, and to effect.[173]

The same is true of military ranks and the hierarchy of command which Professor Roberts is inclined to regard as a product of the reforms of Maurice and his successors. He claimed that in 'the armies of the Landsknechts, for instance, the distinction between officers and men had been faint ... Now all that changed.'[174] However, it was the late fifteenth and sixteenth centuries, not the seventeenth, which saw the emergence of the ranks of colonel (or its continental equivalent, 'camp-master'), sergeant-major, sergeant and corporal and the development of a regular and more elaborate hierarchy command.[175]

On a number of other points Professor Roberts is undoubtedly correct. For instance, weapons did begin to be standardised in the period he is concerned with. In 1626, 1628 and 1635 Charles I's government set out to remedy the situation created by the profusion of weapon sizes in use by prescribing standard types. In the sixteenth century English governments had made no real effort to ensure standardisation.[176] But the overall impression cannot be avoided that his theory of a military revolution from the early seventeenth century poses such a multitude of problems as to make its resurrection a major challenge. Yet this is precisely the task Professor Parker has undertaken.

His thesis is not to be dismissed simply because it incorporated flawed elements of his predecessor's sweeping 'military revolution' theory. As we saw earlier, there is much more to his fine work of 1988. It is time to examine the more substantial alterations Parker made to Roberts's theory. The most important of these is in the field of siege warfare, a topic swiftly skirted in the inaugural lecture of 1956. It was Parker's contention that developments in artillery led to the introduction of a new type of fortification, the *trace italienne*, which resulted in a slowing in the pace of warfare wherever it was present.[177] This is undeniably correct. Only two modifications need to be made to Professor Parker's argument in this key area of siege warfare.

First, he overemphasises the importance of newly built fortifications constructed on the Italian model, replete with ravelins, horn-works and angle-bastions.[178] Repeatedly, in the sixteenth and seventeenth centuries, old-fashioned fortifications held out for very long periods of time.[179] By Professor Parker's argument this is an unlikely phenomenon, as the superior artillery of the new revolutionary age ought swiftly to dispose of them due to their inferior design. In fact, they were able to hold out because of the effectiveness of artillery and the new firearms in defence. As the Spanish engineer Pedro de Navarro observed in the early sixteenth century: 'A city can expect to have more guns than an army can carry with it; whenever you can present more guns to the enemy than he can range against you, it is impossible for him to defeat you.'[180]

It was not necessary to have a freshly built fortress of italianate design to survive. As Professor Parker himself noticed, the cost of such fortifications was prohibitive. Siena was lost in 1555 despite, or rather because of, her new-model fortifications. They had cost so much that insufficient resources remained to conduct the defence effectively.[181] Nor were architects, stone and brick necessary to turn an area into a maze of well-defended positions. Professor Parker has pointed to the twelve entirely new circuits of walls made in the Netherlands between 1529 and 1572. This benefited but a small fraction of the 200 walled towns in the territory, most of which would, in one way or another, feature in the eight decades of war that followed.[182]

An outdated fortification furnished with *ad hoc* improvements, artillery, arquebusiers and musketeers served just as well. The only inhibiting factor was the room available to dig internal trenches for the defenders to defend breaches made in the old-fashioned walls of the fortress they were defending. A small and outdated fortification was a liability. As Peter Whitehorne realised in 1560–2: 'if he that is within, have not space inough to retire, both ditches and rampiers, he is overcum, because he is not abell to withstande the violence of the enemie, who through the breach of the wall, will after enter'.[183] The second point is relatively trivial. The breakthrough in the development of artillery came in the mid-fifteenth century and not, as Professor Parker has suggested, the sixteenth.[184]

Professor Parker's impressively researched military revolution lasts two centuries or, to be exact, 180 years (1530–1710). Within this massive time-span he conflates totally distinct tactical developments: (1) the replacement of the crossbow and longbow by firearms in the sixteenth century and (2) the replacement, in the late seventeenth century, of the pikeman and musketeer by a single weapon fulfilling the functions of both – the bayonet-armed musketeer. It was not until the 1690s that a really effective socket-bayonet evolved. Its predecessor, the plug-bayonet, was experimented with for several decades in the late seventeenth century.[185]

Professor Parker could thus argue that the period 1530–1710 saw the replacement of shock by firepower, which is a difficult position to sustain, whether criticised from a medieval or from a Napoleonic perspective. The Middle Ages is replete with battles won by firepower (archery). Homildon Hill is a classic example (1402).[186] The Napoleonic age abounds with examples of the successful use of shock, whether by infantry or by cavalry. Cavalry formed 19–50 per cent of the force present in fifteen field engagements in the period 1690–1747 for which David Chandler has presented figures. But a large proportion of the cavalry were dragoons, not used for shock.[187] Napoleon made much of the cavalry arm, employing lancers, cuirassiers and other types of cavalry for shock tactics. The French use of infantry columns in the assault in the Napoleonic wars was notorious. They hoped in this way to make up with raw enthusiasm and physical impact what they lacked in discipline and musketry training.[188] The mid-nineteenth century is the point from which the military historian may honestly begin to talk of the eclipse of shock tactics due to the excessive development of firepower on the battlefield. By 1914, cavalry was well and truly redundant. Exceptionally, cavalry performed creditably on Allenby's Palestine campaign of 1917 and was still used to some effect by the German army in swampy areas on the Russian front in the Second World War.[189] However, the experience of the First World War was sufficient to convince all but the most ardent *aficionados*. The 'shock' weapon of both wars was of course the tank, which combined shock and firepower.

Professor Parker quite wrongly assumes that the English victories of the Hundred Years' War were won against mounted knights.[190] It can also be disputed whether, as Professor Parker argues (*loc. cit.*), the French outnumbered the English at Agincourt (1415) by two to one. The English army may well have outnumbered the French.[191] In fact the English, their allies and their enemies tended to fight dismounted with, at most, a small part of the total force fighting mounted.

It was indeed strange, as General Khöler observed, that the cream of English and French chivalry should fight each other on foot: 'The remarkable spectacle, that the French and English knights fought each other on foot lasted into the middle of the fifteenth century.'[192] The former did so to steady their infantry, as at Cravant (1423), when the English and Burgundian men-at-arms dismounted to steady the archers.[193] At Verneuil (1424) and Agincourt (1415) the English did the same as at many other encounters, including Crecy (1346).[194] The French tended to dismount so as not to expose their horses to the English archery, though in a number of their more disastrous encounters they made mounted attacks, as at Crecy and early in the Agincourt battle, when they rode down their own crossbowmen.[195] In the late medieval Empire, the heavy knight almost invariably remained mounted in action in the manner Professor Parker imagined that the French had.[196]

Moreover, Professor Parker, retaining some fraction of Professor Roberts's belief of the significance of Maurice of Nassau, is prepared to argue that Maurice and his associates invented the countermarch in 1594; something Professor Roberts never argued. In fact this tactic, the infantry's version of the caracole, was in use throughout the sixteenth century as a perusal of its military literature reveals.[197] The ancients used the countermarch extensively and several varieties of it are preserved in the tactics of Aelian, which was available in fifteenth- and sixteenth-century editions. Volley fire, which Professor Roberts attributed to an invention of his reformers, was also in common use in the sixteenth century.[198] Bicocca (1522) provides clear evidence of its use by Colonna's arquebusiers in a bastard form.[199]

Yet these problems should not blind us to the very real achievements of Professor Parker's study. His careful consideration of siege warfare in particular lifts his study above Michael Roberts's thesis, with its narrow emphasis on battle tactics. However, it has two fundamental flaws. By explaining but not demolishing Roberts's thesis, he gave it a second lease of life, mixed with some of his own ideas. Second, by covering such a long time-span, his theory of change inevitably loses some of its edge, especially when quite separate and chronologically distanced events become conflated.

In recent years a flood of publications on the 'military revolution' has added further complexities to the debate. Jeremy Black has defined a military revolution of the late seventeenth and early eighteenth centuries, whose significance will no doubt be long argued, but which does not greatly affect the debate on sixteenth-century change, which he dismisses in a few pages of his brief study. There is no reason why an individual cannot combine an enthusiasm both for Black's conception of radical change in the eighteenth century and for my own of an earlier transformation. It would, however, be difficult to combine the Roberts–Parker standpoint and Black's position without making substantial alterations to one in order to accommodate the other.

A characteristic of all three historians – Roberts, Parker and Black – is to concentrate on sweeping changes in society as a result of military change, or vice versa.[200] The interest of Brian Downing's recent study is almost entirely devoted to this aspect of the 'military revolution'.[201] My own analysis avoids doing so for two reasons. First, since the beginning of time governments at war have strained every muscle to raise more money and develop greater military potency. Any argument based on the idea that, at a certain point in time, this need suddenly developed to the point where whole institutions of government had to change overlooks the fact that this pressure has brought about change for centuries and is in no sense revolutionary; rather, it is normal for a nation at war. In our own time the expedients to which governments will turn to finance war have become even more dramatic. But the demands of war will always cause strain of varying degrees depending on the intensity of the conflict.

Second, there are a mass of other, non-military, factors to be considered in any analysis of this type. The need to pay for armies and fleets may have some impact on a society and its government, especially if the financial cost grows. But the nature and efficiency of a government's previous arrangements, the character of its leadership and a wide variety of other elements combine to mould the outcome of these increased pressures in different ways in different countries at different times.

For both these reasons this present study makes no attempt to generalise in this vexed area after the fashion of Roberts, Parker, Black and Downing, though others may find this very aspect of the current 'military revolution' debate so fascinating as to succumb to the temptation to do so. The danger is that we will see a rash of further studies mixing oversimplifications of the military aspects of the period with even more suspicious sweeping statements of political, economic and social linkages to these dramatic and varied visions of 'military revolution'.

Returning to the narrower confines of this present study, it is time to change from criticising previous conceptions and offer something positive in their stead, which other students of the period will doubtless take issue with in their turn. As will have been apparent even from this relatively brief investigation of some of the issues raised by Professor Parker's and Professor Roberts's conceptions of the military revolution, the sixteenth century was a time of particular change. Thus far we have looked only for the problems inherent in existing theories of an early modern military revolution. It is now time to take a more positive tack and begin to elaborate quite a different military revolution from the foregoing.

A military revolution of the sixteenth century is by no means as strange or novel an idea as it might first seem. Sir John Hale saw the years 1519–59 as the most significant period of military change before the age of the Revolutionary Wars and Napoleon.[202] We have already seen G.A. Hayes-McCoy's perception in Chapter 1. Piero Pieri was convinced that between the late fifteenth and the early sixteenth centuries war was transformed.[203] Wilhelm Erben likewise felt that the sixteenth century marked a turning point in military history.[204] None of these writers, one must hasten to say, added flesh and bones to their perceptions. Their statements were more in the nature of asides than rigorous formulations of doctrine. Nor is this surprising, given the multifaceted nature of change during the period. What follows is my own attempt to sum up the momentous sixteenth-century changes in the conduct of war, which swept Europe long before they were properly appreciated in England.

Notes

1. Michael Roberts, *The Military Revolution 1560–1660* (Belfast, 1956).

2. Michael Roberts, *Gustavus Adolphus. A History of Sweden 1611–32* (2 vols, London, 1958), II, pp. 169–85 in particular.

3. Geoffrey Parker, *The military revolution. Military innovation and the rise of the West 1500–1800* (Cambridge, 1988).

4. Geoffrey Parker, 'The "Military Revolution" 1560–1660 – a myth?', *Journal of Modern History*, XXVI (1976), reprinted in *Spain and the Netherlands 1559–1659* (London, 1979), pp. 86–103.

5. John A. Lynn, 'Tactical Evolution in the French Army', *French Historical Studies*, XIV (1985); D.A. Parrott, 'Strategy and Tactics in the Thirty Years' War: "The Military Revolution"' *Militärgeschichtliche Mitteilungen*, XVIII, (1985).

6. Sir George Clark made no attempt to challenge Roberts's ideas in his *War and Society in the Seventeenth Century* (Cambridge, 1958), pp. 96–8. Geoffrey Parker recapitulated several of Professor Roberts's points alongside his own in Parker, *Military Revolution*, p. 24. W.F. Cook takes his terms of reference from Parker and Roberts together, as do Downing and Black. Cook, *Morocco*, pp. 10–11. Downing, *Political Change*, pp. 57–74. Black, *A Military Revolution?*, passim.

7. Neither of these pieces is framed in terms of Roberts's near contemporaneous argument, but both touch on much of the ground in contention. Piero Pieri, *Il Rinascimento e la crisi militare italiana* (Turin, 1952); J.R. Hale, 'Armies, navies and the art of war' in G.R. Elton (ed.), *New Cambridge Modern History*, II (Cambridge, 1958).

8. Jeremy Black, *A Military Revolution? Military Change and European Society 1550–1800* (London, 1991), pp. 7, 10, 67, 93.

9. Brian M. Downing, *The Military Revolution and Political Change. Origins of Democracy and Autocracy in Early Modern Europe* (Princeton, 1992). See especially pp. v, 57–74.

10. W.F. Cook, *The Hundred Years' War for Morocco. Gunpowder and the Military Revolution in the Early Modern World* (Oxford, 1994). See especially pp. 10–11, 60–72, 273–82.

11. David Eltis, 'English Military Theory and the Military Revolution of the Sixteenth Century' (Oxford University D.Phil. Thesis, 1991).

12. Roberts, *Revolution*, p. 5.

13. Ibid., p. 9.

14. Ibid., p. 6.

15. Ibid., pp. 6–7. See Eugen von Frauenholz, *Das Heerwesen des Reiches in der Landsknechtszeit* (München, 1937), p. 67.

16. Ibid., p. 7.

17. Ibid.

18. *Idem, Gustavus*, II, p. 183f.

19. Ibid., II, p. 183. Roberts, *Revolution*, p. 7.

20. Roberts, *Revolution*, p. 7.

21. Ibid.

22. Ibid., p. 10.

23. Sancho de Londoño, *El discurso sobre la forma de reduzir la disciplina militar,*
a meyor y antiguo estado (Brussels, 1589), fos. 3, 9ᵛ–10, 15ᵛ and 42ᵛ.
24. Ibid., p. 8.
25. Ibid., p. 8.
26. Ibid., p. 8.
27. Roberts, *Revolution*, p. 8.
28. Roberts, *Gustavus*, II, p. 180.
29. Michael Roberts, *Essays in Swedish History* (London, 1967), p. 58.
30. Ibid., p. 16.
31. Ibid., p. 12.
32. Ibid., pp. 12–13, 27.
33. Ibid., p. 14.
34. Ibid., p. 21.
35. Ibid., p. 12.
36. Ibid., pp. 23–6.
37. Ibid., p. 28. See also p. 10.
38. Ibid., p. 28.
39. Ibid., pp. 21–2.
40. Parker, *Myth*, p. 89. Parrott, 'Strategy and Tactics', p. 7.
41. John A. Lynn, 'Tactical Evolution', p. 185. See also Hale, *N.C.M.H.*, II,
p. 495.
42. Parker, *Spain and the Netherlands*, p. 89.
43. Parker, *Military revolution*, pp. 4–5.
44. Ibid., p. 12.
45. Ibid., pp. 10–14.
46. Ibid., p. 16.
47. Ibid., pp. 1, 24.
48. Ibid., p. 17.
49. Ernst Richert, *Die Schlacht bei Guinegate 7. August 1479* (Diss. Berlin, 1907),
p. 66. Richard Vaughan, *Charles the Bold* (London, 1973), p. 393. Friedrich Mohr,
Die Schlacht bei Rosebeke am 27. November 1382 (Diss., Berlin, 1906), p. 78.
50. E.G. Heath, *Archery, A Military History* (London, 1980), pp. 2, 137–8, and
158.
51. Richard Czeppan, *Die Schlacht bei Crecy (26. August 1346)* (Diss., Berlin,
1906), pp. 92–3. John F. Guilmartin, *Gunpowder and Galleys. Changing technology*
and Mediterranean warfare in the sixteenth century (Oxford, 1974), p. 148. Jean-
Charles Sournia, *Blaise de Monluc. Soldat et écrivain (1500–1577)* (Paris, 1981), p.
386.
52. T. Reintges, *Ursprung und Wesen der spätmittelalterlichen Schützengilden*
(Bonn, 1963).
53. *Deutsche Reichstagsakten*, IX, no. 410, cited in Max von Wulf, *Die hussitische*
Wagenburg (Diss., Berlin, 1889), p. 42.
54. Gladys Dickinson, 'Some Notes on the Scottish Army in the first half of
the Sixteenth Century', *The Scottish Historical Review* (1949), pp. 135–6, 143.
55. Ibid. Malcolm Vale, *War and Chivalry. Warfare and Aristocratic Culture in*
England, France and Burgundy at the End of the Middle Ages (London, 1981), p.
113. Jim Bradbury, *The Medieval Archer* (Woodbridge, 1985), p. 148.

56. A.R. Williams, 'Metallographic examination of 16th-century armour', *Bulletin of the Historical Metallurgy Group*, VI (1972), p. 15.

57. G. Köhler, *Die Entwickelung des Kriegswesens und der Kriegführung in der Ritterzeit von Mitte des 11. Jahrhunderts bis zu den Hussitenkriegen* (3 vols, Breslau, 1886), II, pp. 367, 382–3.

58. *The Travels of Bertrandon de La Brocquière … 1432 and 1433* (London, 1807), p. 301.

59. Baha al Deen, cited by John Bagot Glubb, *The Lost Centuries From the Muslim Empires to the Renaissance of Europe 1145–1453* (London, 1967), p. 142. Bradbury, *Medieval Archer*, p. 3.

60. Vale, *War and Chivalry*, p. 105. Köhler, *Entwickelung*, p. 383.

61. Jean Giono and Paul Courteault (eds), Blaise de Monluc, *Commentaires 1521–1576* (Paris, 1964), p. 188.

62. Heath, *Archery*, pp. 156–7.

63. Martin de Eguiluz, *Milicia, discurso, y regla militar* (Antwerp, 1595), fo. 80.

64. B. Thordeman, *Armour from the Battle of Wisby, 1361* (Stockholm, 1939), I, pp. 185–7, 190, cited by Vale, *War and Chivalry*, p. 105. Czeppan, *Crecy*, pp. 67, 69. Felix Wodsak, *Die Schlacht bei Kortryk 11. Juli 1302* (Diss., Berlin, 1905), p. 28. L. Douet-d'Arcq, *La chronique d'Enguerran de Monstrelet* (6 vols, Paris, 1857–62), III, p. 106. General Susane, *Histoire de l'infanterie française* (5 vols, Paris, 1876), I, p. 36.

65. Pierre Keller, *Galiot de Genouillac, Grand-maître de l'artillerie de France* (Saint-Cere, 1968), p. 18. E.M. Lloyd, *A Review of the History of Infantry* (London, 1908), p. 91.

66. Sir Roger Williams, *A Briefe Discourse of Warre*, STC 25732 (1590), p. 41.

67. Ibid., pp. 46–7.

68. Raymond de Beccarie de Pavie, Sieur de Fourquevaux, *Instructions for the warres*, trans. Paul Ive [who mistakenly ascribed the work to G. du Bellay], STC 7264 (1589), p. 25.

69. Sir John Smythe, 'An aunswer to contrarie opynyons militarie', British Library, Harleian MS 135, fo. 25ᵛ.

70. Barwick, *Breefe Discourse*, sig. G3ᵛ. Barret, *Theorike*, p. 3. Dudley Digges (ed.), *Foure paradoxes … written long since by Thomas Digges*, STC 6872 (1604), sig. H3ᵛ. L.O. Boynton, *The Elizabethan Militia 1558–1603* (London, 1967), p. 57.

71. Diego de Alaba y Viamont, *El perfeto Capitan, instruido En la disciplina Militar, y nueva ciencia de la Artilleria* (Madrid, 1590), fo. 131. Eguiluz, *Milicia*, fo. 15. Monluc, *Commentaires*, pp. 46–7.

72. Cl. Gaier, 'L'opinion des chefs de guerre français du XVIᵉ siècle sur les progrès de l'art militaire', *Revue Internationale d'Histoire Militaire*, XXIX (1970), p. 733.

73. Gervase Markham, *The Souldiers Exercise* (London, 1639, facs. repr. Amsterdam, 1974), p. 39.

74. Hale (ed.), Smythe, *Certain Discourses*, p. 60.

75. Barret, *Theorike*, loc cit. Barwick, *Breefe Discourse*, sig. C1. Digges, *Paradoxes*, loc cit. Hale (ed.), Smythe, *Certain Discourses*, p. 60. Williams, *Briefe Discourse*, p. 41.

76. Hale (ed.), Smythe, *Certain Discourses*, loc. cit. Gervase Markham, *The*

Souldiers Exercise (London, 1639; facs. repr. Amsterdam, 1974), p. 38. The Italian Mora agreed that much armour was arquebus-proof. Domenico Mora, *Il soldato* (Venice, 1570), p. 143.

77. Gaspard de Saulx, Seigneur de Tavannes, *Memoires* (Paris, 1657), p. 176.

78. De la Barre Duparcq, *L'art militaire pendant les guerres de religion* (Paris, 1864), p. 35. Karl Stallwitz, *Die Schlacht bei Ceresole (14. April 1544)* (Diss., Berlin, 1911), p. 90, n7.

79. Francesco Balbi di Correggio, *The Siege of Malta 1565* (Copenhagen, 1961), p. 84.

80. La Barre Duparq, *L'art militaire*, p. 34.

81. *Contin. altera Chronici de Nangis (Grandes Chron. de France)*, p. 108, cited by Köhler, *Entwickelung*, II, p. 36.

82. Edward Davies, *The Art of War and Englands Traynings* (London, 1619, facs. repr. Amsterdam, 1968), p. 6.

83. Hale (ed.), Smythe, *Certain Discources*, p. 67.

84. Ibid.

85. Jacopo di Porcia, *The preceptes of Warre*, trans. P. Betham, STC 20116 (1544), sig. Evi^v. For a practical example: Ferdinand Lot, *Recherches sur les effectifs des armees françaises des Guerres d'Italie aux Guerres de Religion 1492–1562* (Paris, 1962), p. 118.

86. Barwick, *Breefe Discourse*, sigs. D3 and E2. Barret, *Theorike*, p. 3. Smythe, Harleian 135, fo. 17.

87. Lelio Brancaccio, *I carichi militari* (Antwerp, 1610), p. 9.

88. A number of writers, for instance, recommend keeping the touch-hole under the soldier's armpit in drizzle. William Garrard, *The Arte of Warre*, STC 11625 (1591), p. 82. J.R. Hale (ed.), *On a Tudor Parade Ground. The Captain's Handbook of Henry Barrett, Society for Renaissance Studies, Occasional Papers, No. 5* (London, 1978), p. 43. Thomas Audley: Bodleian Library, Rawlinson MS D363, f 2^v. Robert Hare: British Library, Cotton MS Julius F.v., f 7.

89. British Library, Harleian MS 135, f 103.

90. Heath, *Archery*, p. 216.

91. Mason, *Pro Aris et Focis*, p. 36.

92. David Chandler, *The Art of Warfare in the Age of Marlborough* (London, 1976), p. 76.

93. De la Barre Duparcq, *L'art militaire pendant les guerres de religion* (Paris, 1864), p. 35.

94. Monluc, *Commentaires*, pp. 433–9.

95. Niccolo Machiavelli, *The Arte of Warre*, tr. P. Whitehorne, STC 17164 (1560–2).

96. Piero Pieri (ed.), *N. Macchiavelli Dell'Arte Della Guerra* (Rome, n. d.), p. 71.

97. British Library, Harleian MS 309, f 6^v.

98. Barwick, *Breefe Discourse*, sig. A4^v.

99. Barret, *Theorike*, p. 3.

100. Ibid., p. 75.

101. C. Falls, *Mountjoy: Elizabethan General* (London, 1955), p. 179.

102. John Clarke, *Military Institutions of Vegetius in five bookes. Translated from the Original Latin with a Preface and Notes* (London, 1767), p. 160.

103. R. de Maulde la Clavière (ed.), Jean d'Auton, *Chroniques de Louis XII* (Paris, 1893), III, pp. 169–73. F.L. Taylor, *The Art of War in Italy, 1494–1529* (Cambridge, 1921), p. 110.

104. Paul Kopitsch, *Die Schlacht bei Bicocca 27. April 1522* (Diss., Berlin, 1909), pp. 59–67.

105. J.R. Hale, 'Armies, navies and the art of war' in G.R. Elton (ed.), *New Cambridge Modern History* (Cambridge, 1958), II, p. 498. K. Häbler, 'Die Schlacht bei Pavia', *Forschungen zur deutschen Geschichte* (Göttingen, 1885), XXV, pp. 522–3. M. l'Abbé Lambert (ed.), *Mémoires de Martin et Guillaume du Bellai-Langei* (Paris, 1753), I, pp. 404–5.

106. Ferdinand Lot, *Recherches sur les effectifs des armées françaises des Guerres d'Italie aux Guerres de Religion 1494–1562* (Paris, 1962), pp. 102–4. Another example has been analysed by Vicento Saletta, *La spedizione di Lautrec contro il Regno di Napoli* (Rome, n.d.), p. 33.

107. Ch. Marchand, *Le maréchal François de Scépeaux de Vieilleville et ses mémoires* (Paris, 1893), pp. 102–3.

108. Alaba Y Viamont, *El perfeto Capitan*, f 50. Londoño, *Discurso*, f 25. Hans Delbrück, *Die Strategie des Perikles erläutert durch die Strategie Friedrichs des Grossen* (Berlin, 1890), p. 68.

109. Karl Stallwitz, *Die Schlacht bei Ceresole (14. April 1544)* (Diss., Berlin, 1911), pp. 46 and 61.

110. C.W.C. Oman, *A History of the Art of War in the Sixteenth Century* (London, 1937), pp. 411–12.

111. Oman, *Sixteenth Century*, pp. 447–8 (Moncontour), 435–6 (Jarnac), 564–5 (Gembloux), 578–80 (Turnhout), 256–62 (St Quentin) and 275–8 (Gravelines). Lot, *Effectifs*, pp. 162–6(St Quentin) and 176 (Gravelines).

112. Oman, *Sixteenth Century*, pp. 484–8 (Arques), 553–4 (Heiligerlee), 555–6 (Jemmingen). British Library Royal MS 17 C xxii, f 50ff (Arques). Maximilien de Béthune, Duc de Sully, *Mémoires* (London, 1745), I, pp. 152–3.

113. Sir John Smythe, 'An aunswer to contrarie opynions militarie', British Library Harleian MS 135, f 17. Raymond de Beccarie de Pavie, Sieur de Four-quevaux, *Instructions for the Warres*, trans. Paul Ive [who incorrectly identified the author as G. du Bellay], STC 7264 (1589), p. 25.

114. Humphrey Barwick, *A Breefe Discourse, Concerning the Force and Effect of All Manuall Weapons of Fire*, STC 1542 (?1594), sigs. H2ᵛ and H3.

115. Charles Kohler, *Les Suisses dans les guerres d'Italie de 1506 à 1512* (Geneva, 1897, facs. repr. Geneva, 1978), p. 24.

116. Lelio Brancaccio, *I carichi militari* (Antwerp, 1610), p. 5.

117. Carl von Elgger, *Kriegswesen und Kriegskunst der schweizerischen Eidgenossen im 14., 15. und 16. Jahrhundert* (Lucerne, 1873), pp. 276–7.

118. L.O. Boynton, *The Elizabethan Militia 1558–1638* (London, 1967), pp. 13, 27 and 91–2. *Calendar of State Papers (Venetian)*, VI, part II, p. 1047.

119. G.A. Hayes-McCoy, 'Strategy and tactics in Irish warfare 1593–1601', *Irish Historical Studies*, II (1940–1), pp. 257 and 261–2.

120. Lynn, 'Tactical Evolution', p. 187.

121. Susane, *Infanterie*, I, pp. 54ff.

122. The fullest survey yet compiled of sixteenth-century European military

theory is the work of Max Jähns, *Geschichte der Kriegswissenschaften vornehmlich in Deutschland. Erste Abteilung. Altertum, Mittelalter, xv. und xvi. Jahrhundert* (Munich and Leipzig, 1889). In several fields it has yet to be superseded. Though Jähns is worthless as an authority on English military theory his knowledge of the German and Italian literature is impressive.

123. Juan Barrios, 'La enseñanza militar espanola en tiempo de los austria', *Revue Internationale d'Histoire Militaire*, LVI (1984), p. 98.

124. Eguiluz, *Milicia*, f 73.

125. Oman, *Sixteenth Century*, p. 62. Sir Roger Williams, *A Briefe Discourse of Warre*, STC 25732 (1590), p. 18.

126. Hale, *N.C.M.H.*, II, p. 498. Wiliams, *Briefe Discourse*, p. 18. Edward Davies, *The Art of War and Englands Traynings* (London, 1619, facs. repr. Amsterdam, 1968), p. 130.

127. Buttin, *La lance*, p. 120. Hale, *N.C.M.H.*, II, p. 496. Roberts, *Military Revolution*, p. 6. L.O. Boynton, 'English Military Organization 1558–1638' (Oxford D.Phil thesis, 1962), p. v. Francis Markham, *Five Decades of Epistles of Warre*, STC 17331 (London, 1622), p. 82. Markham, *Souldiers Exercise*, p. 41.

128. François de la Noue, *The Politicke and Militarie Discourses of the Lord de la Noue*, translated by E. A[ggas], STC 15215 (1587), p203.

129. Gaspard de Saulx, Seigneur de Tavannes, *Mémoires* (Paris, 1657), p. 175. See also François Buttin, 'La lance et l'arrêt de cuirasse', *Archaeologia*, XCIX (1965), p. 121.

130. La Noue, *Discourses*, p. 201.

131. La Noue, *Discourses*, p. 201.

132. Cl. Gaier, 'L'opinion des chefs de guerre français du XVIᵉ siècle sur les progrès de l'art militaire', *Revue Internationale d'Histoire Militaire*, XXIX (1970), p. 733. Oman, *Sixteenth Century*, pp. 502 and 581.

133. Monluc, *Commentaires*, p. 814.

134. Williams, *Briefe Discourse*, p. 38.

135. In 1573, the Venetian man-at-arms was required by regulation to use the pistol. J.R. Hale & M.E. Mallett, *The Military Organization of a Renaissance State, Venice c. 1400 to 1617* (Cambridge, 1984), p. 369.

136. La Noue, *Discourses*, p. 203: 'And untill they have learned more steadfastly to keepe order, and to be more carefull of their weapons, they will never worke the like effects with the pistoll as the Reistres.'

137. La Noue, *Discourses*, p. 201.

138. Sully, *Mémoires*, p. 164 (battle of Ivry, 1590).

139. La Barre Duparcq, *L'art militaire*, p. 32. Domenico Mora, *Il soldato* (Venice, 1570), p. 147.

140. Oman, *Sixteenth Century*, p. 406.

141. C.W.C. Oman, 'Walter Morgan's Illustrated Chronicle of the War in the Low Countries', *Archaeological Journal*, LXXXVII (1930), pp. 4–5.

142. M l'Abbé Lambert (ed.), *Mémoires de Martin et Guillaume du Bellai-Langei* (Paris, 1753), V, pp. 296–7. Monluc, *Commentaires*, p. 162.

143. La Noue, *Discourses*, p. 207.

144. Piero Pieri, *Il Rinascimento e la crisi militare italiana* (Turin, 1952), p. 225.

145. Köhler, *Entwickelung*, II, p. 376. Roger Sablonier, 'Rittertum, Adel und

Kriegswesen im Spätmittelalter' in J. Fleckenstein (ed.), *Das ritterliche Turnier im Mittelalter* (Göttingen, 1985), p. 538. Susane, *Infanterie*, I, pp. 65–6.

146. For the Battle of the Spurs see *Mémoires ... du Bellai-Langey*, I, pp. 28–9. *Letters & Papers. Henry VIII*, I, part II, pp. 980–1. For Courtras and Ivry see Sully, *Mémoires*, I, pp. 119–20 and 163–5. Oman, *Sixteenth Century*, deals in some detail with each of the engagements. His study concentrates almost exclusively on the pitched battle of which these are some of the most important exemplars.

147. Heinrich Harkensee, *Die Schlacht bei Marignano (13. u. 14. September 1515)* (Diss., Göttingen, 1909), p. 73. Häbler, *Pavia*, p. 520.

148. A. Essenwein, *Mittelalterliches Hausbuch. Bilderhandschrift des 15. Jahrhunderts mit vollständigem Text und facsimilierten Abbildungen* (Frankfurt a. M., 1887), illustration 55a.

149. Keller, *Genouillac*, pp. 14–17.

150. See British Library Add. MS 34,553, f 23, for but one example.

151. G. Amiaud-Bellavaud, *Un chef huguenot: le captaine Merle et les Guerres de Religion notamment en Auvergne, Gevaudan et Vivarrais* (Uzès, 1958), p. 153. Monluc, *Commentaires*, p. 437. Cook, *Morocco*, p. 10.

152. British Library Royal MS 17 C xxii, f 47^v (1598). William Garrard, *The Arte of Warre*, STC 11625 (London, 1591), p. 11. Carl von Elgger, *Kriegswesen und Kriegskunst der schweizerischen Eidgenossen im 14., 15. und 16. Jahrhundert* (Lucerne, 1873), p. 279.

153. Gervase Markham, *The Second Part of the Souldiers Grammar* (London, 1639, reprinted Amsterdam, 1974), p. 7.

154. Parrott, 'Strategy and Tactics', p. 7f conveniently summarises Geoffrey Parker's chief arguments against Roberts's tactical revolution.

155. Ibid., pp. 9–10.

156. Black, *A Military Revolution*, p. 10.

157. On the reception of Vegetius see J.A. Wisman, 'L'*Epitoma rei militaris* de Végèce et sa fortune au Moyen Age', *Le Moyen Age. Revue d'Histoire et Philologie*, LXXXV (1979), pp. 13–31.

158. Gerhard Oestreich, *Neostoicism and the early-modern state* (Cambridge, 1982), p. 5, n15.

159. Susane, *Infanterie*, I, pp. 74–81. Edgard Boutaric, *Institutions militaires de la France avant les armées permanentes* (Paris, 1863), pp. 337–8.

160. Piero Pieri (ed.), N. Machiavelli, *Dell'Arte Della Guerra* (Rome, n.d.), p. 166.

161. Londoño, *El discurso*, fos. 12^v–13^v, 14, 15 and 20–1.

162. H.J. Hewitt, *The Organization of War under Edward III 1338–62* (Manchester, 1966), p. 115, see also p. 100.

163. M.G.A. Vale, 'Sir John Fastolf's "report" of 1435: a new interpretation reconsidered', *Nottingham Medieval Studies*, XVIII (1973), p. 81.

164. Monluc, *Commentaires*, pp. 62–73.

165. Stallwitz, *Ceresole*, p. 126.

166. P. Contamine, 'The War Literature of the Late Middle Ages: The Treatises of Robert de Balsac and Beraud Stuart, Lord of Aubigny' in C.T. Allmand (ed.), *War, Literature and Politics in the Late Middle Ages* (Liverpool, 1976), p. 112.

167. Alaba Y Viamont, *El perfeto capitan*, f 41ᵛ. Londoño, *Discurso*, f 26. For William Cecil's use of maps see Jane Dawson, 'William Cecil and the British dimension of early Elizabethan foreign policy', *History*, LXXIV (1989), pp. 197–8.

168. Karl Saur, *Die Wehrverfassung in schwäbischen Städten des Mittelalters* (Diss., Freiburg i. Br., 1911), p. 20. F. Mone, 'Über das Kriegswesen im 13.–15. Jahrh. in Rheinpreussen, Elsass, Baden, Bayern, Schweiz', *Zeitschrift für die Geschichte des Oberrheins*, VI (1855), pp. 169–170.

169. Christopher Duffy, *Military Experience in the Age of Reason* (London, 1987), p. 14.

170. Ibid., p. 17.

171. Lot, *Effectifs*, pp. 16, 55, 71 and 161. Siegfried Fiedler, *Kriegswesen und Kriegführung im Zeitalter der Landsknechte* (Koblenz, 1985), pp. 3 and 27.

172. Parker, *Military Revolution*, p. 24.

173. Max Jähns, *Geschichte der Kriegswissenschaften vornehmlich in Deutschland. Dritte Abteilung. Das XVIII Jahrhundert seit dem Auftreten Friedrichs des Grossen* (Munich and Leipzig, 1891), p. 2861.

174. Roberts, *Revolution*, p. 28. See also p. 10.

175. Clements R. Markham, *"The Fighting Veres"* (London, 1888), pp. 53–6. Susane, *l'infanterie*, I, pp. 90, 94–6, 108, 120. Gilbert J. Millar, 'Henry VIII's colonels', *Journal of the Society for Army Historical Research*, LVII (1979), pp. 129–36. Monluc, *Commentaires*, pp. 813–14. Contrast Peter Blastenbrei, *Die Sforza und ihr Heer. Studien zur Struktur-, Wirtschafts- und Sozialgeschichte des Söldnerwesens in der italienischen Frührenaissance* (Heidelberg, 1987), p. 114.

176. Boynton, *Militia*, p. 257.

177. Parker, *Military Revolution*, pp. 7–16.

178. Ibid., pp. 10–14.

179. John Kenyon, *The Civil Wars of England* (London, 1988), p. 65. La Barre Duparq, *L'art militaire*, pp. 87–90.

180. Sir John Hale, 'The Early Development of the Bastion: An Italian Chronology c.1450 to c.1534' in Sir John Hale et al. (ed.), *Europe in the late Middle Ages* (London, 1965), p. 477.

181. J. Hook, 'Fortifications and the end of the Sienese state', *History*, LXII (1977), pp. 372–87 and Parker, *Military Revolution*, p. 12, n114.

182. Ibid. *The Triumphs of Nassau ...*, tr. W. Shute (London, 1613), p. 2.

183. Peter Whitehorne, *Certain Waies for the Orderyng of Souldiers in Battelray*, STC 17164 (1560–2), sig. Iiii.

184. Parker, *Military Revolution*, p. 10. David Eltis, 'Towns and Defence in Later Medieval Germany', *Nottingham Medieval Studies*, XXXIII (1989), p. 93. William H. MacNeill, *The Pursuit of Power. Technology, Armed Force and Society since AD 1000* (Chicago, 1982), pp. 87–8. Carlo M. Cipolla, *Guns and Sails in the Early Phase of European Expansion 1400–1700* (London, 1965), pp. 27–8.

185. David Chandler, *The Art of Warfare in the Age of Marlborough* (London, 1976), pp. 82–3.

186. C.W.C. Oman, *A History of the Art of War in the Middle Ages* (2 vols, London, 1924), II, p. 374. Hans Delbrück, *Geschichte der Kriegskunst im Rahmen der politischen Geschichte. 3. Teil: Das Mittelalter* (2nd revised ed., Berlin, 1923), p. 478.

187. John Childs, *Armies and warfare in Europe 1648–1789* (Manchester, 1982), p. 116. Chandler, *Marlborough*, p. 31.

188. A useful introduction is Michael Glover, *Warfare from Waterloo to Mons* (London, 1980), pp. 21–4.

189. Archibald P. Wavell, *The Palestine Campaign* (London, 1927) for further details on Allenby's use of cavalry.

190. Parker, *Military Revolution*, p. 16.

191. Hans Delbrück, *Geschichte der Kriegskunst im Rahmen der politischen Geschichte* (2nd revised ed., Berlin, 1923), III, p. 486.

192. Köhler, *Entwickelung*, II, p. 379.

193. L. Douet-d'Arcq, *La chronique de Monstrelet* (6 vols, Paris, 1857–62), IV, p. 159.

194. Ibid., III, pp. 105, 108 and 159. Czeppan, *Crecy*, p. 80.

195. Thus the French dismounted at Verneuil (1424). *Monstrelet*, IV, pp. 192–3.

196. Köhler, *Entwickelung*, II, p. 384.

197. William Garrard, *The Arte of Warre*, STC 11625 (London, 1591), pp. 111–15. Sir John Hale, 'On a Tudor Parade Ground. The Captain's Handbook of Henry Barrett 1562', *The Society for Renaissance Studies. Occasional Papers*, V (London, 1978), p. 13.

198. See for instance Tavannes, *Memoires*, p. 178.

199. Jovius cited by Kopitsch, *Bicocca*, p. 46.

200. Black, *A Military Revolution?*, p. 67.

201. Downing, *Military Revolution and Political Change, passim.*

202. Hale, *N.C.M.H.*, II, p. 481.

203. Pieri, *Il Rinascimento e la crisi militare italiana* (Turin, 1952), p. 234.

204. Wilhelm Erben, *Kriegsgeschichte des Mittelalters* (Munich and Berlin), p. iv.

CHAPTER 3

EQUIPMENT, TACTICS AND TRAINING

In the course of the sixteenth century war was revolutionised. Firearms, hitherto ineffective, underwent improvements and emerged as the dominant force on the battlefield and in siege warfare. Strategy, the structure of command, training and organisation underwent profound changes as a result. Infantry and cavalry had now to be trained in unfamiliar formations and techniques when the very idea of collective training was new. A host of other changes in fortification, tactics and armament combined with these developments to transform the conduct of war, laying a groundwork for future change for centuries to come. The idea that the sixteenth century marked a turning point in military history is also put forward by Wilhelm Erben, although without any thorough explanation.[1] Other scholars have also sensed this in their different ways, as we have seen in the preceding chapter. What follows is my own explanation of the significance of the sixteenth century as a period of military transition across Europe.

Improved firearms and artillery lay at the root of these developments. Hand-held firearms had been in use for a long time before the sixteenth century.[2] By the 1470s, large numbers were deployed by the leading armies of the day.[3] The Sforzas had been using them since the 1440s.[4] Their military use stretched back even earlier; for example, Colombus took a number to the New World.[5] But their effect was limited by design failings which were not satisfactorily cured until the early sixteenth century.

In the fifteenth century it was usual to rest firearms against the breastbone before firing. This restricted the amount of powder which could be used before injuring the firer. By the end of the century the shoulder was preferred, allowing greater charges of powder to be used, and thus greater armour penetration.[6] Then, enhanced by new tactics, these weapons came into their own. Cerignola (1503),

Bicocca (1522) and Pavia (1525) were won directly by firearms.[7] In other engagements, such as Agnadello (1509), they proved their worth, although the final outcome was determined by other factors. Agnadello was almost a classic victory of the arquebusier over the cavalryman. Louis XII's personal intervention and the timely arrival of fresh French infantry snatched victory from defeat, though it could not erase the memory of what firearms had done.[8] The governments of Europe were soon at pains to acquire more of these 'fiery weapons' now that their value was plain, ensuring them a firm place in war long into the future. By 1552 c.40 per cent of the French infantry was arquebus-armed. Londoño, in a work written in the 1560s, expected half the Spanish infantry to be equipped with firearms. By the latter part of the century a majority of the Spanish infantry were arquebusiers and musketeers.[9]

When men equipped with firearms achieved their first major successes in the early sixteenth century, Europe was still reeling from the impact of the Swiss. The Swiss had gradually changed their weapons and tactics in the course of the later Middle Ages, adopting the pike phalanx in the course of the fourteenth century.[10] With this formation they had won a series of devastating victories until Marignano (1515)[11] ended their reputation for invincibility. It was not a reputation of long standing. Defeats at Bregenz (1408), Arbedo (1422) and St Jacques (1444) separated the victories of the late fourteenth century.[12] However, further defeats, most notably at the hands of the Spanish arquebusiers at Bicocca (1522),[13] far from sealing their fate, merely led to fundamental changes in infantry organisation and the universal adoption of complex tactics based on the employment of both pikemen and arquebusiers. By the time of the battle of Ceresole (1544) it was already the case that all the infantry present, French, Spanish, German and Italian, used what Karl Stallwitz described as 'the Swiss method of fighting, even if adopted in modified form'.[14] Machiavelli found, a quarter of a century earlier, that all infantry imitated the Swiss, though at that time the use of firearms in conjunction with the pike-square was still in its infancy and sword-and-buckler men were more popular.[15] The Swiss and their rivals, the Landsknechts, and the pike phalanxes they both employed were to remain a factor on the battlefields of Europe for decades to come. However, from the second quarter of the century their pikemen no longer fought alone but in close association with arquebusiers, and later with musketeers. Why was this so? To arrive at an answer to this question it is first necessary to examine the peculiar problems of the early modern battlefield to let the inexorable logic that led to the universal combination of pikes and firearms become clear.

Cavalry was still a formidable force to be reckoned with on the sixteenth-century battlefield. The impressive list of sixteenth-century cavalry victories recounted in the previous chapter should suffice to convince even the most obdurate sceptic of the continuing threat posed by that arm. But the pike-square, when properly formed and well trained, could withstand repeated cavalry charges without breaking. A good example is the successful resistance put up by the German–Spanish square at Ceresole (1544) against Enghien's repeated cavalry charges.[16] Other cases could be listed *ad infinitum*. The Swiss pikemen, as the French theorist and soldier Raymond de Beccarie, Sieur de Fourquevaux remarked in mid-century, placed such trust in their order that they 'dare enterprise upon a whole world of horsemen, as they have made proof at Novare [1513] and at Marignan [1515]'. The battle of Marignano was spread over two days and was lost by the Swiss. Notwithstanding their eventual defeat the Swiss achieved some notable triumphs to which Fourquevaux here refers.[17]

The achievement of the Swiss was to use pikemen offensively, even in the face of horse. At Novara (1513), the Swiss could continue to advance even though attacked by cavalry in flank and rear, such was their discipline and control in formation.[18] This was a remarkable achievement, for, as the Spanish writer Diego de Alaba Y Viamont observed in 1590, horsemen were at their most effective precisely in such flank attacks.[19] François de la Noue, a Huguenot commander of considerable experience, took it for granted that, by keeping good order, a sixteenth-century infantry formation could retreat safely in the face of cavalry blocking its path.[20]

Why did pike tactics on the Swiss model prove so effective against cavalry, the most feared arm of the pre-sixteenth-century battlefield? A hedge of pike-heads or of sharpened stakes, as used by the English and Burgundians in the fifteenth century,[21] deterred a horse in a way that shorter weapons could not achieve. Swiss pikes were 18 feet long; English sixteenth-century pikes 12–18 feet long.[22] As a result, the pike-heads of the fifth rank[23] would protrude beyond the heads of the front rank of the square. When the pike-heads of the leading men and the other three ranks in betweeen are also taken into account, a horseman faced an impenetrable hedge of steel, a 'brazen wall'.[24] 'A squadron of pikes thus couched and handled by resolute and honest men, I cannot see how any troupe of horse dare venture upon them,' confessed Robert Barret at the end of the century.[25] The individual horses would, in the view of Machiavelli, whose military treatise was published in English translation in 1560–2, refuse to encounter the pikes just as they would refuse to be ridden into a stone wall.[26] Thomas Styward agreed: 'for that a horse is a beast and knoweth the perils, and with an ill will, will enter upon the pike'.[27] In Robert Hare's mid-century view the horse had, in any case, no option, as the pike-heads were too dense to let it through.[28]

Any country's foot equipped and trained on the Swiss pattern could act in the same fashion. With good order a resolute stand of pikes had little to fear from cavalry. Don Bernardino de Mendoza, himself a cavalryman of distinction, acknowledged this: 'albeit that in olde time the cavallerie was of more estimation for their furie and redines then the infanterie, experience commeth to discover the contrarie and to put the ground of warr in the squadrons of fanterie, which serve with pikes'.[29] Mendoza's superb leadership of a body of Spanish cavalry at Mook (1574) contributed materially to the Spanish victory over the Dutch. He knew what he was talking about.[30]

This was not to say that any infantry formed up in square could resist cavalry with ease. Arquebusiers without the comfort of a thick, ordered hedge of pikes were unable to halt the onrush of horsemen. If tightly ordered pikemen could fend off cavalry, even well-disciplined arquebusiers could not. Sir John Smythe considered that 1,000 lightly armed cavalrymen 'will in the fields overthrowe and breake above 3,000 or 4,000 harquebuziers or mosquetiers, in case they have no succour of other weapons nor ground of advantage'.[31]

The qualification is important. Though Smythe's contemporaries quite agreed that cavalry would sweep many times their number of unprotected shot off a flat plain, they expected great things of the same arquebusiers with the benefit of some protection, whether a trench or a supporting stand of pikes. As Matthew Sutcliffe put it in 1593:

> the charge of horsemen against shot and targetters [men carrying swords and shields] is mortall, if they be not either garded with pikes, or have the vantage of ditches, or hedges, or woods, where they cannot reach them. In which case the shot gauleth the horse if they come within the levell of the piece.[32]

Robert Barret rammed home the same message five years later, warning that:

> any troupe of shot, though never so brave and expert, being in open field, having no stand of pikes, or such other weapon, nor hedge, ditch, trench or rampier, to relieve and succour them, could not long endure the force of horse, especially Launciers.[33]

Without the advantage of terrain or the protection of a stand of pikes, musketeers would be swept away by cavalry. At Riberac (1568) the Huguenots found that a tightly formed 'bataillon de parade' of arquebusiers was defenceless against cavalry. For all its exemplary order it was simply ridden down.[34] Yet, with the protection of some natural or man-made obstacle, men equipped with firearms could make a stand against horsemen without the need for pikes, as the Spanish arquebusiers did at Cerignola (1503).[35]

Faced with the steady fire of sheltered shot, the cavalry commander found the roles reversed. It was now the cavalryman who stood in mortal danger. 'It is not fit to set the squadron of cavallerie upon any groound subiect to be battered, nor to be hurt with the furie of the enemies harquebuserie or musketrie,' Mendoza warned. In such a position the squadron must either exit the line of fire, demoralising the troops, or itself attack. Either course was perilous. To stay and do neither would risk steady destruction: it was better to stay well clear of protected shot and artillery in the first place.[36] Cavalry could only develop to their full potential in the open field.

Battlefields intersected with ditches and other obstacles were a nightmare for the cavalry commander, as was demonstrated on more than one occasion.[37] The fifteenth century is full of such expedients. The Hussites used wagons in lieu of a natural obstacle to enable their handgunners and crossbowmen to face the onrush of German cavalrymen, setting a European fashion.[38] The English and their Burgundian allies used a hedge of planted stakes to deter the French from attacking home on horseback.[39]

The disadvantage of all such measures was their defensiveness. It was possible to receive charging horsemen after careful preparation by these methods, but not to attack them. The idea that the Hussite waggon columns could also be used offensively is rightly ridiculed by Dr Wulf, one of Hans Delbrück's students.[40] However, the Swiss and those trained in a similar fashion were quite capable of advancing forcefully on a body of horse,[41] a phenomenon which Piero Pieri has argued was quite new on the European battlefield.[42] In fact, pikemen had intermittently achieved successes against cavalry in the Middle Ages, Courtrai (1302) and Bannockburn (1314) being notable examples. At Courtrai, the Flemish pikes advanced to attack the French cavalry.[43] However, these northern pikemen never achieved the repeated success of the Swiss and consequently failed to leave a lasting mark on the general picture of European military development. The Flemings, who had made something of a tradition of fighting with the pike, suffered repeated defeats at the hands of cavalry-dominated armies at Cassel (1328), Rosebeke (1382), Othée (1408), Gavre (1453) and Brusthem (1468).[44] At Courtrai (1302) their pikemen were able to take advantage of difficult terrain to defeat their mounted opponents.[45] The outcome at Bannockburn (1314) was similarly influenced by the nature of the ground. The Swiss ability to prevail without a terrain advantage was one of the chief reasons for their more lasting success.

The widely copied Swiss pike tactics gave infantry the ability to face cavalry in the open field with confidence. A clear indication of this was the spread of first horse armour and then cavalry pistols in the sixteenth century, as the mounted arm desperately struggled to find ways of defeating the pike-square.[46] Yet pike-armed infantry were powerless against firearms skilfully deployed. Sixteenth-century firearms were fairly inaccurate weapons; the sporting rifle was the only accurate gun at this time.[47] For the remainder it might be said, as Colonel Hanger observed in 1814 of the English infantry musket, that 'a soldier must be very unfortunate indeed who shall be wounded by a common musket at 150 yards provided his antagonist aims at him'.[48] When fired at men in open order at a distance, as was the case in most sixteenth-century skirmishes, they did little damage. Forquevaux noted how 'in a skirmish wherein tenne thousand Harquebussados are shot, there dieth not so much as one man'.[49] At Ceresole (1544), so little damage was done by the skirmishers of both sides when they met that their clash lasted from daybreak to 11 a.m. without decisive result.[50] However, when fired into the seething human mass of a pike-square at close range, their leaden projectiles could not fail to do terrible damage, as the Swiss found to their cost at Bicocca (1522) and Pavia (1525).[51]

But the true effect of firearms and artillery did not lie simply in the men they killed, maimed and injured. It was also psychological. Monluc, with decades of experience on Europe's battlefields behind him, considered that artillery 'is what causes more shock and very often more fear than harm'. The impact of a single cannon-ball, however, often killed twelve to twenty-five men in a densely packed formation. At Ravenna (1512) one shot allegedly disposed of thirty men-at-arms.[52]

The sound of a mass discharge of these weapons of fire was unnerving.[53] Werner Schodeler struggled in his contemporary chronicle to find the words to express the psychological shock at Marignano (1515) when the French fired on the advancing Swiss with artillery and hand-held guns:

> thus the enemy engaged and let off all their guns of all calibres and all their hand-held firearms. That was such a thing that one might have thought that the skies had opened with every fury and that heaven and earth were breaking apart under the enemy fire.[54]

The Spanish artillerist Collado confirmed the terror of Schodeler's picture of what it was like to be under fire: 'every moment you felt cannon balls and arquebus shot whistling past your ears and every hour you saw the ground sown with the minute pieces of the shattered bodies of your companions.'[55]

It was not unheard of for men to break and run after being fired on rather than approach to push of pike. The English soldier and writer, Robert Barret, commented that:

> it is rarely seene in our dayes that men come to hand-blowes, as in old time they did: For now in this age, the shot so employeth and busieth the field (being well backed with a resolute stand of pikes) that the most valiantest and skilfullest therein do commonlie import the victorie ... before men come to hand-blowes.[56]

He exaggerated. However, it was undeniably true that a mixed force of pikes and shot had the edge over infantry armed only with pikes. This was especially true when, as at Cerignola (1503) and Bicocca (1522), the pikemen could be held up by an obstacle such as a trench and thereby left exposed to fire without the possibility of an effective reply. Pikemen were terribly vulnerable once they had lost their order and gaps appeared in the serried rows of pikeheads.

The psychological effects of artillery and arquebus fire helped to break up the order of a pike-square even faster than mere casualties alone would have done. The effect of shot and artillery in unhinging formations could already be seen in some fifteenth-century engagements.[57] At Gavre (1453), 'as soon the said artillery had settled and began to fire, the men of Ghent opened their ranks and disjointed their order'.[58] By the sixteenth century it was such a common problem that the Swiss specifically provided the death penalty for men who left order under fire.[59]

If the mounted threat rendered shot helpless without protecting pikes or an advantage of ground, the pikemen were themselves terribly vulnerable to enemy shot without their own to protect them. The psychological effect of firearms was so great that they could decide the issue if unchecked by their own kind, 'for many times it hath beene seene that battailes have beene gotten by shotte onely, without push of Pyke, or stroke of weapons'.[60] The pikemen, encumbered by their armour, the massive pikes they bore and the dictates of their closely ordered formation, could never close with their oppressors, who buzzed like flies around them.

Were they to manage to close, there was no doubt in the minds of contemporaries that pikemen could defeat arquebusiers and musketeers no matter what the odds.[61] But they could not usually hope to close the more mobile shot. The only real security they could enjoy against harassment by enemy shot was to possess their own. Robert Barret concluded, naturally enough, that:

> As the armed pike is the strength of the battell, so without question, is the shot the furie of the field: but the one without the other is weakend the better halfe of their strength. Therefore of necessitie (according to the course of the warres in these dayes) the one is to be coupled and matched with the other in such convenient proportion, that the advantage of the one may helpe the disadvantage of the other.[62]

Combined pike and shot tactics were an inescapable consequence of the coming of age of firearms in the sixteenth century. Though firearms were devastating in their effect on horse and foot alike, they needed the support of pikemen to avoid being swept away by enemy cavalry. If the enemy lacked cavalry it was safe to reduce the number of pikemen and maximise the proportion of arquebusiers and musketeers.[63]

Thus, while pikemen could not easily deal with concentrations of artillery and arquebusiers without shot of their own, the arquebusiers were helpless in the face of cavalry without protective terrain or the support of a stand of pikes. Each needed the other. The shot would be ridden down in open ground without the protection of the pikes, while the pikes without their own shot to protect them would be helpless in the face of the enemies' arquebusiers, as the Imperial pikemen found at Pavia (1525).[64] This was the new orthodoxy, and it became more and more deeply entrenched as the military revolution took hold. Pikes and shot could be mixed on every level from the company to the army. Most writers followed Thomas Audley and Robert Barret in recommending that each company carry its just proportion of each weapon type, the distribution sanctioned by practice.[65] The English theorists Leonard and Thomas Digges were unusual in their view that companies should contain only a single weapon type. They recommended this, however, not to enable each weapon type to fight separately but to facilitate their combination in large formations several companies strong.[66]

This necessary cooperation between pikemen and shot could take many forms. Men with arquebuses could be inserted into the pike-square itself to fire behind the shelter of their comrades' pike-heads as was done to some effect at Ceresole (1544). Monluc thought he was the first to think of putting 'a rank of arquebusiers in between the first and second rank [of pikemen] to kill the captains in the first rank'. In fact the enemy at Ceresole had hit on the same idea and, when the rival pike-squares approached, 'there was a great killing; not a single shot failed to tell'. Leonhart Fronsperger recommends exactly the same proceeding in his military treatise written in 1565: 'and a rank of the best arquebusiers is introduced after the first or foremost rank of long weapons'.[67]

Alternatively, groups of arquebusiers could be deployed on the flanks of the pike-square, able to fire before contact, but also free to run to the rear if threatened. Thomas and Leonard Digges likened the pikes in this combination to the walls of a town and the shot to the flanking bastions whose fire would prevent the enemy approaching the walls:[68] an arrangement described in European theorists of all nations in the latter half of the century.[69]

Thus, though some might extol the 'puissant pike'[70] more than the arquebus or musket or vice versa,[71] all came to recognise that it was only in the careful combination of the two that victory was to be obtained. A new system of infantry tactics had arisen. The new tactics put a premium on training which was also quite new. In the past it had been enough to train men individually in the use of their weapons without practising *en masse*. The complex pike and matchlock tactics of the sixteenth century required rigorous training both of the men in the use of their weapons[72] and of the body of pikemen and their supporting arquebusiers and musketeers as a coordinated group.

Individual training with pike and sword was considered worthwhile in the late Middle Ages, as was practice at the butts. The tournament offered an excellent opportunity for the individual to practise his skills. In 1412 Christine de Pisan felt that jousts and tourneys should be proclaimed twice or thrice a year to keep France at a high pitch of military preparedness.[73] The late medieval commander and his subordinates were required to demonstrate their worth by fighting as individuals, rather than by mastering large bodies of theoretical knowledge in order to train and organise others. Waurin, a highly experienced man of war, comments that both Bedford and the Earl of Salisbury fought as individuals at the battle of Verneuil (1424), setting an example to their men by their physical prowess.[74]

In the sixteenth century these skills were no longer enough. The new infantry tactics required trained troops in order to be effective. The most striking aspect of the literature generated by the military revolution in sixteenth-century England was its emphasis on the achievement of classical standards of order, discipline and training. Pikemen needed all these qualities if their large and cumbersome formations were not to disintegrate into formless masses of confused humanity.

An emphasis on training, whether or not inspired by Roman models, was an inescapable consequence of the complex pike-and-shot tactics of the century. Untrained troops were a liability. Henry Barrett found pike-training invaluable.[75] It was, as Sir John Smythe observed, easier to organise bows and bills for battle than to use modern weapons, pikes and firearms effectively.[76] Pikemen needed careful training:[77] 'They must oftentimes practise to traile, push, warde, couch, crosse … as for the necessitie of the skirmish or battaile apperaineth,' Thomas Styward observed.[78]

The organization and training of pikemen posed particular problems. Whereas arquebusiers and musketeers were expected to operate loosely in small groups of under a hundred men,[79] pike-squares could number several thousand in the sixteenth century. At Fornovo (1495), the Swiss packed 3,000 men into a 60–metre square.[80] By 1522 they were employing 7,500-man squares, each measuring 75 × 100 men for the attack on the Imperialist lines at Bicocca.[81] Nor were these 75–rank-deep formations extraordinary. Writers played with pike-squares of far greater dimensions. Ten thousand men was the highest number mentioned by the more cautious theorists,[82] although some, like the Italian Mora, entertained the idea of vast bodies of 16,000 men or more.[83] That there should be 2,000–7,000 men in a single pike-square was quite normal.[84] Indeed, some writers strongly counselled against the use of pike formations of fewer than 3,000 men in battle.[85]

The 35-man-deep Spanish squares at Dreux (1562) were, if anything, on the small side by contemporary standards.[86] As the Spanish veteran Francisco de Valdes pointed out, it was quite normal for three to four regiments to join up to create a single square.[87] These vast squares gave greater security against cavalry apart from the obvious psychological and material advantage of being in the larger formation. But they also required careful training and posed new problems of organization and control.

Among the duties of command now came the organization and training of pikemen and shot, together with the mastery of an ever-growing literature on their use, not to mention the growing technicalities of siege warfare. Group training, particularly of the pikemen, placed heavy demands. But it could not be shirked, for the resulting order and discipline, as the Italian military theorist Ascanio Centorio degli Hortensii observed in 1568, was more important than bravery[88] – or, indeed, numbers. As Captain Francesco Ferretti put it eight years later:

> You must always remember that it is not the superiority in number of soldiers over the enemy that promises certain victory, but if there is good order in dispositions and ready obedience is observed and true understanding of discipline in executing [it] ...[89]

Works of theory published in England in the course of the century rammed home the same message. Captain Barnaby Rich insisted in 1574 that: 'Captaynes should use great diligence in ye trayning of their men, considering that an Army is not to be chosen for the multitude, or bicause in ye same be hardy [brave] men, but bicause they be wel trained and in their orders wel apointed'.[90]

Good order was not an ideal. It was a cruel necessity for the enormous pike-squares of the century. 'For if discipline and entertainment faile, the more men there be, the more is the disorder and confusion,' François de la Noue observed.[91] The moment the leading pikes shuddered apart in confusion, creating gaps for the enemy to exploit, the pike-square was vulnerable. As Robert Barret noted, 'it doth much import that the Front be gaillard and strong: for the front once broken, the battell stands in hazard'.[92] Thomas Digges's countrymen fell so far short of the necessary discipline that 'a thousand horse is able to defeat five times as many such footmen'.[93]

Sixteenth-century pike-squares were made up of several layers. In the exact centre of the pike-square stood the ensign. Around him men with halberds formed an inner square, protecting him against attack from all four directions. Outside this central box of halberdiers stood the pikemen, who lacked defensive armour, then came a layer of pikemen with corslets of armour plate and finally the outer coating of muskets and arquebusiers, whose job it was to shelter under the pikes of their companions ready to discharge when the time came.[94] The unarmoured pikemen were called *picche secche* in Italian military parlance. Their job in battle was to push on the backs of the *picche armate* in front and push forwards into their places if they were killed. If there was a shortage of corslets *picche armate* were paced only on the front and rear of the pike-square and not on the sides.[95] To form such a complex body out of a multiplicity of individual companies in line of march, each with a share of the several types of men, was a difficult task not lightly undertaken. It required a good understanding of mathematics and systematic records. Knowledge of multiplication and division and square roots were essential. Yet these skills were far from widespread in early modern Europe. This is an as yet little-charted field. Sir Keith Thomas has made an initial survey, but much more research would be needed to give even a remotely clear picture.[96]

As a result, a new military hierarchy from the sergeant-major of an army to the company corporal emerged across Western Europe.[97] Their purpose was to tackle these new technical aspects of war while leaving the more traditional tasks of command to the existing military hierarchy, from the general to the company lieutenant. The corporal, the sergeant, the sergeant-major, the sergeant-major-general, the corporal-of-the-field and the colonel were all ranks brought to England by the military revolution of the sixteenth century.[98] On the continent their hierarchical counterparts, from the *maestro de campo* to the *cabo de esquadra,* came of age with the revolution.[99]

The sergeant-major was the coping-stone of the new hierarchy. On his talent – or lack of it – depended the fate of entire formations. When the Spanish veteran de Valdes compiled his *El Espejo* in the 1560s at Alva's request and thereby furnished his comrades with one of the most important books of the century on war, he had effectively written a treatise on the office of the sergeant-major.[100] It was the sergeant-major's task to create order in action.

The sergeant-major's rank was a novelty born of the military revolution. Francisco de Valdes commented that it was:

> so called, because in every regiment (which is as much as a Romane legion) there is a Sergeant who is superintendent and Heade over all the other Sergeants that are in his regiment: and as every Sergeant in ech company taketh the ... order of his Captaine or lieutenant, so the Sergeant Maior receaveth it of the Captaine Generall, or Coronell, or master of the camp, and afterwards from him it passeth to the other Sergeantes of the same regiment.[101]

It was also for him to 'appoint unto everie Capteine their severall places within everie battaile', as Sir Robert Constable observed in 1576.[102] In this, as in all his other dealings with captains, he was to be obeyed, as Gerrat Barry emphasised to his pre-Civil War readership.[103]

However, it was a matter of concern to contemporaries that the Romans, whom they in many senses admired as a model, had made no use of sergeant-majors. Robert Barret solved the problem by claiming that the Roman *tesserarios*, used to 'ensigne and teach their people of warre the use and managing of their armes at all idle and vacant times', corresponded to the sergeant-majors of the sixteenth century.[104] But the sixteenth-century sergeant-major was responsible for his men not merely during training, but in action as well. The English writers Thomas and Leonard Digges resolved the problem by pointing out that: 'everie [Roman] Colonell for his owne bandes was a Serieant major, and for the ordering of the whole, in the day of Battaile, the Generall himself discharged it'[105]

There could be no question of the average sixteenth-century colonel or general performing such a task, as he would lack knowledge of the techniques involved. Francisco de Valdes, a *maestro de campo* under Alva, admired the Romans and Spartans for their ability to dispense with specialised sergeant-majors:

> the Captaine Generall and Chiefe head of the Armies, understanding and perceiving of howe great moment and importance the good order and perfection of the Squadron or Battaile is, in which consisteth all the force of the whole Armie, they would trust no particular men with this office, but themselves disposed theyr Armies.[106]

Captain John Shute despaired of the ability of his countrymen to follow the Romans in this respect, while on the continent innumerable captains existed who were quite 'able to be colonells,

Sergeant generall of the armie' and so on.[107] His optimism as far as the continent was concerned exceeded that of Valdes, who was perhaps in a better position to know. Certainly, none of the major European powers felt able to dispense with the services of a specialist hierarchy ranging from the sergeant-major of an army to the sergeant of its smallest company in order to meet the demands of the changed tactics of the revolution. These ranks persisted well beyond the sixteenth century as later generations found need of the same supports to solve not dissimilar problems.

The sergeant-major was ultimately responsible for the discipline and order of the army, and in particular of its pike-squares. To achieve his tasks he demanded and received the unconditional obedience of the captains and colonels of the army. If, Thomas Styward noted, 'that be denied him, no diligence that he can use may availe him any iot to give any hope of good successe in his great office'.[108] In the end only he was held to account, as de Valdes wryly observed: 'I have alwaies seene that not only the common judgement of all men, but also the Captains and Generals do use to praise or blame the Sergeantes Maior, because they leade their Regments in good or ill order.'[109]

But what were the particular skills that the sergeant-major had which most sixteenth-century captains so conspicuously lacked? In the view of the Isle of Wight militia captain, Sir George Carey, a mere sergeant needed to be 'of some skill in Arithmeticke', and able to read and write.[110] The demands on a sergeant-major were similar, but of a higher order. He needed to possess full records of the composition of the force under his command, usually obtained by working over submissions from lower officials of the strengths of their subordinate commands.[111] Using his well-developed mathematical skills,[112] the sergeant-major worked out the distribution of the different types of infantrymen within his chosen formation, the number of men per rank and file of each layer and a myriad other details.

William Garrard, with fourteen years' service in Spanish armies behind him, felt that in order to succeed, the sergeant-major needed to 'ioyne practise with Theorike, which is reading, specially in Algorisme, Algebra and the platformes of battailes'.[113] Besides knowledge of algebra and arithmetic, 'which are set out by M. Digges in his *Stratioticos*', Garrard expected his ideal sergeant-major to memorise the details, which would enable him to form any battle with rapidity. The list was endless: 'how manie maniples or sleeves everie battaile may be resolved into, how many pikes in the front, back and flanckes, how many rankes of Halberds to gard the Ensigne ....' [114]

To help him ready reckoners, tables and solutions to standard problems were offered by the theorists themselves, together with detailed diagrams illustrating finished formations on which the place of every single individual was clearly marked by letters denoting their weapon type. A capital 'A' denoted an 'Ansaigne' [ensign], a small 'a' an archer, 'h' an 'harquebusier', and so forth. [115] The Italian theorist Giovanni Mattheo Cigogna recommended in 1583 that the tabular aids available in printed form should be memorised for additional convenience. [116] The most heavily used military tables in sixteenth-century Europe were those of Girolamo Cataneo, which became available to English readers from 1574, less than a decade after their first Italian edition. [117] However, Cataneo's were by no means the only ones to be had. In fact, such tables existed in embarrassing profusion, with each major theorist offering his own.

In the middle third of the century Thomas Audley, Robert Hare and Henry Barrett all offered tables in their manuscript treatises to aid in drawing up pike-squares. [118] They were soon followed by a string of printed theories as the century drew to a close, ranging from those of Thomas Styward and Barnaby Rich in the 1580s to Robert Barret's in 1598. [119] The main function of these tables was to help calculate the number of men per side of a pike-square or any of the commoner formations in use. With this information at his fingertips, it was possible for a sixteenth-century sergeant-major to perform rapidly a number of simple drills and create a square or rectangle suitable for deployment in the field or on the march.

Quick-reckoning aids of this kind saved a certain amount of tedious calculation and would expedite operations on the training ground and in the field. Some tables were very simple and pre-supposed a high degree of knowledge in the user, while others came complete with paragraphs of explanation to enable the reader to interpret them correctly. [120] But their basic function was the same. From his knowledge of the dimensions of a formation in men per side it was relatively easy using a rule of thumb of 3 feet per man in rank and 7 feet per man in file to calculate the space it would occupy on the ground. [121] An experienced sergeant-major, however, would be able to judge that with his eye from memory, without having to do the calculations and then laboriously pace out the space available. [122]

Diagrams had the advantage over tables in that they more easily stuck in the memory.[123] They also made it easier to visualise the end result. The system of identifying men by the first letter of the weapon they carried provided a remarkably clear way of presenting information. Its origins were pre-sixteenth century.[124] To name a few English writers, the Digges, Thomas Styward, Giles Clayton, William Garrard and Robert Barret all made prolific use of diagrams. In this way their manuals presented the European revolution in tactics and organization in easily accesible form.

The purpose of these manuals was simple: to make order possible in the field. If it could not be achieved the consequences were dire. A disordered pike-square or cavalry squadron was already lost. Girolamo Cataneo, whose *Tavole brevissime* (Brescia, 1567) was translated into English in 1574, echoed universal opinion when he commented that disordered troops can 'with a lesse number of people [be] assaulted, put out of order and overthrowen'.[125] The most likely occasion for such a disaster was on the march when there was a natural tendency for the men to string out and lose formation unless the sergeant-major kept them under constant control.[126] If the sergeant-major was incompetent it did not take the strains of a march to dissolve his troops into a confused, milling mass. Alva's chief sergeant-major during the invasion of Portugal created complete chaos when he tried to create a new battle formation out of the assembled tercios. The task went beyond his ability.[127] In battle, a disordered pike-square would be swept away by cavalry and easily dispatched by well-ordered pikemen. Arques (1589) provides an amusing example of the consequences of order and disorder to an infantry formation, a body of Landsknechts. Other occasions can be multiplied *ad infinitum*; for instance, the unfortunate case of the disordered Swiss at Bicocca (1522).[128]

Given the importance of the sergeant-major to the fresh tactical world of the sixteenth century, the prestige of his rank will come as no surprise. As we have seen, he was obeyed by captains and, in the case of the sergeant-major of an army, by colonels.[129] Brantôme cites with approval the case of a French sergeant-major, La Burthe, who struck a noble dead for arguing with him.[130] Unlike the late medieval commanders, the sergeant-major did not seek to fight in person.[131] His job was solely to see that order was kept, in which function he more closely resembled Roman officers than the leaders of chivalry. As Monluc pointed out, in his myriad battles Caesar rarely fought physically himself.[132]

The idea of the importance of order was not unique to Antiquity and the sixteenth century; it enjoyed intermittent life throughout the Middle Ages and especially at those moments when infantry were used as the heart of an order of battle. In the later Middle Ages the English, the Swiss and the Hussites[133] depended in their different ways on order as an element in their success. It should also be realised that discipline – in the looser sense of not leaving a force to plunder without permission – was a commonplace in medieval military ordinances.[134] As Sir Clement Edmunds rightly remarked in 1600, such provisions had existed since the 'verie infancie of warres'.[135] However, none of these forces had to train *en masse* to be able to handle their peculiar problems of order. The Swiss and Charles the Bold of Burgundy[136] took the first steps towards training in the fifteenth century, but for all their importance their achievements had their limitations. Their medieval forces never developed the full sophistication of the parallel hierarchy of command of camp-masters, sergeant-majors, sergeants, corporals and file-leaders subsequently developed by sixteenth-century armies, including their own. Nor did they possess the complicated mathematical tables later used to draw up men in formation. Theirs was a more primitive discipline. However, it should not be forgotten that it was the Swiss and the success of their simple pike tactics which gave much of the impetus to the changes that swept Europe.[137] Though Louis XI briefly tried to have troops trained on the Swiss model, full-scale European imitation of Swiss methods was a sixteenth-century phenomenon. The Swiss use of drums to control pikemen on the move was copied across Europe. The Elizabethan William Garrard wrote with pardonable exaggeration that it was 'ye Switzers who first invented drums'.[138] In fact, precedents for the use of drums stetched back many centuries.[139] Yet for all its superiority, Swiss influence was only slowly extended. The first battle between two armies in which both used Swiss-style pike tactics did not occur until 1499.

Other fifteenth-century armies afforded an even greater contrast with what was to come. Theirs was a primitive discipline indeed. In 1791, an English visitor to a Moghul camp found that:

> the traces of order, discipline and science are so faint as to be scarcely discernible, except in the outward appearance of the men, the management of their horses, and their dexterity in the use of the spear and sabre, which individually gives a martial air.[140]

Much the same could be said of most late medieval armies.

In the sixteenth century collective training became as important as individual prowess, and the most disciplined had a decisive edge. When two bodies of pikes clashed, greater cohesion and self-confidence won the day. Monluc found at Ceresole (1544) that 'as our pike-square continued to push, the enemy gave way and turned'. Even in the better-ordered phalanx, Monluc found it difficult maintaining his balance and sometimes sank on his knees. Still, he recovered on each occasion.[141] Scattered or disordered individuals had little chance against a fast-moving, tightly packed formation. Order told every time.

Order was also the keynote of the military literature which accompanied the military revolution of the sixteenth century. It also lay at the heart of Roman military doctrine as exemplified by the treatise of Vegetius on war. Therefore, it may come as no surprise that the young Alva learnt Vegetius off by heart by the age of thirteen in an effort to master his future profession.[142] Roman calls for intense training and strict, almost obsessive maintenance of order spoke directly to the modernisers. They had long extracted lip-service from medieval writers, but scarcely altered their habits of indiscipline or lack of training.[143]

As Alva's disciple Francisco de Valdes observed: 'that Armie which is best ordered, though it be least in number of men, shall alwaies (according to reason) become victorious'. For 'Iulius Caesar being Proconsull, subdued unto the Empire of Rome many and rude barbarous Nations ... And I praie what made him victorious, but the good order and discipline he used?' In the same way 'in our daies Hernando Cortes ... onely by the good order he used he did subdue the whole kingdom of Mexico'. He also gives the example of the defeat of Louis of Nassau's force in Friesland by Alva's more disciplined but vastly smaller army.[144] Discipline was decisive.

In the medieval manuscript tradition that preceded the rebirth of military theory in the sixteenth century, Vegetius and other classical writers were copied and sometimes translated, but by scribes who had never held command in war.[145] Their efforts served to keep a faint memory of Roman and Greek military methods alive in the minds of contemporaries, but no more. The military theory of the later Middle Ages consisted almost entirely of translations of classical writers undertaken by scholars rather than military men. There were exceptions, such as the work of Philip of Seldeneck[146] and the late medieval military engineers. Valturius's mid-fifteenth-century work is particularly impressive, describing all manner of devices from battering rams to calthrops. [147] However, it remains a fact that what was written on war before 1500 did not compare, either in volume or in quality, with what was to follow. [148]

The new literature treated military problems in a practical way and was written almost entirely by experienced soldiers. It was the credo of the new age that reading was a key to success in war as in other spheres of life. As the early modern editor of von Schwendi's military treatise argued: 'At least you learn so much ... through application in reading that you are not easily surprised by something that happens; and thus nothing, be it so new or strange, that happens, can occur of which you have not read something almost the same.' [149] The ideal sixteenth-century commander had, like Piero Strozzi, full mastery of the wars of the ancients and was conversant with the art of fortification and a good mathematician to boot. [150] Printed histories of past and present wars complemented military theorists both ancient and modern as the guides of the mid-sixteenth-century warrior. He was therefore as curious about the Turkish methods of war as he was about those of his own forbears. Pietro Bizari's history of the Turkish wars was as eagerly read by Elizabethans as by the Italian audience it was originally intended for. [151] The Turkish achievement of a discipline that in some respects rivalled the Romans helped to stimulate the century's curiosity. [152]

The extraordinary wealth of military matter published in the course of the century did more than just support interest in the past and present nature of war. It spread new tactical methods, and through tables and visual aids helped commanders to enact them on the field. [153] Giles Clayton, for instance, in a work he published in 1591, provided lavish information with which to construct standard formations with varying numbers of men. A typical section is the following. It furnishes the number of men who will form the sides of a bastard pike-square and a broad pike-square if the force to be put into formation numbers 500:

> 500. The square roote is 22. 16 unplaced;
> bastard square, 23 in front, 21 in flanke,
> 17 unplaced; broad square, 31 in front,
> 16 in flanke, 4 unplaced ... [154]

The most commonly used tables of this kind in Europe were Girolamo Cataneo's *Tavole brevissime* (Brescia, 1567), which were used alike by Elizabethans and Spaniards, not to mention their intended audience. The English translation went through two editions: STC

4790 (1574) and 4791 (1588). As Eguiluz pointed out in his work of 1595, de Valdes's excellent treatise relied on Cataneo for its tabular component: 'And there are some who turn to the dialogue of Valdes, for it contains the reckoner of Cataneo Novares of the state of Venice, from whom it was taken, showing how to make formations from 100 to 20,000 men ...'[155] By means of such mathematical appendices the reader is spared the need to calculate the relevant figures himself. Diagrams showing the exact position of each man in a formation of a given size made the soldier's task still easier. A letter coding system (p = pikeman, d = drummer, etc.) enabled contemporary writers to show the place of each man in formation. A line of ten pikemen would be represented thus:

PPPPPPPPPP

There were of course limitations to what the military literature of the sixteenth century was able to achieve. Much of what was spelt out in seventeenth-century texts was left to the imagination of the reader in the previous century. A good example is the treatment of drums in the military literature of these centuries. Their use in ensuring the orderly movement of large, tightly formed bodies of troops was indispensable. And, if mid-sixteenth-century theorists like Henry Barrett refused to be drawn into the details of their function, they were still adamant that these should be fully mastered if chaos were not to ensue.[156] In this they differed little from their seventeenth-century successors, most of whom found it sufficient to insist that the sounds of the drum be learnt, without themselves supplying the necessary details.[157] But if sixteenth- and seventeenth-century writers approached the use of drums in a similar fashion, they were very different indeed in their treatment of verbal orders.

Some writers in the 1590s began the trend by giving their own choice of command words for particular orders. Hitherto, no one had thought to list standardised orders with which to control the evolutions of men in formation in both training and action. By the mid-seventeenth century such formulae were a routine part of the military theory pouring off the English presses. Even Thomas Styward's late-sixteenth-century treatise – in William Garrard's view the best published training manual in any European language – failed to render word for word the commands necessary to control pike and shot in the field.[158] Sir John Smythe's *Instructions, Observations and Orders Mylitarie* of 1594 was the first manual in England to attempt to give specific words of command.[159] It was not as if sixteenth-century officers were at a loss for words to control their troops either in training or on operations. The problem was that, lacking a uniform system of phrases of command, each officer chose his own *vocabula artis*. When William Wade offered his own system of words of command in a manuscript of 1597 he hoped they would come to replace all others in use. Mere generation of additional systems of words of command without standardisation across England would merely breed confusion. It was essential to settle on 'some certaine wordes which being once learned, shall still serve for direction'.[160]

In addition to their careful and increasingly standardised use of words of command, the training manuals of the seventeenth century could further simplify the task of operating modern pike and musket tactics by a new invention, the use of numbered postures. Although only three commands were needed to order men to load, aim and fire a musket while standing,[161] some twenty to fifty individual stages, or postures, were involved.[162] Fewer postures were involved in the manipulation of a pike in action,[163] but these too could be individually numbered and illustrated as an aid in training. None of the theorists published in England during the century bothered to depict or even list such postures, although the technique of instruction by numbered postures was used by theorists of fencing during the century.[164]

The English use of postures in training began to follow the Dutch example with the translation in James's reign of Jacob de Gheyn's *Wapenhandlingen van roers, musquetten ende spiessen*.[165] Sir Thomas Kellie readily conceded that it was easier to learn the use of pike and musket with the aid of 'the figures which are set down in his Excellence the Grave Maurice [the same Maurice of Nassau singled out by Professor Roberts], his Booke of postures'.[166]However, he cautioned that such aids could not substitute for actual practice.[167] Results depended, in the seventeenth century as in the sixteenth, on patient training by experts. Military literature only offers part of the picture. The sixteenth-century introduction of training *en masse* for the infantry across Europe and the practical developments that this involved was the decisive step; the final perfection of these techniques needed to portray them on the printed page was a later refinement.

The cavalry also went through important changes in the sixteenth century, although the military literature of the period paid them scant attention compared to the infantry, whose transformation we have already examined. This was most clear in the matter of armament. Firearms transformed the world of cavalry just as they transformed infantry tactics and siege warfare. When the infantryman handed in his crossbow and longbow for the arquebus and later the musket,[168] the cavalryman began his adventure with firearms.

Muskets in the sense of longer and more powerful arquebuses featured at the battles of Ravenna (1512) and Mühlberg (1547). Their emergence as a lasting feature of the military scene dates from Alva's introduction of the musket and forked rest in the late 1560s. Pistol-armed cavalry appeared in numbers on the battlefield from the 1540s, more than a generation after the arquebus first made itself felt at Cerignola (1503). The use of the pistol never eclipsed shock action in the cavalry repertoire,[169] but none the less altered the nature of cavalry combat. Whereas, previously, cavalry encounters often lasted several hours, the killing power of pistols tended to make them shorter. The horseman lightly galloped off rather than stay the full course on the field with the constant risk of death from a pistol fired at close range. As Tavannes noticed: 'The large pistols make ... close action so dangerous that everyone wants to leave, making the fights shorter.'[170]

The use of the caracole[171] by pistol-armed cavalry imitated the tactics used by infantry arquebusiers to reduce the damage done by the length of time required to reload their weapons. When one rank or a group of ranks had fired simultaneously they ran to the rear, their places being taken by men behind, who in turn ran off after firing. By the time the last ranks of skirmishing arquebusiers had fired, the first would have reloaded, ready to take their places. Using the same tactic with mounted men was not always a success: sometimes the rearward movement of those horsemen who had fired was taken for flight.[172] At other times the retiring pistoleers intermingled with and disordered other troops on their flank as they fell back to reload.[173]

Firearms also led to the emergence of a further type of cavalry, the argoletiers or arquebus-armed dragoons of the sixteenth century. Taking advantage of the firepower of the arquebus and the tactical mobility of the horse, they proved ideal for seizing advanced positions and holding them dismounted.[174] At a pinch they could also fire while mounted and skirmish to the flanks of their heavier brethren, retiring if seriously pressed.[175] However, the older types of cavalry – stradiots, men-at-arms, demi-lances and lancers – continued to exist alongside the new, much as the older ranks of lieutenant and captain maintained their ground alongside the new hierarchy of corporals, sergeants, sergeant-majors and camp-masters in the hierarchy of command. Some of these ranks, for instance the camp-master or colonel and the corporal, even found their way into the cavalry.[176]

Tight order was almost as important for the mounted arm as it was for Europe's infantry in the sixteenth century, but it could be achieved with less careful training than the pike-squares demanded. François de la Noue, a senior Huguenot cavalry commander, pointed out how the advantage of the German pistoleers, when fighting French men-at-arms, lay in their deeper, tighter order. Despite the bravery of the men-at-arms their thin disorderly formations betrayed them.

> Herein wee must say that the Germaines exceed all other nations, because they seeme to bee not onely close but even glewed each to other ... whensoever they be broken, in their retire and flight they still remaine unseparate and ioyned together: which the speares [French men-at-arms] do not.[177]

Simply, 'those that keepe themselves closest and doe strike with the whole body conioyned, doe worke to the greatest effecte'.[178] The veteran Monluc also found the German deep order preferable to the casual line of men-at-arms.[179] Order was almost as important to the success of sixteenth-century cavalrymen as it was to a square of pikes; without it they were at the mercy of even an inferior opponent. François de La Noue expresses this memorably in the class-conscious fashion of the French nobility of the time: French men-at-arms, the cream of French society, could be beaten by a troop of varlets if the varlets used tight order and discipline. This recalls Cromwell's remark about his troopers' social state half a century later.[180] A well-trained eye, such as that of Tavannes at Jarnac (1569), was quick to spot the signs of disorder in a cavalry formation.[181] Pikes that waved in disorder and broken lines of horse offered incalculable opportunities to the observer who knew how to exploit them.

Obviously the effective use of cavalry for shock impact on disordered troops was not something that had to wait until the late fifteenth and early sixteenth centuries to be discovered. It is not in the least revolutionary, but has a long medieval tradition. What *was* new was the adjustment in thinking caused by the perfection of firearms for use on horseback. The introduction of firearms-based tactics to the cavalry succeeded in dividing contemporaries. As we saw in Chapter 2, by no means all pistol-armed cavalry adopted the much-criticised caracole. Nor was it an unmitigated disaster. Garrard provided an excellent description of the caracole for his readers:

> I have seene skirmish a guidon of horsemen rutters [reiters], who comming to the fight in their accustomed squadres and thence picking forward some of the first rankes and threds to provoke the enemie, and when these of thee first ranks have discharged their Pistolets, making Carier and being charged, they place themselves againe at the backe of their owne squadre, from whence at the same instant time others of the first ranks to disband themselves, and give charge upon the enimie: but being charged themselves of the enemie, retyring they convey themselves behind their own people ...[182]

He was himself very taken with 'this speciall order'.[183] François de la Noue found the caracole, with its inbuilt retrogade movement, liable to be taken for flight and too easily turned into a rout.[184] The Digges, however, felt that the caracole was a splendid tactic for use against a pike-square, and quite superior to the lance.[185] Yet both Mendoza and Williams were certain that, in a cavalry-versus-cavalry encounter, lance-armed cavalry would make short work even of greater numbers of reiters.[186]

However, there was more to the impact of firearms on cavalry than the caracole. Even the men-at-arms found themselves adopting the pistol, though they still relied on the lance for their initial impact.[187] La Noue, who was critical enough of the caracole, was willing to state that 'it is a miracle if any be slaine with the speare'.[188] The pistol, with the ability to penetrate plate armour at close range,[189] was a far more formidable weapon, and did not have to be used in the cumbersome caracole in order to have effect. The force of reiters in their thick formations in simple charge was, in La Noue's estimation, enough to secure them victory over the French men-at-arms of his day, who obstinately used the thin line as their fighting formation.[190] The old method of concentrated shock was enough to achieve results without the support of the new firearms. But the 'fiery weapons' had left their mark on both cavalry and foot, neither of which could any longer operate as they had for most of the Middle Ages.

Notes

1. Wilhelm Erben, *Kriegsgeschichte des Mittelalters* (Munich and Berlin, 1929), p. iv.

2. For an introduction to the subject see M. Reinaud and M. Favé, *Histoire de l'artillerie 1re partie*. *Du feu grégeois des feux de guerre et des origines de la poudre à canon d'après des textes nouveaux* (Paris, 1845), especially p. 211.

3. Ernst Richert, *Die Schlacht bei Guinegate 7. August 1479* (Diss., Berlin, 1907), p. 68. Ch. Brusten, 'L'armée bourguignonne de 1465 à 1477', *Revue Internationale d'Histoire Militaire* (1959), p. 462. Eugen von Frauenholz, *Das Heerwesen der Schweizer Eidgenossenschaft in der Zeit des freien Söldnertums* (Munich, 1936), pp. 96 and 105. *Idem, Das Heerwesen des Reiches in der Landsknechtszeit* (Munich, 1937), p. 53. Maury D. Feld, 'Middle-Class Society and the Rise of Military Professionalism: The Dutch Army 1589–1609', *Idem, The Structure of Violence* (London, 1977), p. 182.

4. Peter Blastenbrei, *Die Sforza und ihr Heer* (Heidelberg, 1987), pp. 178–9.

5. James D. Lavin, *A History of Spanish Firearms* (London, 1965), p. 43.

6. J.F. Guilmartin, *Gunpowder and Galleys. Changing technology and Mediterranean warfare at sea in the sixteenth century* (Oxford, 1974), p. 274.

7. Auton, *Chroniques*, III, pp. 169–73. Taylor, *Art of War*, p. 110. Kopitsch, *Bicocca*, pp. 59–67. Hale, *N.C.M.H.*, II, p. 498. Häbler, 'Pavia', pp. 522–3. Lambert (ed.), *Bellai-Langei*, I, pp. 404–5.

8. Ferdinand Lot, *Recherches sur les effectifs des armées françaises des Guerres d'Itale aux Guerres de Religion 1494–1562* (Paris, 1962), p. 33.

9. General Susane, *Histoire de l'infanterie française* (5 vols, Paris, 1876), I, p. 93. Sancho de Londoño, *El Discurso sobre la forma de reduzir la disciplina militar a meyor y antiguo estado* (Brussels, 1589), f 18. Domenico Mora, *Il soldato* (Venice, 1570), p. 82. Francisco de Valdés, *The Sergeant Maior*, trans. J. Thorius, STC 24570 (1590), sig. D3.

10. For an overview see Carl von Elgger, *Kriegsween der schweizerischen Eidgenossenschaft im 14., 15. und 16. Jahrhundert* (Lucerne, 1873), pp. 104–5

11. Heinrich Harkensee, *Die Schlacht bei Marignano (13. u. 14. Sept. 1515)* (Diss., Göttingen, 1909), pp. 85–8 and 103–7. M. l'Abbé Lambert, *Mémoires de Martin et Guillaume du Bellai-Langei* (Paris, 1753), I, pp. 73–5. See also the section from Werner Schodeler's chronicle printed in Frauenholz, *Schweizer Eidgenossenschaft*, pp. 113–14.

12. Piero Pieri, *Il Rinascimento e la crisi militare italiana* (Turin, 1952), p. 241. Susane, *L'infanterie*, I, p. 52. Richard Vaughan, *Charles the Bold* (London, 1973), pp. 210, 387–93 and 429–32.

13. See the preceding chapter for further detail and sources.

14. *Die Schlacht bei Ceresole (14. April 1544)* (Diss., Berlin, 1911), p. 71. Compare Jean Giono and Paul Courtéault (eds), Blaise de Monluc, *Commentaires 1521–1576* (Paris, 1964), p. 158.

15. Piero Pieri (ed.), N. Machiavelli, *Dell' Arte Della Guerra* (Rome, n.d.), p. 40.

16. Stallwitz, *Ceresole*, p. 97.

17. Stallwitz, *Instructions for the Warres*, tr. Paul Ive, STC 7264 (1589), p. 26.

[This work was falsely ascribed to G. Du Bellay by its sixteenth-century English translator.] Heinrich Harkensee, *Die Schlacht bei Marignano (13. u. 14. Sept. 1515)* (Diss., Göttingen, 1909), pp. 85–8.

18. Georg Fischer, *Die Schlacht bei Novara 6. Juni 1513* (Diss., Berlin, 1908), p. 137.

19. Diego de Alaba Y Viamont, *El perfeto Capitan, instruido En la disciplina Militar y nueva ciencia de la Artilleria* (Madrid, 1590), p. 68.

20. François de la Noue, *The Politicke and Militarie Discourses of the Lord de la Noue*, STC 15215 (1587), p. 204.

21. As for instance at Cravant (1423). L. Douet-d'Arcq (ed.), *La chronique d'Enguerran de Monstrelet* (6 vols, Paris, 1857–62), IV, p. 160.

22. Charles Kohler, *Les Suissses dans les guerres d'Italie de 1506 à 1512* (Geneva, 1897; facs. repr. Geneva, 1978), p. 24. G.A. Hayes-McCoy, 'Strategy and tactics in Irish warfare 1593–1601', *Irish Historical Studies*, II (1940–1), p. 259.

23. Machiavelli and Clayton considered the sixth rank of eighteen-foot pikes would protrude also. Piero Pieri (ed.), Niccolo Machiavelli, *Dell'Arte Della Guerra* (Rome, n.d.), p. 75. Giles Clayton, *The Approoved Order of Martial Discipline*, STC 5376 (1591), p. 45.

24. Robert Barret, *The Theorike and Practike of Moderne Warres*, STC 1500 (1598), p. 47.

25. Ibid., p. 76.

26. Pieri (ed.), Machiavelli, *Arte Della Guerra*, p. 47.

27. Thomas Styward, *The Pathwaie to Martiall Discipline*, STC 23413 (1581), p. 157.

28. Robert Hare, Military treatise (1557), British Library, Cotton MS Julius F.v., f 33.

29. Bernardino de Mendoza, *Theorique and Practise of Warre*, tr. Sir E. Hoby, STC 17819 (1597), p. 54.

30. Max Jähns, *Geschichte der Kriegswissenschaften vornehmlich in Deutschland. Erste Abtheilung. Altertum, Mittelalter, XV. und XVI. Jahrhundert* (Munich and Leipzig, 1889), p. 568. C.W.C. Oman, *A History of the Art of War in the Sixteenth Century* (London, 1936), pp. 561–3.

31. Sir John Smythe, 'An aunswer to contrarie opynions militarie', British Library, Harleian MS 135, f 11.

32. Matthew Sutcliffe, *The Practice, Proceedings, and Lawes of Armes*, STC 23468 (1593), p. 109.

33. Barret, *Theorike*, p. 69.

34. Oman, *Sixteenth Century*, p. 406.

35. F.L. Taylor, *The Art of War in Italy 1494–1529* (Cambridge, 1921), p. 110.

36. Bernardino de Mendoza, *Theorique and Practise of Warre*, tr. Sir E. Hoby, STC 17819 (Middelburg, 1597), p. 109.

37. Lot, *Effectifs*, p. 34 (Ravenna, 1512) and p. 38 (Novara, 1513).

38. Max von Wulf, *Die husitische Wagenburg* (Diss., Berlin, 1889), pp. 42 and 51. Joseph Würdinger, *Kriegsgeschichte von Bayern, Pfalz und Schwaben von 1347 bis 1506* (2 vols., Munich and Augsburg, 1868), II, p. 380f. Philip of Cleve, 'Kurtzer bericht der fürnemsten mittel weg und Ordnung von Krieg zu Land und Wasser', Staatsbibliothek, Munich, cod. bav. 1682 / cod. germ. 1682, fos. 13ᵛ and 50.

Leonhart Fronsperger, *Kriegsbuch* (3 vols, Frankfurt, 1596), I, pp. XLIII–XLIX.

39. William Hardy (ed.), Jehan de Waurin, *Recueil des Croniques et anchiennes istoires de la grant bretagne* (Rolls Series, London, 1864–91), V, iii, p. 65. Samuel Bentley, *Excerpta Historica* (London, 1831), p. 42. Other instances can be multiplied. John Keegan presents an interesting theory of the manner of their deployment at Agincourt (1415). John Keegan, *The Face of Battle* (London, 1976), pp. 91–2.

40. Wulf, *Wagenburg*, pp. 13–21.

41. As at Novara (1513). Georg Fischer, *Die Schlacht bei Novara 6. Juni 1513* (Diss., Berlin, 1908), p. 130.

42. Piero Pieri, *Il Rinascimento e la crisi militare italiana* (Turin, 1952), pp. 218 and 234.

43. Felix Wodsak, *Die Schlacht von Kortryk 11. Juli 1302* (Diss., Berlin, 1905), p. 90.

44. Ibid., pp. 69 and 81. Friedrich Mohr, *Die Schlacht bei Rosebeke am 27. November 1382* (Diss., Berlin, 1906), pp. 73–85. Roger Sablonier, 'Rittertum, Adel und Kriegswesen im Spätmittelalter' in J. Fleckenstein (ed.), *Das ritterliche Turnier im Mittelalter* (Göttingen, 1985), p. 537.

45. Wodsak, *Kortryk*, pp. 41 and 90.

46. J.G. Mann, 'Notes on the Armour of the Maximilian Period and the Italian Wars', *Archaeologia*, LXXIX (1929), p. 241.

47. A.R. Hall, *Ballistics in the Seventeenth Century* (Cambridge, 1952), p. 8.

48. B.P. Hughes, *Firepower. Weapons' Effectiveness on the Battlefield, 1630–1850* (London, 1974), p. 26.

49. Fourquevaux, *Instructions*, p. 25.

50. Bellai-Langei, *Mémoires*, V, p. 293.

51. Kopitsch, *Bicocca*, pp. 59–67. Hale, *N.C.M.H.*, II, p. 498. Häbler, 'Pavia', pp. 522–3. Lambert (ed.), *Bellai-Langei*, I, pp. 404–5.

52. Monluc, *Commentaires* , p. 158. Maximilien de Béthune, Duc de Sully, *Mémoires*, (London, 1745), I, 119. *Mémoires de Messire Pierre de Bourdeille, Seigneur de Brantôme contenans Les Vies des Hommes Illustres et grands Capitaines estrangers de son temps* (Leyden, 1665), p. 115.

53. François de Rabutin, *Commentaires sur le Faict des dernières Guerres en la Gaule Belgique, entre Henri second treschrestien Roy de France, et Charles cinquième Empereur* (Paris, 1555), V, f 61ᵛ.

54. Frauenholz, *Schweizer Eidgenossenschaft*, p. 114.

55. Luigi Collado, *Pratica Manuale di Artiglieria* (Venice, 1586), p. 8.

56. Robert Barret, *The Theorike and Practike of Moderne Warres*, STC 1500 (1598), p. 75.

57. M.G.A. Vale, *War and Chivalry. Warfare and Aristocratic Culture in England, France and Burgundy at the End of the Middle Ages* (London, 1981), p. 114.

58. H. Beaune and J. D'Arbaumont (ed.), *Mémoires d'Olivier de La Marche* (3 vols, Paris, 1884), II, pp. 320–1.

59. Diego de Alaba Y Viamont, *El perfeto Capitan* (Madrid, 1590), f 131.

60. Clayton, *Approved Order*, p. 25. Captain John Bingham repeated the same sentiment in his *Aelianus, The Art of Embattailing an Army* (London, 1629; facs. repr. Amsterdam, 1968), sig. A4.

61. La Noue, *Discourses*, p. 199.

62. Barret, *Theorike*, p. 69.

63. Francisco de Valdes, *The Sergeant Maior*, tr. J. Thorius, STC 24570 (1590), sig. C2.

64. K. Häbler, 'Die Schlacht bei Pavia', *Forschungen zur deutschen Geschichte*, XXV (Göttingen, 1885), p. 522.

65. Thomas Audley, Military treatise, Bodleian Library, Tanner MS 103, f 31. Barret, *Theorike*, p. 46.

66. Leonard and Thomas Digges, *An Arithmeticall Militare Treatise Named Stratioticos*, STC 6848 (1579), p. 97.

67. Jean Giono and Paul Courtéault (eds), Blaise de Monluc, *Commentaires 1521–1576* (Paris, 1964), p. 162. Fronsperger, *Kriegsbuch*, I, p. XLII.

68. Thomas and Leonard Digges, *An Arithmeticall Militare Treatise Named Stratioticos*, STC 6848 (1579), p. 102.

69. Bernardino de Escalante, *Dialogos del Arte Militar* (Brussels, 1595), f 46. Londoño, *El Discurso*, fos. 11 and 17ᵛ. Francesco Ferretti, *Dell'Osservanza Militare* (Venice, 1576), p. 101.

70. The phrase is Shakespeare's from the scene in the English camp before the battle of Agincourt in *Henry V*. The English theorists Giles Clayton and William Garrard both gave the pike pride of place as did the Spaniard Londoño. Giles Clayton, *The Approoved Order of Martiall Discipline*, STC 5376 (1591), p. 16. H.J. Webb, *Elizabethan Military Science. The Books and the Practice* (London, 1965), p. 88. Londoño, *El Discurso*, f 9ᵛ.

71. Charles V once remarked that the power of his empire resided in the lighted matches of his Spanish arquebusiers. Cl. Gaier, 'L'opinion des chefs de guerre français du XVIᵉ siecle sur les progrès de l'art militaire', *Revue Internationale d'Histoire Militaire*, XXIX (1970), p. 742.

72. See pp. 56–7 above.

73. M.H. Keen, *Chivalry* (London, 1984), p. 236. William Caxton had the same thought. A.T.P. Byles (ed.), William Caxton, *The Book of the Ordre of Chyvalry* (E.E.T.S., 1926), p. 124 cited by Juliet Barker and M.H. Keen, 'The Medieval English Kings and the Tournament', J. Fleckenstein (ed.), *Das ritterliche Turnier im Mittelalter* (Göttingen, 1985), p. 227.

74. Waurin, *Recueil*, V, iii, pp. 113–14.

75. Hale (ed.), *Henry Barrett*, pp. 45–6.

76. Hale (ed.), Smythe, *Certain Discourses*, p. 52.

77. Lelio Brancaccio made this point well in his treatise *I carichi militari* (Antwerp, 1610), p. 5.

78. Styward, *Pathwaie*, p. 45.

79. Jean Giono and Paul Courtéault (eds), Blaise de Monluc, *Commentaires 1521–76* (Paris, 1964), p. 122. Barret, *Theorike*, p. 88. Rich, *Path-way*, sigs. K3–K3ᵛ. Digges, *Stratioticos*, pp. 84 and 105. Clayton, *Approoved Order*, p. 67.

80. Piero Pieri, *Il Rinascimento e la crisi militare italiana* (Turin, 1952), p. 343. Also see p. 236.

81. Paul Kopitsch, *Die Schlacht bei Bicocca 27. April 1522* (Berlin, Diss., 1909), . p. 51.

82. Kurt Neubauer (ed.), *Das Kriegsbuch des Philipp von Seldeneck vom Ausgang*

des. 15. Jahrhunderts (Diss., Heidelberg, 1963), p. 91. Sutcliffe, *Practice*, p. 107.
British Library, Additional MS 34,553, f 16. Styward, *Pathwaie*, p. 123.

83. Mora, *soldato*, p. 119.

84. Rich, *Path-way*, sig. K3. Reinhard Count of Solms, *Dises Buch und Kriegs-beschreibung*, Bayerische Staatsbibliothek Rar. 986 (1559), VIII, f 2.

85. Clayton, *Approoved Order*, p. 66. Charles Hughes (ed.), Sir Henry Knyvett, *The Defence of the Realme. 1596* (Oxford, 1906), pp. 22 and 64.

86. De la Barre Duparcq, *L'art militaire pendant les guerres de religion* (Paris, 1864), p. 36.

87. Valdes, *Sergeant Maior*, sig. C1ᵛ.

88. Ascanio Centorio degli Hortensii, *Discorsi di Guerra* (Venice, 1568), p. 13.

89. Francesco Ferretti, *Della Osservanza Militare* (Venic, 1576), p. 53.

90. Barnaby Rich, *A Right Exelent and Pleasaunt Dialogue, betwene Mercury and an English Souldier*, STC 20998 (1574), sig. Eiiiᵛ.

91. La Noue, *Discourses*, p. 170.

92. Barret, *Theorike*, p. 46.

93. Dudley and Thomas Digges, *Foure Paradoxes*, STC 6872 (1604), sig. G3.

94. François de La Noue, *The Politicke and Militarie Discourses*, translated by E. A[ggas], STC 15215 (1587), pp. 207–8.

95. Ferretti, *Osservanza*, p. 99.

96. K.V. Thomas, 'Numeracy in Early Modern England', *Transactions of the Royal Historical Society*, V series, XXXVII (1987), p. 109.

97. Markham, *Fighting Veres*, pp. 53–6. Also see 'sergeant major', 'colonel', 'sergeant' and 'corporal' in Sir James Murray (ed.), *A New English Dictionary on Historical Principles* (Oxford, 1914). Susane, *infanterie*, I, pp. 90, 94–6, 108 and 120.

98. See in particular Millar, 'Henry VIII's colonels', pp. 129–36.

99. The continental equivalent of the colonel was the camp-master. Monluc, *Commentaires*, pp. 813–14.

100. His English translator J. Thorius renamed the book, in Spanish 'The Mirror', *The Sergeant Maior*, STC 24570 (1590).

101. Valdes, *Sergeant Maior*, sig. B2.

102. Sir Robert Constable, 'The order of a Campe or Army Royall with the dutie of everie officer belonging to the same' (1576), British Library, Harleian MS 847, f 54ᵛ.

103. Gerrat Barry, *A Discourse of Military Discipline*, STC 1528 (Brussels, 1634), p. 51.

104. Barret, *Theorike*, p. 37.

105. Digges, *Stratioticos*, p. 106.

106. Valdes, *Sergeant Maior*, sig. B4.

107. British Library, Royal MS 17 C xxii, f 3. William Bourne thought the embatteling of a large force to be a matter beyond the ability of English captains and understood only by generals. William Bourne, *Inventions or Devises. Very necessary for all Generalles and Captaines, or Leaders of men, as wel by Sea ass by Land*, STC 3420 (London, 1578), sigs. *1–*1ᵛ

108. Styward, *Pathwaie*, p. 20.

109. Valdes, *Sergeant Maior*, sig. E3.

110. British Library Lansdowne MS 40, f 14ᵛ.

111. Eguiluz, *Milicia*, f 45ᵛ. Valdes, *Sergeant Maior*, sigs. C1–C1ᵛ. Gutierrez de la Vega, *Compendious treatise*, f 9ᵛ.

112. Mora, *Soldato*, p. 55: 'deve essere buon Arithmetico et abachista per potere in un subito sommare con la memoria ogni grande numero ...'

113. Garrard, *Arte*, p. 161.

114. Ibid., p. 171.

115. See for instance Thomas Styward's key. Styward, *Pathwaie*, p. 43.

116. Giovan. Matteo Cigogna, *Il Primo Libro del Trattare Militare* (Venice, 1583), f 2ᵛ. Fifty years later Gerrat Barry felt that to do so was humanly impossible, though the sergeant-major would be well advised to make full use of the tables themselves. Barry, *Discourse*, p. 42.

117. Girolamo Cataneo, *Tavole brevissime* (Brescia, 1567). Idem, *Most Brief Tables to Knowe Redily Howe Manye Ranckes of Footemen Go to the Making of a Just Battayle*, tr. H.G., STC 4790 (1574).

118. Bodleian Library, Rawlinson MS D363, fos. 45–62ᵛ: 'This table proporcioned by rank and ray from thre men in a rank unto xxi men in a rank ...' Ibid., f 45. Hale (ed.), *Henry Barrett*, p. 37. British Library, Cotton MS Julius F.v., fos. 40–7.

119. Styward, *Pathwaie*, sig. A4 and unpaginated table attached to the end of the work. Rich, *Path-way*, sigs. I4 and L2. Barret, *Theorike*, p. 49.

120. Cataneo, *Most Brief Tables*, sigs. Aiiii-Aiiiiᵛ.

121. Barret, *Theorike*, p. 52. Garrard, *Arte*, p. 218.

122. Cigogna, *Primo Libro*, f 16ᵛ.

123. Fisher, *Warlike Directions*, sigs. A2–A2ᵛ.

124. For an introduction see J.R. Hale, 'A humanistic visual aid. The military diagram in the Renaissance', *Renaissance Studies*, II (1988), pp. 280–98.

125. Girolamo Cataneo, *Most Brief Tables to Knowe Redily Howe Manye Ranckes of Footemen Go to the Making of a Just Battayle*, STC 4790 (1574), sig. Aiii.

126. Valdes, *Sergeant Maior*, sig. E3. Robert Barret, *The Theorike and Practike of Moderne Warres*, STC 1500 (1598), p. 102.

127. Ibid., p. 94.

128. Oman, *Sixteenth Century*, p. 489. Bellai-Langei, *Mémoires*, I, p. 268.

129. Escalante, *Dialogos*, f 40. Ferretti, *Osservanza*, p. 90. Thomas Styward, *The Pathwaie to Martiall Discipline*, STC 23413 (1581), p. 20.

130. Etienne Vaucheret (ed.), Brantôme (Pierre de Bourdeille), *Discours sur les colonels de l'infanterie de France* (Paris, 1973), p. 130.

131. Escalante, *Dialogos*, f 50.

132. Monluc, *Commentaires*, p. 779.

133. See Zizka's ordinance of war of 1423 printed in Frauenholz, *Landsknechtszeit*, p. 123.

134. See for instance Richard II's Durham Ordinances. Sir Travers Twiss (ed.), *The Black Book of the Admiralty* (Rolls Series, London, 1871), I, pp. 453 and 457.

135. Sir Clement Edmunds, *Observations upon the Five First Bookes of Caesars Commentaries*, STC 7488 (1600), p. 88.

136. Charles's ordinance of 1473 is of particular interest. Richard Vaughan, *Charles the Bold*, (London, 1973), pp. 209–10.

137. Susane, *L'infanterie*, I, pp. 52–5. Pieri, *Rinascimento*, p. 250.

138. William Garrard, *The Arte of Warre*, STC 11625 (1591), p. 204.

139. Henry Farmer, *Military Music and its Story. The Rise and Development of Military Music* (London, 1912), pp. 2–15.

140. William Irvine, *The Army of the Moghuls* (London, 1903), p. 185.

141. Monluc, *Commentaires*, p. 159.

142. William S. Maltby, *Alba. A Biography of Fernando Alvarez de Toledo, Third Duke of Alba, 1507–1582* (London, 1983), p. 10.

143. For one medieval tribute to Roman discipline among many see P.S. Lewis (ed.), *Écrits politiques de Jean Juvenal des Ursins* (2 vols, Paris, 1978), I, p. 75.

144. Valdes, *Sergeant Maior*, sigs. B4ᵛ–C1.

145. J.A. Wiseman, 'L'Epitoma rei militaris de Végèce et sa fortune au Moyen Age', *Le Moyen Age. Revue d'Histoire et de Philologie*, LXXXV (1979). Matthias Springer, 'Vegetius im Mittelalter', *Philologus*, CXXIII (1979). Paul Meyer, 'Les Anciens Traducteurs Français de Végèce et en particulier Jean de Vignai', *Romania*, XXXV (1896), pp. 401–23. Robert Bossuat, 'Jean de Rouvroy. Traducteur des Stratagèmes de Frontin', *Bibliothèque d'Humanisme et Renaissance*, XXII (1960), pp. 273–86 and 469–89. Lewis Thorpe, 'Mastre Richard a Thirteenth-Century Translator of Vegetius', *Scriptorium*, VI (1952), pp. 39–50. Diane Bornstein, 'Military Manuals in Fifteenth-Century England', *Medieval Studies*, XXXVII (1975).

146. For the text of Seldeneck's work and details of two important Czech military writings see Kurt Neubauer, *Das Kriegsbuch des Philipp von Seldeneck vom Ausgang des 15. Jahrhunderts. Untersuchung und kritische Herausgabe des Textes der Karlsruher Handschrift* (Diss., Heidelberg, 1963), p. 33.

147. Bayerische Staatsbibliothek (Munich), cod. lat. 23467, fos. 155–158ᵛ and 124. For an exhaustive inventory of similar works in Italy and Germany see the bibliography of Bert S. Hall's *The so-called "manuscript of the Hussite Wars' engineer" and its technological milieu: a study and edition of codex latinus monacensis 197, part I* (University of California, Los Angeles, Ph.D., 1971).

148. Ferdinand Lot rightly pointed to the significance of this development. Lot, *Effectifs*, p. 9. Other writers have been slower to do so.

149. *Herrn Lazari von Schwendi ... Kriegs Diskurs* (Dresden, 1676), p. *6ᵛ.

150. Brantôme, *L'infanterie de France*, p. 199.

151. His work was curiously dedicated to the Earl of Bedford: *Historia di Pietro Bizari, Della guerra fatta in Ungheria dall'invictissimo Imperatore de Christiani, contra quello de Turchi* (Lyons, 1568), sig. *2.

152. E.S. Forster, *The Turkish letters of Ogier Ghiselin de Busbecq* (Oxford, 1927), p. 62. Peter Whitehorne, *Onosandro Platonico, Of the Generall Captaine*, STC 18815 (1563), sig. Aiii. Garrard, *Arte*, p. 30. Barret, *Theorike*, p. 12.

153. Sir John Hale, 'A humanistic visual aid. The military diagram in the Renaissance', *Renaissance Studies*, II, pp. 280–98.

154. Giles Clayton, *The Approoved Order of Martiall Discipline*, STC 5376 (1591), p. 81.

155. Martin de Eguiluz, *Milicia, discurso, y regla militar* (Antwerp, 1595), f 22.

156. Hale (ed.), *Henry Barrett*, pp. 40 and 51.

157. As for instance Thomas Trussell's *The Souldier ...* , STC 24298 (London, 1626), pp. 59–60. Kellie, *Pallas Armata*, p. 22.

158. Garrard, *Arte*, p. 79. Omitting Wade and Smythe, Charles Hughes claimed in his edition of Sir Henry Knyvett's *The Defence of the Realme. 1596* (Oxford, 1906), p. 75 that before 1600 'there could not be said to be such a thing as a drill-book in the English language'.

159. Smythe, *Instructions*, pp. 22–3.

160. British Library, King's MS 265, f 275ᵛ.

161. Kellie, *Pallas Armata*, p. 26. *Directions for Musters wherein is showne the order of Drilling for the Musket and Pike* (Cambridge, 1638), sig. A3ᵛ.

162. Ibid. Peacham, *Compleat Gentleman*, pp. 230–1. Fisher, *Warlike Directions*, pp. 10–12. Kellie, *Pallas Armata*, pp. 25–6.

163. Peacham, *Compleat Gentleman*, p. 232.

164. Maury D. Feld, 'Middle-Class Society and the Rise of Military Professionalism: The Dutch Army 1589–1609'. Feld, *The Structure of Violence. Armed Forces as Social Systems* (London, 1977), p. 175.

165. Ibid. Geoffrey Parker, *The military revolution. Military innovation and the rise of the West, 1500–1800* (Cambridge, 1988), p. 20. Copying of the Dutch example was not limited to manuals for the musket and pike. John Cruso included a series of 24 postures for the use of a cavalryman armed with pistols. John Cruso, *Militarie instructions for the cavallrie*, STC 6099 (Cambridge, 1632), pp. 38–9.

166. Kellie, *Pallas Armata*, p. 27.

167. Ibid.

168. R.C. Clepham, 'The Military Handgun of the Sixteenth Century', *The Archaeological Journal*, LXVII (1910), p. 138. Hale, *N.C.M.H.*, II, p. 496. Brantôme, *l'infanterie de France*, p. 166.

169. See above.

170. Gaspard de Saulx, Seigneur de Tavannes, *Mémoires* (Paris, 1657), p. 174.

171. See above.

172. La Noue, *Discourses*, p. 201.

173. Saulx, *Mémoires*, pp. 367–8.

174. Edward Davies, *The Art of War and Englands Traynings* (London, 1619; facs. repr. Amsterdam, 1968), p. 130.

175. Sir Roger Williams, *A Briefe Discourse of Warre* STC 25732 (1590), p. 35.

176. Monluc, *Commentaires*, p. 807. *Count Mansfields Directions of Warre. Given to all his officers and souldiers in generall* (London, 1624), pp. 17ff.

177. Christopher Hill, *God's Englishman. Oliver Cromwell and the English Revolution* (London 1970), pp. 64–7.

178. Ibid., p. 200.

179. Monluc, *Commentaires*, p. 814. The events of Ivry (1590) and Turnhout (1597) proved him right. Oman, *Sixteenth Century*, pp. 502 and 581.

180. La Noue, *Discourses*, pp. 188–9.

181. Oman, *Sixteenth Century*, p. 449.

182. Garrard, *Arte*, pp. 118–19.

183. Ibid.

184. La Noue, *Discourses*, p. 201. Tavannes made much the same criticism, though he was more concerned with the disorder the tactic created in the reiters' ranks, which rendered them peculiarly vulnerable to counter-attack. Gaspard de Saulx, Seigneur de Tavannes, *Mémoires* (Paris, 1657), pp. 367–8.

185. Digges, *Stratioticos*, p. 144.
186. Williams, *Briefe Discourse*, p. 38. Mendoza, *Theorique*, p. 51.
187. La Noue, *Discourses*, p. 202. J.R. Hale and M.E. Mallett, *The Military Organization of a Renaissance State. Venice c.1400 to 1617* (Cambridge, 1984), p. 369.
188. Ibid., p. 201. Tavannes felt much the same. Tavannes, *Mémoires*, p. 176.
189. Tavannes, *Mémoires*, p. 175.
190. La Noue, *Discourses*, p. 186.

CHAPTER 4

THE NEW SIEGE WARFARE
AND ITS IMPLICATIONS

Developments in infantry and cavalry tactics, important as they were, were not the sum total of military change in these years. The growing emphasis on training and the changing nature of military theory have already been touched on – as has the transformation of the hierarchy of command in the course of the century. Yet more important, perhaps, than any other single development was the revolution in siege warfare, which by the mid-sixteenth century had profoundly altered the face of war in Europe.

As the battles of the Italian Wars demonstrated in the first quarter of the century, even a simple trench defended by firearms and artillery was a formidable obstacle.[1] How much more so a fortress specifically designed to give full play to these weapons of fire. In the course of the fifteenth century, Italian engineers created a new fortress design which did just this.[2] The bastioned defence which they developed could be used in two ways. A new fortification could be constructed of stone or brick at great expense, replete with bastions, geometrically arranged walls, ditch and glacis and counterscarp, or much the same effect could be achieved by using wood and earth to create an *ad hoc* fortification which would show off the besieged's artillery and firearms to good advantage. Earth served as well against cannon shot as stone and brick and its cost could be ten times less.[3] The town of Ghent was given ravelins, ditches and counterscarps for less than 300,000 florins, despite the enormous circuit of its walls, which compared to that of Paris. This was a perishable defence using earth and wood. But if, as François de La Noue pointed out, 'the King of Spayne should have made this fortification according to the written rules, he must have spent above six millions and twentie yeares at the least'.[4]

Both kinds of fortification, cheap and expensive, sprouted across

Europe in the course of the century. The first to employ angle-bastions at regular intervals along all walls was constructed around the papal port of Civitavecchia in 1515.[5] Their particular advantage lay in their thick, squat walls and use of a high counterscarp to mask the walls from artillery fire. Medieval fortress designs allowed the walls to rise very high indeed. Their very height was a problem to the besieger, who was forced to use longer and more cumbersome scaling ladders and taller and more unwieldy siege towers in consequence. If they were high enough they also presented some obstacle to incendiary arrows, a commonly used way of smoking a defender out. During the siege of Neuss (1474) the Burgundians fired up to thirty fire-arrows an hour.[6]

The artillery at the besieger's disposal posed no real threat until, in the course of the fifteenth century, the development of iron projectiles and cannon cast in one piece[7] produced the formidable siege artillery with which Charles VII recaptured Normandy[8] and Charles VIII invaded Italy.[9] Torsion engines of ancient design were still in use right up to that time.[10] They were little inferior to the primitive bombards of the fourteenth and early fifteenth centuries. A stone cannon of c.1420 had a powder:projectile weight ratio of 1:13. More powder risked the destruction of the cannon itself. Such a feeble powder load inevitably reduced the performance of early cannon. Within half a century a ratio of 1:2 became possible and the cannon had come of age.[11]

The thin, tall, medieval defences of Europe's towns and castles were quite inadequate when put to the test by the new artillery of the late fifteenth century. They offered a huge target to cannon fire, and were unstable if damaged and far too thin to resist the new artillery.[12] If the defender attempted to mount his artillery on them it could not be brought to bear on men at the base of the walls, where a huge blind spot existed.[13] The medieval use of projecting towers created further lateral blind spots in addition to those created vertically by the very height of the walls. A man standing in one tower, or on the wall, was prevented from seeing an enemy at work at the base of another tower of the fortification by the projecting bulk of the walls of the tower he was working at.

At first, a partial remedy was discovered by Europe's soldiers. They piled up earth behind the medieval walls in order to increase their thickness. This afforded more comfort against artillery fire and provided the defender with a greater surface on which to place his artillery in defence. An English writer of the mid-sixteenth century

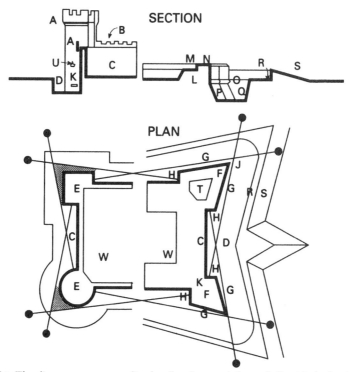

Note: The diagram contrasts medieval wall and tower defences (left) with the bastion and rampart system (right). Lines of fire illustrate how the triangular trace avoids blind spots.

Key: A: Machicolations or machicoulis gallery, bracketed upper-level works allowing defenders to drop heavy objects to the foot of the wall. B: *Merli* (Italian) or merlons (English), solid protective components between embrasures. C: Curtain, section of wall or rampart between towers or bastions. D: Ditch. E: Towers, with hatching indicating blind spots. F: Bastions, solid gun platforms projecting from the curtains. G: Face of the bastion. H: Flank of the bastion. J: Salient or pointed tip of the bastion. K: Gorge or throat of the bastion. L: Rampart. M: Terreplein or gun platform. N: Parapet. O: Cordon, moulding dividing vertical and battered sections of a rampart or bastion. P: Scarp, battered (sloping) lower section of rampart/ bastion. Q: Counterscarp, outer wall of ditch. R: Covered way, protected infantry position outside the ditch. S: Glacis, gently sloping earth bank concealing the covered way and all but the uppermost defensive works. T: Cavalier, raised gun platform on rampart or bastion. U: Keyhole gunport. V: Letterbox gunport. W: Enceinte, area enclosed (literally 'belted') by a fortification.

Figure 4.1 Medieval and early modern fortification
Source: The diagram and the accompanying key are reproduced from Simon Pepper and Nicholas Adams, *Firearms and Fortifications. Military Architecture and Siege Warfare in Sixteenth-Century Siena* (Chicago and London, 1986), p. 4.

proposed just this, when he suggested that the defender 'dygge up the erthe to the heyght of the walles, for gonnes and other ingynes'. This method of defence was used at Metz (1552). The towers were filled with earth.[14] The problem was, as Duke Philip of Cleves pointed out in the first quarter of the sixteenth century, that when a breach was made the earth which had been piled up to thicken the wall poured out, making a tidy slope for the attacker to clamber up.[15]

The real solution came with the Italian invention of the angle-bastion. Hidden behind a massive glacis and ditch, a bastioned fortification used earthen or brick walls as thick as contemporaries could make them: 'le fortezze, che hoggidi si fanno, hanno il ciglio, o spalto molto rilevato in modo che a pena il parapetto della mura si discuopre [the fortresses made nowadays have a glacis or ditch raised to such a height that the parapet of the wall is scarcely visible]'.[16] At each corner a tapering angular bastion was placed in lieu of a tower. The bastion protruded slightly from the walls it emerged from, and cannon could be placed in these protruding flanks. From this position they could fire along the length of the adjoining wall, past the flank and along the outer face of the bastion at the other end of the wall. This geometrical design reduced blind areas to a minimum, as can be seen from Figure 4.1.

An angle-bastioned defence left no substantial space where the attacker could mass unscathed. The bastions were kept close together and the stretches of wall between them kept short to ensure that the length of ground the cannon had to sweep did not exceed its effective range.[17]

For a fraction of the cost of such a stone or brick angle-bastioned fortress, ad hoc fortifications could be dug, which for a few years could fulfil the same functions, until wind and rain swept them away. Such earthen defences withstood professionally conducted sieges just as well as their stone or brick counterparts.[18] Their chief vulnerability was the ease with which the attacker's pioneers could dig them away should they ever come within reach of the wall.[19] In William Garrard's view the best defence against artillery was earth, 'beeing well compounded and made of good matter, rather then in stone walles'.[20] Cannon were so powerful that walls constructed on the wrong principles could offer no defence.[21]

Thin, high, medieval walls, designed to frustrate escalade[22] and keep out fire-arrows, could not withstand battery by modern siege artillery as effectively as could thick, squat, earthen or brick structures. In the mid-seventeenth century Richard Norwood considered 20-foot-deep earthen walls to be effectively cannon-proof.[23] Most medieval town walls were one-third as thick.[24] As Robert Barret put it in 1598, cities were strong if they had 'thicke walles, great Terraplenes, and broad and deepe ditches'.[25]

An angle-bastioned fortification could be dug with surprising ease. A huge ditch was excavated following the geometrical pattern (square, pentagonal, hexagonal, etc.) selected for the defensive perimeter. The earth excavated from the ditch formed the walls, glacis and counterscarp. The only obstacles were the quality of the soil, the cost of labour and the availability of timber to shore it up. The theorist Richard Norwood even provided exact details for the seventeenth-century reader anxious to build one himself.[26] The Netherlands saw such fortifications sprout like mushrooms in the course of the eighty-year conflict with Spain.

The value of the angle-bastioned fortification lay not so much in the physical obstacle they placed in the path of the attacker, or in their resistance to his cannon, as in the excellent fields of fire they opened up for the defenders' artillery and firearms. As Peter Whitehorne realised in 1560–2, the new fortifications with their low parapets presented less of a hindrance to the movement of the enemy's troops than did the precipitous walls of the traditional kind.[27] Nor did the angle-bastioned fortifications offer complete security against the besiegers' cannon.

Room in which to make fresh defences behind a breach in the outer wall and massive ditches completed the demands of the new age. The first point was amply explained by Peter Whitehorne, who realised in 1560–2 that 'if he that is within, have not space inough to retire, both with diches and rampiers, he is overcum, because he is not abell to withstande the violence of the enemie, who through the breach of the wall, will after enter'.[28] The functions of the huge ditches advocated by contemporaries were multiple. For a start, they could hide the bulk of the fortification from the enemy's cannon, if their height approximated to that of the new-style low walls. A vast trench resulted, of which one side was formed by the wall itself, the other by the outer bank of the ditch. William Garrard had just this in mind when he advocated the use of deep ditches 'in the which the fortification may remaine covered, and closely hid ... to thee intent the Parapettes be onely seene and no other'.[29] The logic behind this was simple enough. It is 'a most sure rule in matter of fortifications', the Spaniard Bernardino de Mendoza assured his readers, 'that whatsoever is seene the defendant looseth, by shooting of the artillerie in direct line as the sight goeth'.[30]

The primary function of the ditch, however, remained the ancient task of impeding the attacker's progress on foot both above and below the surface. How well it performed this role depended very much on its type. Water-filled ditches were generally preferred to the dry variety because they impeded the digging of mines by the besieger[31] and virtually ruled out surprise attacks by escalade.[32] The problem was that they also ruled out sallies[33] and expeditions to clear debris from the ditch floor, which blocked the line of sight of the defender's guns in the event of an assault.[34] Water also tended to cause sanitary problems in summer and to freeze over in winter, giving the attacker a solid operating surface.

The protection against mining offered by a water ditch was very welcome in an age which used the mine as much as artillery to break open a breach in the defences to be exploited by assault.[35] The mine was age-old. Byzantine military treatises from the early Middle Ages understood the techniques involved – and the best countermeasures – as well as their sixteenth-century successors.[36] Whereas in the pre-gunpowder age the wall was demolished by burning through the wooden props holding up the mine-shaft below it, from the fifteenth century an explosion beneath the foundations could be arranged.[37] Safety dictated that the mine itself twist and turn to reduce the blast of the explosion on the escaping miners as they fled after lighting the fuse.[38] Gunpowder brought new risks as well as the obvious benefit of greater damage to the defences above the mine. If the besieger had dug a mine or two under the walls filled with explosive, he would time the explosion for a few seconds before the assault in order to gain maximum surprise. But the risks were great. The English assault on Corunna (1589) reached the tower under which their mine had been placed so quickly that several were killed by debris from the explosion.[39]

Gunpowder artillery had an impact far greater than the gunpowder mine on siege warfare, wrenching it out of the past. We have already seen the effect of improved cannon on fortress design beginning to be registered in the printed literature of the later sixteenth century in England: the appearance of illustrations featuring angle-bastions and the growing preference for vast ditches, shielding massive earthen walls from the besiegers' fire. But the impact of artillery was not restricted to the siege cannon at the attackers' disposal. Cannon were the mainstay of the defence of towns from the later Middle Ages.[40] The skill was in placing them at points where they were as free as possible from the danger of enemy fire, yet in a position to sweep the length of the walls to prevent the enemy from approaching the breaches. The sixteenth-century introduction of the angle-bastion solved the second part of the problem. It also solved the first. If the guns in the neck of the bastion were pulled back a few feet, the outer wall of the bastion would protect them against all shots save those fired along the length of the curtain wall between the bastions by siege-guns placed close to the neighbouring bastions: a most unlikely proceeding.[41] Barring such a siting, the siege batteries could do little against the defending cannon until they had demolished a sizeable part of the outer wall of the bastion in which they were placed.

A good siege-train could demolish 120 feet of old-fashioned wall in under twenty-four hours.[42] The walls of a more up-to-date fortification would take much longer to demolish. At Alkmaar in the early 1570s, Alva's men were willing to expend 7,000 cannon balls to achieve a single breach. The Italian, Busca, reckoned that 15,000 cannon balls were required to create a large assaultable breach.[43] The design of the new fortifications often made it hard for the besieger to bring his guns to bear. But, in the end, a breach would be created even if it was first necessary to bring up labourers and pioneers to cut away the protective counterscarp before the besiegers' guns could see the wall they were to perforate. The Turks were forced to do precisely this during the siege of Fort St Elmo at Malta (1565).[44]

Instead of making a breach and simply assaulting, the sixteenth-century besieger was increasingly forced to make three breaches: one in the wall and one in each of the two bastions flanking it in order to knock out the defending artillery, or else face the massacre of his assaulting troops.[45] The anonymous author of *A Myrrour for English Souldiers* (1595) explained the problem. The

> flankers [enfilading gun positions] of the bulwarks [angle-bastions] of a town of war (being wel made and wel used) are the special strength for defence of the same town, for no enemie from without the town can make any breach to be assaulted in any part of any bulwarke, or in any part of any curten wall betweene two bulwarkes, but the assaulters of that breach must passe within the deadly and extreame danger of the said flankers, if the said flankers shall not be first damned (as they call it) by the enemie.[46]

His personal contribution was to suggest that instead of trying to silence the hidden enfilading guns with fire on the outer surface of their bastion, the attacker could just as well pile up earth to block their line of fire. The obvious disadvantage of such a solution was the 'infinite labor of pioners' under fire that it entailed.[47] In practice there was no alternative to the slow and steady destruction of the flanking gun positions by cannon fire.

When it came to more general questions, such as how to lay out siege artillery, how many breaches to create, what quantity of guns were required and how to protect them against enemy fire, contemporaries were well served with advice from a range of manuals and published accounts. However, the treatment of these issues, as with all aspects of siege warfare, was patchy in comparison to more basic matters, such as infantry organization and training. There was little point in making only a single breach, since to do so allowed the defender to concentrate his response in anticipation of the inevitable assault. A choice of breaches meant a dispersal of the defender's resources and either multiple simultaneous assaults or feints and a genuine attack at what was judged to be the weakest point. Sir Roger Williams, a veteran of the Spanish Army of Flanders himself, admired the Spaniards, who 'lightlie ... give their assaults generall at once, I meane at all their breaches and mines, if the ground serve to mine'.[48] Assaulted at several points simultaneously, the defenders were always forced to think of their backs, a fear which Williams's former comrades exploited ruthlessly by employing 'messengers of credite on horsebacke ... which runne from breach to breach, crying courage the Tertia de Leige is entered. So at the other breaches the like, that the Tertias, of Lumbardy or Naples, or others are entred, when there is no such matter.'[49]

To achieve such a psychological effect and make maximum use of the besieger's superiority in manpower, the more breaches there were the better. Bernardino de Mendoza felt that at least two breaches, each eight to nine men wide, were the bare minimum. Even though each would require a separate assembly of guns to batter the enemy fire positions and create the large breaches he desired, the effort was worth the trouble.[50] In the mid-seventeenth century Richard Norwood reckoned on 1,000 shots for one breach.[51]

If multiple breaches were required, the logistic effort to marshal the barrels of powder, wagons of shot, hundreds of gunners and all the necessary cannon would be immense. Giovanni Ruscelli's *Precetti della milita moderna* (Venice, 1568) gives some idea of the scale of the problem. A healthy siege-train of forty guns of different calibres would require 442 gunners and helpers and 1,050 non-specialist labourers and pioneers. Each of the larger pieces would use up well over a thousand pounds of powder each day to fire a paltry forty shots.[52] Contemporary theorists responded to the problem by providing checklists of items needed. Both Thomas Styward and Robert Barret supplied lengthy lists of the supplies required by contemporary artillery, the powder, shot and all the other myriad items essential for a major siege.[53] Barret expected a siege-train of seventy guns firing shot of 20 pounds weight or more and seventy-two lighter pieces, which together would require 5,000 quintals of powder and some 30,000 cannon shot of all calibres. Putting aside the horses and oxen required to haul the wagons of powder and shot, the cannon alone needed between eight and thirty animals each, depending on their weight and size.[54]

Barret's estimate of what was necessary was on the high side. The Spanish theorist Escalante was happy with a mere thirty heavy pieces, Norwood with ten.[55] But Matthew Sutcliffe shared Barret's desire for a vast artillery train, equal to the tasks that would face it. 'He that employeth lesse than twenty cannons, and other pieces', he assured his readers, 'cannot looke for any good effect.' The Turks at Vienna used over sixty cannon; contemporaries should strive to do the same.[56] The gunners and their pieces, once assembled before the walls and fire positions they were to demolish, were vulnerable to musketry and arquebus fire as well as to the attention of any heavy guns the defenders had trained on their positions. They were also open to sallies, unless careful precautions were made for their protection. The ordinary soldier massing for the assault, or merely employed to guard against sallies, also needed to be shielded from hostile fire.

The problem was that it was not just one breach that was required. If the attacker contented himself with creating a breach and did not bother to destroy the cannon in the angle-bastions overlooking the breach he had made, his men would be massacred by scatter-shot fired from those pieces in the event of an assault.[57] Eliminating these flanking cannon was much harder than creating a breach in the wall between them and greatly slowed the pace of the siege. They were customarily placed in recesses (retired flanks) in the necks of the bastions, almost hidden from view and very hard to hit.[58] It was thus necessary to assign guns to destroy the defender's flanking cannon as well as to create the multiple breaches which contemporary writers considered necessary if the assault was to succeed.[59] If the besieger lacked enough cannon to perform all these tasks he would be faced with the alternatives of either making an assault across a space swept by cannon-fire, or abandoning the siege. Very few sixteenth-century forces had the number of breaching-cannon required to do the job quickly and efficiently. As we have seen, Matthew Sutcliffe took it as axiomatic that a besieger who used 'lesse than twenty cannons and other pieces' could not hope for success.[60] The French needed between twenty-six and twenty-eight heavy guns to achieve results against Novara in 1513.[61] Many sixteenth-century sieges depended for their success on the use of more.

Nor would the defender be standing idly by while the besieger proceeded with his ponderous battery and marshalled his men for the assault. Every breach would be repaired by the defender with materials gathered for the purpose, infinitely prolonging the besieger's task if he did not maintain so constant a fire on the breach as to prevent repair parties from working by day or night. During the siege of Metz (1552), Charles V's artillerists maintained a fire of 60–100 shots a day but this did not prevent the defenders from making substantial repairs to the areas that had been hit.[62] The work of the artillerists was also made far more dangerous by the arquebusiers and musketeers among the garrison. Whereas in the later Middle Ages it had been usual to place cannon only a few dozen paces from the walls,[63] by the sixteenth century a distance of several hundred yards was considered sensible in order to be out of arquebus range.[64] If the commander none the less wished his battery to be close in, he was forced to pay danger money to his men, as the Duke of Suffolk did at Boulogne (1544).[65] Frequently it was not merely the hazards of musketry that delayed the besieger, but the defender's unsilenced artillery firing on his own. The sieges of Gaeta (1503),[66] Siena (1555)[67] and Thionville (1558) were classic examples of the effectiveness of artillery in this role. Of the latter, Monluc remarked in amazement: 'I never saw a more furious counter-battery.'[68] At Malta (1565), the garrison paid a heavy price for the severe shortage of ammunition which prevented their cannon firing on the Turks as they went about their battery.[69] If it had been available, the Grand Master could have delayed the Turks for many extra weeks and possibly saved Fort St Elmo from capture.

Under fierce fire the early-modern besieger was forced to delay the pace of his advance by digging trenches to protect his men.[70] Nor could the trenches take the shortest possible line to the besieged. They needed to zigzag every few dozen yards to prevent the defending artillery from enfilading them and firing down their length.[71] Wickerwork gabions filled with earth provided additional protection for the artillerymen and for the trench system.[72] The entire trench complex took weeks to construct, especially if there were additional embellishments of the kind Monluc recommended.[73]

The guns were best shielded by wickerwork gabions filled with earth to absorb the impact of heavy shot.[74] William Bourne, in his book *Inventions or Devises* (1578), proposed the use of a sheet to hide the men when not firing if gabions could not be found. It was his view, as it was of all his contemporaries, that the gabion was the only satisfactory solution.[75] Trenches, zigzagging every few yards to prevent the enemy firing enfilade down their full length, were essential to shield troops and artillerymen as they moved about, and to provide cover for the marksmen who swept the enemy walls.[76] If the ground was too stony to be worked the besieger had a serious problem. If he used heaps of stones as shelter they would shatter on impact, increasing rather than lessening the danger.[77]

Two English soldiers published in the 1590s, William Garrard and Sir Roger Williams, both wanted their gun batteries sited within 160 yards of the walls.[78] This put the gunners within bow, arquebus and musket range, making some form of protection indispensable. Bernardino de Mendoza had no sympathy for those who put their artillery at the mercy of small arms fire, although, as he conceded, the further away the siege-cannon were placed the harder it was to obtain accuracy. Putting the guns right by the brim of the ditch, as some preferred, was merely to tempt sallies.[79]

Fourquevaux, whose mid-century treatise was translated by Paul Ive for English publication in 1589, proposed bringing trenches right up to the walls, getting the siege artillery swiftly into position and then creating and assaulting a breach so quickly that the defenders would never have a chance to repair it.[80] The risk of the enemy repairing the breach shortly before an assault was enough to ensure that the besieger took elaborate precautions even if he did not adopt Fourquevaux's lightning approach. It was regarded as good practice to keep up a constant fire on the breach, day and night, to deter repair parties.[81] The repair of breaches was, in the view of an anonymous English writer of c.1540, a critical point which made the difference between success and failure, contributing to the loss of Rhodes in 1522 when the besieged chose to continue a divine service rather than immediately shore up the defences.[82] Even if the besieger took great care to fire continuously to deter repairs, he was foolish if he did not reconnoitre the breach immediately before an attack[83] and take careful note of the appropriate length of scaling ladders.[84] These little precautions were worth many lives in the event of an assault, as the English army found to its cost before Leith (1560) and at Rhé off La Rochelle (1627), where it used ladders that were too short.[85] This latter defect was a common one, in Mendoza's view, 'many townes having missed being wonne, by reason their ladders were to short, having taken measure to the iust height of the wal, but not from that parte of the ground where the ladders were faine to stand'.[86] Only an expert reconnaissance could answer that question satisfactorily.

Once the breaches had been made, the defending guns silenced and the mines prepared for demolition, the assault loomed. Every effort would be taken to drive the enemy's musketeers from the walls so as to allow the assaulting troops to reach the breach without loss.[87] What awaited them there was another matter. An assault was a more fearful affair in the sixteenth century than at any time before in the history of siege warfare.

The defenders would not have been idle. Behind the breach there would now be a defensive trench, variously termed a *retirata*, a retrenchment or a half-moon. In it, and in the windows of houses of the town overlooking the breach, would be posted men with firearms able to fire point-blank into the breach.[88] Also posted to fire into the breach were the defender's artillery pieces, loaded with scattershot. Both the arquebusiers and the artillery were hidden from view until the attacker stepped into the breach. At such close range every musket shot told and all defensive armour was useless.

As Sir John Smythe appreciated, in assaults, muskets and arquebuses 'doe kill or hurte 10, 20 or 30 for every one that they kill or hurte in services of the field'. But when, as at Cerignola (1503), similar conditions could be duplicated on the field of battle as in an assault firearms proved every bit as lethal.[89]

The odds in a sixteenth-century assault were stacked heavily in a competent defender's favour. Waiting behind the breach, the attacker would find artillery and marksmen protected by a semicircular ditch crowned with an earthen or improvised parapet. Whoever survived their remorseless point-blank fire stood to be swept away by the defender's massed pikes. If the outer circuit of the defences was sufficiently large, it was easy enough to find room inside by demolishing houses and using open spaces to dig the 'half-moon' called for by contemporary orthodoxy.[90]

The half-moon gave the defender protection and a height advantage: the 'deeper the ditch [of the half-moon] is, and the higher the bank is raised, the better the work prooveth'.[91] In the ditch of the half-moon the attackers who had survived the point-blank musketry and cannons filled with 'cut off Pikes, chained bullets, Dice of steele covered with lead' and 'all the vilest shot they can invent'[92] were now expected to survive the 'garlands and balles of wild fire, molten leade, scaulding oyle and such like' as they struggled to climb out and face their tormentors on even terms.[93]

When Alva's men made repeated assaults on Haarlem in the course of the famous siege (1573), they stepped over the breach each time only to be confronted with the 'half moone, I mean the trench which the defendants made overthwart the breach within'. Then, as Sir Roger Williams explained, 'they were murdered like dogges. The defendants had divers fowlers [small artillery pieces] and other [artillery] peeces loaden with nailes and small shot' and many men with firearms who wrought terrible execution on them.[94] The remainder of the attacker's force would be driven away by push of pike by the defender's massed infantry.[95]

It is not surprising that successful assaults were rare in the sixteenth century. Towns tended to fall through a shortage of defenders, a lack of powder or artillery, or scarcity of food, rather than by assault.[96]

There was little a besieger could do to improve his chances. One trick was to try to gain a height advantage over the defence by building mounds overlooking the breaches, 'mounts' and 'cavaliers' in the parlance of the time. In addition to diversions and a 'rolinge trenche to advance the ladders', Sir Robert Constable recommended that an attacker who had decided on an assault should create 'a mount in such a place to anoye them that shall defend the assault'.[97] The guns on it would be able to fire over the rubble in the breach into the defences of the half-moon beyond. Bernardino de Mendoza also recommended the use of 'raysed platformes and cavaliers without, wherby to domnere over the walles'.[98] Apart from carefully surveying the breach before the assault there was little else that could be done. By posting musketeers and arquebusiers in the trenches close to the walls, the enemy could be kept off the parapets as the assaulting troops marshalled. Sir Robert proposed just this in his manuscript treatise of 1576, namely that 'the generall placeth harquebusiers and archers withe the rest of his souldiors to scowre the toppe and the lowpes of the walles, and that being done he with the Captenees and rest of the souldiors passe the dykes and attempt the assault'.[99] This was also advised by William Garrard and Mendoza.[100]

Once the assault failed, as the overwhelming majority of sixteenth-century assaults did, a well-prepared attacker could draw some comfort in defeat if the defenders overreached themselves in the moment of triumph. The bowmen, arquebusiers and musketeers who had swept the walls before the assault would have found targets hard to obtain. It was another matter after all was lost. 'For', as the English soldier William Garrard explained, 'it is the custome of the besieged, at the repulse of an Assault, the souldiors more willingly doo show themselves, and appeare carelessly at the breaches ... for they thinke that no man can hurt them.'[101] It was also wise to keep substantial reserves in case the defenders rushed out *en masse* in the wake of their victory. Without marshalled reserves the retreat from the breach could become a rout, which would infect the entire camp. It was unwise to assume otherwise, given that 'in case the besieged putt backe the men from the assault, if they retire it is easilie to be beleeved that it will be with disorder and scattering', as Mendoza pointed out.[102]

Such pessimism was not out of place. The breach and half-moon were the terror of the sixteenth-century military world. Muskets were devastating enough at close range. But as Humphrey Barwick, a musketeer of long experience, explained: 'within holdes or trenches there may be used, as the maner is, peeces of better force, more to offend the enemies then muskets: as Fauconits, Robinets and Organ-pipes' and indeed all manner of other artillery pieces, all firing from 'small loupes made that the enemies shall not discerne the same, before the shooting thereof, which may not be done, but upon good occasion', as during the assault itself.[103]

Improvements in firearms and their use in conjunction with artillery-based defences weakened the attacker of a fortified place no less than the attacker on the battlefield in the sixteenth century. In both cases, firearms and artillery behind earthworks and *ad hoc* defences prevailed on more occasions than the courage of those thrown against them with consequent deterrent effect. The pattern of war itself had changed.

The hopelessness of assaults against a well-equipped defender rapidly assumed the status of conventional wisdom. Don Bernardino de Mendoza, a Spanish soldier of great experience, explained in his late sixteenth-century treatise, written for the benefit of the future

King Philip III of Spain, that fortified places fell 'through want of men, powder, artillery, munition and victuals' rather than by assault.[104] As François de La Noue recognised, it took many months of assault and battery to take a place fortified in the Italian fashion. This held just as true for cheap bastioned fortifications improvised out of earth and wood as it did for the expensive prestige defences of the period. La Noue considered that even the Duke of Parma, 'The skilfullest assaulter of townes that I know', would be forced to spend months on an assault. Inferior commanders could easily 'labour two moneths about the winning of a Raveline [an outwork]'.[105]

Yet to take a fortification by assault was the quickest method and one which relied, as de Mendoza recognised, on the defender lacking all the necessaries to conduct an efficient defence. Otherwise, the siege would drag on still longer as the attacker would have no more effective a method than to starve the defender into submission.

This was by no means easy. The defender had to be cut off from resupply. The Spanish in the Netherlands were greatly disadvantaged by their failure to establish command of the sea. They could not follow Henry V's successful policy at Harfleur (1415) of combined land and sea blockade when faced with the siege of seaports.[106] As so many of the towns that resisted siege had access to the open water,[107] it was not surprising that the Eighty Years' War in the Netherlands furnishes one of the most striking examples of the decelerating effect of the new conditions of siege warfare on the pace of war. Even a commander so fortunate as to deal with a town with no sea access still faced a protracted siege, which he might at any point be forced to abandon due to the approach of a hostile army.[108] The mere news of Parma's approach was enough to cause Henry IV to break off his siege of Rouen (1591–2) for fear of the threat Parma would pose to his own supply lines as he waited to starve the town into submission.[109] Less astute commanders were often forced to break off lengthy sieges when their stocks of food ran out, not because of enemy action but because of administrative incompetence and lack of foresight.[110] The besieger faced the same problem in earlier ages and was sometimes forced, like the Archbishop of Cologne during the Soest feud of 1444–9, to abandon sieges for lack of supply.[111] Repeatedly, sixteenth-century commanders failed to maintain land cordons sufficiently tightly to intercept all the supplies sent to the besieged by their external allies.[112] Even with a successful blockade it could take nine months to achieve the capitulation through starvation of a badly stocked town like Siena (1555).[113]

There was a quicker method of taking towns in the sixteenth century which, so far, has not been mentioned – being let in by the inhabitants. Treachery, bribery, fear and collusion all helped to speed operations by allowing towns to be swiftly taken with the co-operation of those inside. The Spanish captured several towns in the Netherlands by bribing their garrison commanders to defect.[114] The inhabitants might even let in their enemies involuntarily by opening their gates to let in their own men fighting outside and thereby allowing the enemy to stream in with them, as happened at Cadiz (1596) and on other occasions in the Anglo-Spanish war of 1585–1604.[115] Occasionally, an escalade made without collusion from within might lead to the capture of a strong place in a single night – indeed, this was how the Huguenot, Captain Merle, took the small town of Issoire (1575);[116] but with a good watch this rarely happened. Barring such good fortune there was no alternative but to wait patiently for months before taking each place that had been fortified in the modern way.

This revolution in siege warfare was to have serious implications for strategy and the conduct of war. William Davison observed after the Spanish victory at Gembloux (1578) that the battle would avail Philip II's governor in the Netherlands little. For he still needed to besiege and capture 'one towne after another the least of a number whereof cannot cost him less than halfe a yeres siege with an infinite charge, loss of men and hazard of his fortune and reputation bycause (as men of warr are wont to say) one good town well defended sufficeth to ruyn a mightie army'.[117] Rapid progress, such as Parma made in the southern Netherlands in the early 1580s, was only possible if one side, for political reasons, lacked the will to fight. Failing a political collapse the commander was forced to besiege town after town at great cost before he could enjoy the possession of the territory he sought to conquer. The explanation for the slow progress of Charles V's invasions of France and Philip II's difficulty in reasserting his authority in the Netherlands lay in the enormous number of fortified places, all of which presented formidable obstacles in the changed conditions of the sixteenth century. Gone were the days when Henry V could win the crown of France *de jure*[118] and many of its richest provinces by *de facto* occupation in less than a decade of astute campaigning. As Blaise de Monluc observed, even if a commander won a string of victories he would sink in a morass of siege problems before conquering France. Merely taking Paris was not enough:

il y a tant d'autres villes et places en ce royaume, qui seroient bastantes pour faire perdre trentes armees, de sorte qu'il seroit aise se ralier et leur oster celle-la, avant qu'ils en eussent conquis d'autres, si le conquerant ne vouloit despeupler son royaume pour repeupler sa conqueste [there are so many other towns and places in this kingdom, which would suffice to absorb thirty armies, that it would be easy to recover and drive them back out of one before they had taken more, if the conqueror did not wish to depopulate his kingdom to populate his conquest].[119]

This was precisely the dilemma of strategy in the new era. If a commander gathered the forces necessary to capture the enemy's strong places he risked losing his own. Providing garrisons on the scale necessary to secure the Netherlands from attack consumed a sizeable percentage of Philip II's revenues in the later sixteenth century. This expenditure also left less money available for offensive operations. It was not surprising that in eighty years of war and peace the warring parties in the most fortified area in Europe, the Netherlands, remained deadlocked. There were simply not enough men, nor was there enough money available both to garrison one's own territory and to acquire more. When Philip II denuded the Netherlands' garrisons to provide an offensive force for operations in France he promptly lost to Maurice of Nassau several towns (1590–4), whose defence had been weakened by the withdrawals.[120] On the other hand, when Leicester parcelled much of his large force into separated garrisons during his tenure in the Netherlands he was criticised for inactivity and denuding the field army to the point where offensive operations were crippled.[121]

In other theatres of war the same dilemma existed, but it was not as stark.[122] The density of fortified places was lower and their defence was, on average, more difficult.[123] For the easily worked earth and high water-table of the Netherlands were the military engineer's dream. A water ditch was a more effective obstacle than a dry ditch even if the latter were furnished with casemates for its protection. Casemates, ranging from the purpose-built to simple loop-holes added as an afterthought to an existing fortification, were a common enough sight in the sixteenth century.[124] The water made mining and escalade almost impossible, thereby greatly complicating the besieger's task.[125] Though the Italian theorist Carlo Theti noted that a water ditch froze in winter in cold climates and nurtured disease in hot weather, he too recognised its formidable advantages.[126]

Even without the peculiar advantage of the terrain of the

Netherlands and in areas where no new purpose-built Italianate fortifications existed, ordinary old-fashioned defences still posed formidable obstacles in the new age. A breach could be rapidly made in a wall of antiquated design, but it remained only a breach. To take the town an assault was still necessary, and firearms and artillery were no less deadly in defence of a half-moon behind a medieval wall than in defence of one behind a more modern fortress wall. The only question was whether enough room existed behind the breach to dig the half-moon. This was the criterion that divided the indefensible sites from the defensible in the sixteenth century.[127]

Thus changes in the performance of firearms and artillery had, by the early sixteenth century, begun to transform war in Europe. They led in the course of the century to several new developments, which taken together constitute a revolution in the conduct of war in western Europe. A new system of infantry tactics, using pikemen in conjunction with men equipped with firearms became universal. The new tactics engendered a new approach to military organisation and a new emphasis on training *en masse*, as distinct from the training of the individual in the use of his weapon, as was familiar in the late Middle Ages. New ranks were created across Europe in the course of the century with the uniform intent of facilitating the training and control of men in the use of the new tactics. Order in the Roman sense – merely paid lip-service in the Middle Ages – at last came into its own after centuries of neglect, embodied in a new military literature, unparalleled in medieval experience. A major exception should be made for the armies of Byzantium, at least in the early Middle Ages. They were trained and disciplined in the use of relatively complex tactics, as surviving military manuals reveal. However, western Europe had not seen anything of the kind for centuries. The literature nurtured the new European tactical order that had given it birth with practical aids, propaganda and the dissemination of information and techniques.

Firearms left their mark on cavalry tactics, although their influence was less significant than in other fields. The mounted arquebusier, the precursor of the dragoon, spread across Europe. Pistoleers rivalled the men-at-arms of old for battlefield domination and drove their rivals to acquire pistols alongside their more traditional weapons. The caracole was used alongside more traditional shock tactics by Europe's new firearm-equipped cavalry.

But it was in the field of fortification and siege warfare that the improvements in firearms wreaked their most profound effects, distorting strategy and turning the capture of even the most trivial town into a major undertaking. When Montmorency captured the castle of Avigliana he hung its garrison as a lesson to those 'who fight on in places of little importance'. The gesture was in vain.[128] The nature of war in Europe had changed, and it was to remain bound by the constraints of these developments initiated in the sixteenth century until the age of Napoleon.

These developments did not take place at a uniform pace across Europe. Some regions, the British Isles foremost among them, were slower than others in adopting the new methods, weapons, hierarchy and techniques. It is in order to observe this hesitant but inevitable progression towards the acceptance of the military revolution that we now turn to sixteenth-century England.

Notes

1. F.L. Taylor, *The Art of War in Italy, 1494–1529* (Cambridge, 1921), p. 110.

2. Sir John Hale, *Renaissance Fortification. Art or Engineering?* (Norwich, 1977), pp. 12–14. Sir John Hale, 'The Early Development of the Bastion: An Italian Chronology *c*.1450–*c*.1534'. Sir John Hale, J.R.L. Highfield, B. Smalley (eds), *Europe in the Late Middle Ages* (London, 1965), pp. 466–91. Doris Bellebaum, *Die Befestigungen der Stadt Wesel in ihrer Entwicklung 1349–1552* (Cologne, 1961), p. iii.

3. Georg Ortenburg, *Waffe und Waffengebrauch im Zeitalter der Landsknechte* (Koblenz, 1984), p. 157.

4. La Noue, *Discourses*, p. 217. See also the preceding chapter.

5. Geoffrey Parker, *The Military Revolution. Military Innovation and the Rise of the West* (Cambridge, 1988), p. 10.

6. Nicolaus Bömmels, 'Die Neusser unter dem Druck der Belagerung', *Neuss, Burgund und das Reich* (Neuss, 1975), p. 277.

7. Viktor Poschenburg, *Die Schutz und Trutzwaffen des Mittelalters* (Wien, 1936), p. 184.

8. Volker Schmidtchen, *Bombarden, Befestigungen, Büchsenmeister* (Düsseldorf, 1977), p. 122, n329.

9. Max Jähns, *Handbuch einer Geschichte des Kriegswesens von der Urzeit bis zur Renaissance. Technischer Theil.* (2 vols, Leipzig, 1880), II, 1154.

10. Rudolf Schneider, *Die Artillerie des Mittelalters. Nach den Angaben der Zeitgenossen dargestellt* (Berlin, 1910) provides an excellent introduction to the varieties of medieval siege artillery.

11. Karl Jacobs, *Das Aufkommen der Feuerwaffen am Niederrhein bis zum Jahre 1400* (Bonn, 1910), p. 13.

12. Jähns, *Handbuch*, II, p. 1148. Hale, *Art or Engineering?*, pp. 12–13.

13. Heinz Waschow, *4000 Jahre Kampf um die Mauer. Der Festungskrieg der Pioniere. Geschichte der Belagerungstechnik* (Bottrop, 1938), p. 17.

14. *An Order Whych a Prince in Battayl Muste Observe*, STC 18842 (1540?), sig. Bvᵛ. Hale, *N.C.M.H.*, II, p. 492.

15. Christopher Duffy, *Siege Warfare. The Fortress in the Early Modern World 1494–1660* (London, 1979), p. 2. Schmidtchen, *Bombarden*, p. 123.

16. Gabrielo Busca, *Della Espugnatione et Difesa delle Fortezze* (Turin, 1585), p. 72.

17. Paul Ive, *The Practise of Fortification*, STC 14289 (1589), sig. B3.

18. François de la Noue, *The Politicke and Militarie Discourses of the Lord de la Noue*, tr. E. A[ggas], STC 15215 (1587), p. 217.

19. Matthew Sutcliffe, *The Practice, Proceedings and Lawes of Armes*, STC 23468 (1593), pp. 263f.

20. Garrard, *Arte*, p. 285.

21. Ive, *Practise*, sig. F4. Humphrey Barwick, *A Breefe Discourse Concerning the Force and Effect of All Manuall Weapons of Fire*, STC 1542 (1594?), sig. C2ᵛ.

22. Whitehorne, *Certain Waies*, sig. Iiiii.

23. Richard Norwood, *Fortification or architecture military*, STC 18690 (London, 1639), p. 126.

24. M. Romeiss, 'Die Wehrverfassung der Reichsstadt Frankfurt a. M. im Mittelalter', *Archiv für Frankfurts Geschichte und Kunst*, XLI (1953), p. 11.

25. Barret, *Theorike*, p. 124.

26. Richard Norwood, *Fortification, or architecture military*, STC 18690 (London, 1639), pp. 92–6.

27. Peter Whitehorne, *Certain Waies for the Orderying of Souldiers in Battelray*, STC 17164 (1560–2), sig. Iiiii.

28. Whitehorne, *Certain Waies*, sig. Iiii. Francesco Ferretti, *Della Osservanza Militare* (Venice, 1576), p. 79.

29. Garrard, *Arte*, p. 284.

30. Mendoza, *Theorique*, p. 119.

31. Mora, *Soldato*, p. 180. Ive, *Practise*, sig. A4. Bourne, *Inventions*, p. 46.

32. Gabrielo Busca, *Della Espugnatione et Difesa delle Fortezze* (Turin, 1585), p. 9. Ive, *Practise*, sig. A4.

33. Garrard, *Arte*, p. 289. Busca, *Fortezze*, p. 9.

34. Ive, *Practise*, sig. A4.

35. Evans (ed.), *Works*, p. 229. Simon Pepper, 'The underground siege', and J.B. Bury, 'The early history of the explosive mine', *Fort*, X (1982).

36. George T. Dennis (ed.), *Three Byzantine Military Treatises* (Washington D.C., 1985), pp. 37–9

37. Ortenburg, *Waffe und Waffengebrauch*, p. 169. Jähns, *Handbuch*, II, p. 1153.

38. Sutcliffe, *Practice*, p. 224. Bourne, *Inventions*, p. 50. Whitehorne, *Certain Waies*, sig. Kiiᵛ.

39. *Calendar of State Papers (Foreign) Jan–July 1589*, p. 353.

40. David Eltis, 'Towns and Defence in Later Medieval Germany', *Nottingham Medieval Studies*, XXXIII (1989), pp. 92–4.

41. *A Myrrour for English Souldiers: Or, An Anatomy of an accomplished man at Armes*, STC 10418 (London, 1595), sig. G1. Whitehorne, *Certain Waies*, sig. Eii.

42. Jähns, *Handbuch*, II, p. 1154. Also see Georg Fischer, *Die Schlacht bei Novara 6. Juni 1513* (Diss., Berlin, 1908), pp. 80–3.

43. J.X. Evans (ed.), *The Works of Sir Roger Williams* (Oxford, 1972), p. 134. Busca, *Espugnatione*, p. 21.

44. Francesco Balbi di Correggio, *The Siege of Malta 1565* (Copenhagen, 1961), p. 61.

45. British Library, Harleian MS 847, f 63. Styward, *Pathwaie*, p. 14. Garrard, *Arte*, p. 280. Barret, *Theorike*, p. 138. Sutcliffe, *Practice*, p. 230. Whitehorne, *Certain Waies*, sig. Eii. Williams, *Briefe Discourse*, p. 20.

46. *Myrrour*, sig. F3ᵛ.

47. Ibid., sig. F4.

48. Williams, *Briefe Discourse*, p. 21.

49. Ibid.

50. Mendoza, *Theorique*, pp. 87 and 96.

51. Norwood, *Fortification*, p. 135.

52. Ruscelli, *Precetti*, f 13.

53. Styward, *Pathwaie*, pp. 11–13. Barret, *Theorike*, pp. 133–6.

54. Ibid. Compare C.S.L. Davies, 'The supply services of English armed forces, 1509–1550' (unpublished Oxford D.Phil., 1963), p. 231.

55. Bernardino de Escalante, *Dialogos del Arte Militar* (Brussels, 1595), f 66. Norwood, *Fortification*, p. 135.

56. Sutcliffe, *Practice*, p. 231.

57. Sir John Hale (ed.), Sir John Smythe, *Certain Discourses Military* (1590) (Ithaca, 1964), p. 22.

58. Duffy, *Siege warfare*, p. 17. Domenico Mora, *Il soldato* (Venice, 1570), p. 203.

59. Mendoza, *Theorique*, pp. 87 and 96.

60. Matthew Sutcliffe, *The Practise, Proceedings and Lawes of Armes*, STC 23468 (1593), p. 231.

61. Fischer, *Novara*, p. 105.

62. F.M. Chabert (ed.), *Journal du Siège de Metz en 1552* (Metz, 1856), p. 67. François de Rabutin, *Commentaires sur le Faict des dernières Guerres en la Gaule ...* (Paris, 1555), IV, f 83.

63. Philippe Contamine, *La Guerre au Moyen Age* (Paris, 1980), p. 343.

64. Busca, *Espugnatione*, p. 71.

65. S.J. Gunn, 'The Life and Career of Charles Brandon, Duke of Suffolk, c.1485–1545', (Oxford D.Phil., 1986), p. 294.

66. Camille Monnet, *Petite histoire veridique des faits et gestes du capitaine Bayard avant et pendant les guerres d'Italie* (Grenoble, 1970), p. 64.

67. Monluc, *Commentaires*, p. 311.

68. Ibid., p. 426.

69. Balbi, *Malta*, p. 62.

70. Monluc, *Commentaires*, pp. 328 and 433. Busca, *Espugnatione*, p. 67.

71. Staatsbibliothek (Munich), Cod. bav. 1682, f 32ᵛ. Battista della Vale di Venafro, *Vallo libro continente appertinente a Capitanii, retenere et fortificare una Citta con bastioni [etc.]* (1531), f 20ᵛ.

72. Du Bellay, *Instructions*, p. 242. Carlo Theti, *Discorsi delle Fortificationi, Espugnationi, et Difese delle Citta et d'altri Luoghi* (Venice, 1589), p. 12. Della Vale, *Vallo*, sig. Aiiiiᵛ.

73. For the significance of Monluc's embellishments see the introduction to Ian Roy (ed.), Blaise de Monluc, *The Habsburg–Valois Wars and the French Wars of Religion* (London, 1971), p. 17.

74. Thomas Smith, *The Arte of Gunnerie*, STC 22855 (160), pp. 68–9.

75. Bourne, *Inventions*, p. 57.

76. Ibid., pp. 56–7. Garrard, *Arte*, pp. 284 and 295. British Library, Harleian MS 847, f 61ᵛ. Barret, *Theorike*, p. 138.

77. Mendoza, *Theorique*, p. 89.

78. Garrard, *Arte*, p. 295. Evans (ed.), Williams, *Works*, p. 134.

79. Mendoza, *Theorique*, p. 90.

80. G. du Bellay [actually Raymond de Beccarie de Pavie, Sieur de Fourquevaux, not du Bellay wrote the work in question, *pace* Ive], *Instructions for the Warres*, tr. Paul Ive, STC 7264 (1589), p. 243.

81. Bourne, *Inventions*, p. 53. Smith, *Gunnerie*, p. 69. Mendoza, *Theorique*, p. 94.

82. *An Order Whych a Prince in Battayll Muste Observe*, STC 18842 (1540?), Bviv.

83. Williams, *Briefe Discourse*, p. 21.

84. Mendoza, *Theorique*, p. 145. Sutcliffe, *Practice*, p. 225.

85. *C.S.P. (Spanish) 1558–67*, p. 159. G.G. Langsam, *Martial Books and Tudor Verse* (New York, 1951), p. 160. Kenneth Ferguson, 'The Expedition to Rhé, 1627', *The Irish Sword*, XIII (1979), p. 371.

86. Mendoza, *Theorique*, p. 145.

87. William Garrard, *The Arte of Warre*, STC 11625 (1591), p. 301.

88. *A Myrrour for English Souldiers: Or an Anatomy of an Accomplished Man at Armes*, STC 10418 (London, 1595), sigs. F1ᵛ–F2.

89. British Library, Harleian MS 135, f 107.

90. *Order Whych a Prince*, sig. Bvᵛ. Jacopo di Porcia, *The Preceptes of Warre*, tr. P. Betham, STC 20116 (1544), sig. Hviii. Barret, *Theorike*, p. 124. Whitehorne, *Certain Waies*, sig. Iiiii.

91. Sutcliffe, *Practice*, p. 250.

92. Williams, *Briefe Discourse*, p. 21.

93. Mendoza, *Theorique*, pp. 135–6.

94. Evans (ed.), *Works*, p. 124.

95. C.R. Markham, 'The Fighting Veres,' *Lives of Sir Francis Vere … and of Sir Horace Vere* (London, 1888), pp. 108–10.

96. Ibid.

97. British Library, Harleian MS 847, f 60.

98. Mendoza, *Theorique*, p. 99.

99. Harleian MS 847, f 61ᵛ.

100. Garrard, *Arte*, p. 301. Mendoza, *Theorique*, p. 97.

101. Garrard, *Arte*, p. 303.

102. Mendoza, *Theorique*, p. 96.

103. Barwick, *Breefe Discourse*, sigs. E1–E1ᵛ.

104. De Mendoza, *Theorique*, pp. 135–6.

105. La Noue, *Discourses*, p. 219.

106. Benjamin Williams (ed.), *Henrici Quinti Angliae Regis Gesta* (London, 1850), pp. 20–1.

107. Sutcliffe, *Practise*, p. 203.

108. This had long been a problem of siege warfare. R.C. Smail, *Crusading Warfare 1097–1193* (Cambridge, 1956), pp. 24–5 and 38.

109. R.B. Wernham, 'Queen Elizabeth and the siege of Rouen, 1591', *Transactions of the Royal Historical Society*, 4th series, XV (1932), p. 174. In August 1590 Parma's appearance caused Henry to break off his siege of Paris. Ibid., p. 164.

110. For some sixteenth-century examples see Paul Kopitsch, *Die Schlacht bei Bicocca 27. April 1522* (Diss., Berlin, 1909), p. 38. Monnet, *Bayard*, pp. 165–6.

111. Bömmels, 'Neusser,' p. 286.

112. For examples see Balbi, *Malta*, p. 62. Häbler, 'Pavia', p. 517.

113. Monluc, *Commentaires*, p. 302.

114. Geoffrey Parker, *The Dutch Revolt* (Norwich, 1981), pp. 221–2. Anon., *A briefe cronicle and perfect rehearsall of all the memorable actions hapned not onelie in the Low Countries, but also in Germany, Italy, Fraunce and other countries since the yeare 1500* (1597), sig. E1.

115. Julian S. Corbett, *Drake and the Tudor Navy with a History of the Rise of England as a Maritime Power* (2 vols, London, 1917), II, p. 37.

116. G. Amiaud-Bellavaud, *Un chef Huguenot: le capitaine Merle et les Guerres de Religion notamment en Auvergne, Gevaudan et Vivarais* (Uzès, 1958), p. 153.

117. Geoffrey Parker, *The Army of Flanders and the Spanish Road 1567–1659. The Logistics of Spanish Victory and Defeat in the Low Countries' Wars* (Oxford, 1972), p. 10.

118. He won the right to inherit by the treaty of Troyes.

119. Monluc, *Commentaires*, p. 170.

120. Oman, *Sixteenth Century*, pp. 551 and 569–75.

121. *C.S.P. (Foreign) 1586 June–1587 March*, pp. vi and 49. For a defence of Leicester's conduct see Anon. [?Thomas Digges], *A Briefe Report of the Militarie Services Done in the Low Countries by the Erle of Leicester*, STC 7285 (1587).

122. See Parker, *Military Revolution*, pp. 39–40.

123. Oman, *Sixteenth Century*, p. 408. Geoffrey Parker has much to contribute on this aspect. Parker, *Military Revolution*, pp. 24–33.

124. Staatsbibliothek (Munich), cod. bav. 1682, f 69. Busca, *Espugnatione*, p. 79. The lack of casemates at St Elmo was said to have contributed to its loss (1565). Balbi, *Malta*, p. 27.

125. Busca, *Espugnatione*, pp. 109 and 9–10.

126. Theti, *Discorsi*, p. 25. See also Ive, *Practise*, sigs. A3ᵛ–A4.

127. Whitehorne, *Certain Waies*, sig. Iiii.

128. Lot, *Effectifs*, p. 67.

CHAPTER 5

ENGLISH MILITARY
DEVELOPMENT

'The art of war is now such that men are fain to learn it anew every two years end,' Philip II's faithful servant Granvelle claimed with some exaggeration in 1559.[1] Only a power in near constant conflict could hope to keep fully abreast of the technical and organisational change in the rapidly changing field of war. However, there was very little continuity in the Tudor military experience before Elizabeth's commitment to the rebel provinces in the Netherlands took shape from 1585. From 1585, English troops were constantly engaged, whether in the Netherlands and France, or in expeditions to the Iberian peninsula and the Indies. Before 1585, peace and military decay prevailed, with some notable exceptions. Seventy-seven of the 100 years from 1485 until 1585 were spent at peace.[2] As captain John Shute pointed out in 1598, a good captain could not be made in the life of a butterfly.[3] Long years of military experience, or at least a period of systematic training, were required. Before 1585, the former could only be gained if the soldier was willing to serve in the armies of foreign powers to make up for the lost experience his own could not provide. Systematic training only began in the final decades of the century.

The English lack of a substantial standing army compounded the problem. The yeomen of the guard,[4] a few scattered garrisons in England[5] and Ireland[6] and at Calais provided a limited reservoir of skilled personnel. The Calais garrison, particularly important for its close contacts with the soldiers of the Netherlands, was lost to a skilful French attack in 1558, depriving the country of one of its few centres of military expertise.[7] Schemes were floated in the reigns of Henry VIII,[8] Edward VI[9] and Elizabeth,[10] which, had they been implemented, would have generated a standing army of many thousand men. But nothing came of them.

This deficiency coupled with the long periods of peace before

1585 led to a military decay, which was noticed by sensitive contemporaries.[11] For Europe, 1585 marked no divide. The intense
military activity of the Valois–Habsburg wars was scarcely concluded
by the Peace of Câteau Cambrésis (1559) before the first of a long
series of French civil wars erupted. From the late 1560s a war began
in the Netherlands, which was to last with intermissions for eighty
years. The struggle with the Turk turned the Mediterranean and
eastern Europe into theatres of war for much of the century.

England fell far behind the leading powers of the continent, in
both training and experience, until the last decades of the century.
Whereas training was commonplace on the mainland in response to
the new weapons and techniques of the military revolution, the
English were ignorant of it. This lack of 'warlike discipline' adversely
affected imperial veteran Lazarus von Schwendi's opinion of England
in the 1550s, shared quite independently by a Venetian observer in
a report of 1557.[12] The English problem was one not of lack of
courage, but of lack of training and experience.[13] With a leavening
of veterans who had learned their trade in other nations' armies,
improvement would be swift.[14]

The history of English military development in the sixteenth
century is, in part, a history of the impact of precisely these soldiers
of fortune. Complemented by foreign specialists in fortification and
other advisers they gradually spread the new ideas of the military
revolution, bringing the government to adopt the pike and arquebus,
introduce mass training and new patterns of fortification, and
transform the command structure in use in the field. By their
writings and translations of key foreign works they introduced their
countrymen to the latest methods in use on the continent. In the
1550s this process had barely begun. It was only in the final decade
of the century that it could be said to be complete. As late as 1578
Captain Barnaby Rich found England lucky not to have been put
to the test of invasion, considering its chronic shortage of experienced soldiers to lead and train men in the new pattern.[15]

The time has come to examine the general impact of the military
revolution on English military development. Although we shall be
concerned with changes in military practice it will be necessary to
make a brief examination of English military theory from two points
of view – first, because the emergence of a practically oriented
military literature was, as we have seen in Chapter 3, one of the
hallmarks of the military revolution, and second, because English
military theory aided the introduction of training, thereby con-

tributing to the spread of the revolution itself rather than passively reflecting it.

Among the first signs of the military revolution in England was the appearance of firearms. Until Mary's reign their numbers were few. Humphrey Barwick, reminiscing of his youth among the archers of the Edwardian army, commented that 'at that time there were not in most bands of 100 men above 10 or 15 [arquebusiers] and in many none at all'.[16] Only 7 per cent of Henry VIII's native troops had arquebuses during his large-scale invasion of France in 1544.[17] The French, by Spanish standards slow to acquire firearms, used them to equip a full third of their infantry by mid-century.[18]

The chief reason for this backwardness was continuing faith in the merits of the longbow. Not merely was it a much cheaper[19] weapon and already plentifully available, but it evoked memories of the great victories of the Hundred Years' War, Crecy, Poitiers and Agincourt. These were kept alive by propagandists[20] as well as by the monarch himself. Henry VIII practised with the bow, as did Edward VI and, much later, Mary Queen of Scots.[21] Henry VIII's pride in the weapon is well evidenced in his support for Roger Ascham, an enthusiastic proponent,[22] and the many proclamations his government issued to encourage the bow and curb the use of cross-bows and firearms.[23] The preamble to a proclamation of 1528, one of many enforcing the archery legislation of Edward III, gives some indication of his feelings. It was through the longbow that Henry's 'noble progenitours not only ... defended this his said realm and subjects thereof against the danger and malice of their enemies, but also with a mean and small number and puissance, in regard and comparison to their enemies, have done many notable exploits and acts of war to the discomfiture of their said enemies.'[24] Bishop Latimer developed this line further in a sermon of 1549, speaking of the longbow as 'God's instrument'. It was in fact 'a gift of God that he hath given us to excel all other nations withal'.[25] This sentiment was not universal. Humphrey Barwick in the late sixteenth century and Sir Walter Raleigh in the early seventeenth felt that English successes in France should be attributed to superior morale and not the bow.[26]

Henry VIII himself, for all his romantic attachment to the bow, hedged his bets in the course of the 1540s by building up a large stockpile of foreign arquebuses and pikes.[27] This policy was continued by his daughter Mary I, who made the arquebus compulsory alongside the longbow in all save a few counties of the realm.[28] On paper, men with firearms now formed almost one-fifth of the foot in the Marian militia; a greatly improved percentage.[29] In practice, progress was slow and, by the time of the rebellion of the northern earls, very few if any of the militiamen of the northern counties were armed with the modern pike and arquebus rather than the traditional bow and bill.

Long after Mary's reign many remained reluctant to see the longbow replaced by firearms. A variety of compelling arguments could be found to show why the weapon of Crecy, Poitiers and Agincourt should be retained.[30] Sentiment and inertia combined to see the bow employed well into the 1580s and beyond, though in diminishing numbers. Thus 3,577 men of the Essex footbands in 1590 included 1,177 archers and billmen as well as 2,400 men armed with pikes and firearms in the continental fashion.[31] Elizabethan expeditionary forces of the same period were invariably furnished with modern weapons, although as late as the mid-1580s we still find a company of archers serving under Leicester in the Netherlands.[32] Humphrey Barwick felt his countrymen were novices with firearms in the 1590s.[33] Yet at this very time the Elizabethan regime was taking steps to ensure that the trained bands contained only pikemen and men equipped with firearms.[34]

The romanticism of the bow penetrated well into the seventeenth century. Bowmen were sent on Buckingham's ill-fated expedition to La Rochelle (1627) and enrolled in royalist Oxford during the Civil Wars.[35] Charles I signed a commission intended to reactivate Henry VIII's archery legislation in March 1629.[36] As late as 1798 a tract appeared arguing for the retention of the bow as a national weapon in combination with the pike;[37] an idea Charles I had enthusiastically supported to the point of ordering his countrymen, unavailingly, to adopt it by proclamation.[38]

Given the persistence of respect for the bow, the achievement of the Elizabethan regime and its military advisers in finally brushing it and the bill aside to make way for the new weapons of the continent is all the more remarkable. Their case was not helped by the success of English bowmen against continental mercenaries during the suppression of the Western Rising (1549)[39] and the devastating defeat inflicted on the Scots pikemen at Flodden (1513) by English billmen, whose axe-heads clove off the points of the Scottish pikes wreaking fearful slaughter.[40] At Pinkie (1547) the Scottish pike-squares were again massacred, although this time in part by modern weapons.[41] But none of these cases could prevent the eventual wholescale adoption of pikes and firearms for both expeditions and home defence.

The adoption of the caliver[42] (arquebus) was, as we have seen, a gradual process. Departing expeditions could often be issued with equipment in government stock even when the armouries in the localities where they had been raised were unable to provide them with modern weapons. It is thus quite pointless to try to identify a date from which England went over to modern weapons when, in fact, for most of the century it employed both new and old, such that in 1569 Cornwall was happily paying for a mixture of bows, bills and calivers.[43] The adoption of the caliver's more powerful brother, the musket, was equally messy. The musket was far heavier than the caliver, using one-and-a-half times more powder to propel its bullet over a greater distance with superior penetration on impact.[44] While Philip II's armies were using it enthusiastically from the late 1560s the first appearance of a musket in an English company dates from the late 1580s, although the weapon appeared in private use a decade earlier.[45] The government made up for its initial dilatoriness in recognising the importance of the musket by ordering the counties to provide large numbers in the final decades of the century. Norfolk was ordered to equip 15 per cent of its foot with the weapon in 1588.[46] By 1597, the government hoped to see two-thirds of the foot armed with muskets.[47] Even the Spanish armies in the Netherlands failed to achieve anything like this proportion.[48] Progress towards the Privy Council's target was naturally slow and calivers existed alongside muskets in county arsenals well into the seventeenth century.

As we have seen, the tactical combination of pikemen and infantry armed with firearms lay at the heart of the European military revolution. The developments stimulated a new military literature, led to the introduction of a new hierarchy of command and, most important of all, the spread of training *en masse*. The half-hearted adoption of firearms in England and the persistence of the longbow delayed the full impact of the military revolution in England until the final third of the century. Only four of the forty-two editions of sixteenth-century English military theory reviewed in my 1991 thesis fall into the first two-thirds of the century.[49] Regular training of bodies of troops began in the counties in 1572–3.[50] The new ranks of sergeant,[51] camp-master,[52] colonel,[53] corporal[54] and sergeant-major[55] came into general use in the second half of the century, long after continental armies had first adopted them.[56] Just as the bow and bill continued alongside more modern weapons well into the final third of the century the antiquated rank of 'vintener' or commander of twenty men continued in use alongside the new continental rank of corporal.[57] This imperfect reception of the ideas and methods of the military revolution from the continent, and the juxtaposition of old and new for decades on end, would have been avoided had English exposure to war been more continuous during the century. The magic of the old methods crowned with success in the Hundred Years' War further delayed innovation. Memories of the inadequacy of continental pike tactics in the face of bows and bills at Stoke (1487) and Flodden (1513) may well have remained at mid-century when Mary made the first moves to bring the pike into regular English use. Firearms had made a poor showing during the Wars of the Roses, which may also have been remembered.

The supporters of the military revolution and of up-to-date continental pike and firearm tactics needed to battle against opposition to their ideas as late as the 1590s. This peculiarity renders English military literature in the period particularly interesting. There is no continental equivalent to the English literary battle over the relative merits of bow and musket. The continent had few glorious memories of the crossbow, a weapon which underperformed disastrously at Crecy (1346) and did not shine in other engagements.[58] The continental works are also less in the nature of manifestos for change than their English counterparts. Sir Roger Williams's *A Briefe Discourse of Warre* (1590)[59] is a classic example of this English tendency. It is not enough to explain the techniques of the changed European battlefield. Williams also felt obliged, even at that late date, to justify them to a sceptical nationalistic audience. Characteristic of his writing is the insecure and aggressive explanation of the merits of continental cavalry armament towards the end of the work, which concludes:

> I persuade my selfe, that al the warriers in Europe, saving our selves and the Scots will bee of my minde. I am sure the Earle of Essex, Generall Norris, the Lord Willoughbie, Sir Richard Bingham, with the most of all that served against the great Captains, I mean the Prince of Parma and his followers, will say and confesse as I doo.[60]

Against this faction, which was prepared to accept continental methods unreservedly and counted in Williams, Essex, Norris and Willoughby some of the most important English commanders of the century, stood a highly disparate opposition ranging from the

London bowyers and fletchers[61] to Sir John Smythe, captain, publicist and political malcontent, whose treatise in defence of the bow was suppressed by the authorities in 1590.[62] The opposition scored some notable triumphs, scotching schemes which would have led to a trained force of 4,000 arquebusiers in the late 1560s[63] and maintaining legislation in defence of archery well into Elizabeth's reign.[64] The sheer cost of training men in the new weapons and procuring the weapons themselves found the bow lobby allies in the counties, who were genuinely shocked at the 'overburdenous', 'importunate' and 'unwonted charges' involved in modernisation.[65] When the trained militia was eventually introduced in 1572–3 their worst fears were indeed realised. Their strenuous resistance to reform continued long after the measures were in place.[66] However, by this time it was less a matter of disagreement with the adoption of firearms and the introduction of training, as concern at the ruinous effects of the local taxation on the poorer elements of county society that supported it.[67]

This element of struggle renders the establishment of the military revolution in England particularly interesting. Very far from being a quiet backwater in the long and often eventful development of English arms, the sixteenth century was actually a decisive turning point.[68] We have seen how the military revolution transformed English armies through the introduction of new weapons. Continuing our examination of the impact of the military revolution in England we shall survey, in turn, the introduction of mass training and England's struggle to keep abreast of changes in siege warfare. But before examining the growth of training in England it is as well first to sketch a picture of the country's military organisation and recruitment in order to place the government's efforts to train a portion of the militia from 1572–3 in perspective – the first real attempt to come to grips with the challenge of new weapons and tactics.

As we have seen, there was no adequate standing army in sixteenth-century England. The only permanent troops were 2,000–3,000 men in garrisons scattered among the royal fortifications in England and abroad and the sovereign's personal guard.[69] They were shabby but professional.[70] When the government needed men to mount an expedition they could drain a few hundred experienced men from the garrisons, as Elizabeth did from Berwick at the height of the rebellion of Shane O'Neill.[71] The vast bulk had to be found elsewhere. At first, the Tudor government wrote to selected individuals in the counties to assemble certain numbers of men in a private capacity with which to serve the Crown in the field. This method was used by Leicester as late as 1585 for his expedition to the Netherlands.[72] In the course of the century official channels developed at the expense of this personal approach to private individuals. The tested, late medieval system of indentured retinues[73] was gradually abandoned in favour of selection of individuals by a bureaucracy of commissioners, sheriffs and Lords Lieutenant and their deputies.[74]

The Crown could either instruct its agents to draw on their local militia for the soldiers needed or leave them greater discretion in the matter. Henry VIII and Mary both issued calls for militiamen to be sent in the mid-Tudor years.[75] However, by Elizabeth's reign the government had become reluctant to send good county men abroad. In 1602–3, the Privy Council directed the Lords Lieutenant and sheriffs of eighteen counties to gather vagabonds and masterless men to be sent to fight in the Low Countries.[76] By that date the government could have ordered the same officials to send trained men from the select militia or, at least, ordinary citizens enrolled in the general militia, which was regularly mustered but not trained. But it chose not to.

Nor was the government's action in 1602–3 unusual. Captain Barnaby Rich criticised the English tendency 'to scoure both Towne and Cuntrie of Rogges [rogues] and vagabons' to fill up their ranks in time of war. 'In other Countries,' as he commented bitterly, 'where they use the service of malefactours, they admit them not for souldiers, but they send them to their Gallies and to other places of like slavery; and those captains that hath made triall of such Souldiours would gladly be ridde of his charge to be eased of his trouble.'[77] The practice of sending felons to serve on expeditions is attested by numerous Elizabethan examples.[78] The commanders themselves sometimes contrived to procure men of the lowest quality, as Sir John Perrott did for his operations in Ireland in 1571.[79] The net effect was that Elizabethan military expeditions were composed of some of 'the meanest companies, which might be chosen out of the Queenes Maiesties forces'.[80]

Ideally, as the Elizabethan theorists pointed out, the government should have followed the path of antiquity and enlisted their expeditionary forces 'not of ye base, loose, abiect, unhonest sort by Cornelius Tacitus well termed *purgamenta urbium suarum*, but of the honest, well-bred, and renowned Burghers and other country inhabitants'.[81] In practice, the 'honest' citizenry was anxious to avoid enlistment by any possible means on account of the conditions of service. Corruption was rife. All captains were entitled to embezzle six men's wages out of every company of 100 men. These 'dead pays' were officially accepted by the end of Elizabeth's reign.[82] But many captains took more, leaving the men in their charge underpaid and starving. Captains who started with men who were neither beggars nor criminals in former life often reduced them to that state, or simply stood by as they died for lack of money and food.[83] The moralising translator of Plutarch's *Lives*, Sir Thomas North, lacked any moral conscience in his treatment of the men under his command in Ireland. By embezzling their pay and neglecting their welfare he reduced them to abject misery. Many died.[84] It was reported to the Privy Council that of 'all the captains in Ireland Sir Thomas North hath from the beginning kept a most miserable, unfurnished, naked, and hunger-starven band'.[85] Naturally enough, those who could sought to avoid service, and the officials entrusted with the task of selecting men were careful not to pick men of standing. As Captain Barnaby Rich observed in 1574, when the parish constable was required to send his quota of men for service overseas, he was naturally 'loth that anye honest man through his procurement should hazarde himselfe'. How much more logical to see the advantage for the community in being rid of 'any idle fellow, some drunkard, or sediciouse quariller, a privye picker, or such a one as hath some skill in stealing of a goose'.[86] After his unhappy experience at Rouen in the early 1590s, where the troops he was sent lacked training and tended to 'beggar themselves and fall into disorder',[87] Essex felt that the only way to raise men of any quality was to bypass the county officials and send his own 'superintendents' to pick individuals from the trained select militia and elsewhere for service in 1597.[88] Ordinarily, the trained militiamen, many of whom were 'chosen of the better sort', could expect to be exempted from the hazards of service abroad.[89] Only a tiny fraction of the 105,800 men raised and sent on expeditions in the years 1585–1603 were drawn from the trained bands of the select militia.[90]

The militia itself rounded off the Tudor armed forces, complementing the small professional core army based in garrisons, the foreign mercenaries so heavily used in the mid-Tudor years[91] and the men the government could raise for service abroad in wartime. The clearest sign of the impact of the military revolution in England was the transformation of the county militia. The militia was, as we have seen, a largely untapped resource for the conduct of war outside the realm, but remained the country's mainstay in the event of invasion. In 1588, in the event of invasion militia detachments were to man the coastal defences and operate a scorched-earth policy[92] until the main militia armies could defeat the invader and drive him into the sea.[93]

After this brief review of Tudor military organisation we are in a position to examine the introduction of training into the English military system and the role played by military theory in facilitating this development. Mass training was, as we have seen in Chapter 3, a necessary consequence of the Europe-wide transition to pike-and-firearm tactics in the course of the century. Until 1572–3, no attempt was made to train the English militia. From its earliest existence in Henry VIII's reign the militia was mustered periodically in order to furnish the government with statistics and allow its officers to form an impression of the quality of the force and the state of its equipment.[94] Queen Mary's legislation of 1558 fixed statutory levels of equipment for the militia but made no provision for training.[95] The break-point came in 1572–3, when the government separated the militia into two sections.[96] A select militia, consisting of only 26,000 men in 1588,[97] was to be trained and equipped with the most modern weapons on the continental pattern. The other, far larger part, numbering almost one-third of a million men in 1577, was to make do with a few modern weapons and large numbers of antiquated bows and bills; even then, many of its members were to be without any recognised weapons at all.[98] It was not to be trained, but musters enabled the government to keep track of its strength.[99]

The creation of a trained militia was the Elizabethan regime's single most important reaction to change in the European conduct of war. It was, as Sir Francis Walsingham pointed out, 'a thing never put into execution in any of her Majesty's predecessor's time'.[100] The measures of 1572–3 were only the hesitant beginnings of reform. Real progress came a decade later in the charged atmosphere of war and anticipation of war. Between 1573 and 1580 the number of men trained in Cornwall increased by a factor of ten from 400 to 4,000.[101] In 1584, the government ordered the President of the Council of the North to train 10,000 men in Yorkshire alone, a tenfold increase on its demand of 1573.[102] By 1588 the greatly expanded forces under training and the cost of dispatching troops on expeditions abroad was costing the Elizabethan ratepayer vast sums. In that year, Burghley assured Walsingham that 'whole towns pay as much as four subsidies' in meeting the cost of local defence. Exeter paid more than five.[103] Between 1577 and 1600 the cost of Hertfordshire's training more than quadrupled from £20–£40 a day to £150 a day.[104]

This growth in the provision of training in the decades after 1572–3 was a clear victory to those who, like Sir Roger Williams, had come to understand the value of the reforms in organisation, equipment and the introduction of training carried out by the major European powers decades earlier. Williams, who had served in the Spanish Army of Flanders in the 1570s, was in an excellent position to explain to contemporaries the changed nature of modern war.[105] By the mid-1580s his advice was taken very seriously by the government and, in the course of the ensuing hostilities, he and other like-minded reformers held high commands in every theatre of war.[106] Theirs were not the first voices to preach the necessity of training. Thomas Audley, theorist and veteran of Henry VIII's wars, desired it,[107] as did the government's continental agent, Sir Thomas Gresham, early in Elizabeth's reign. 'If', he pointed out, 'this were put presently in use, and good captains appointed to train them up, the news of that once spread through Christendom would be terrible.'[108] The early beginnings of militia training in the 1570s were largely the victory of an older generation. However, the expansion of training and the introduction of muster-masters and increasing numbers of Deputy Lieutenants to administer from the mid-1580s,[109] and the gradual elimination of bow and bill from county arsenals were in large part the achievement of a younger generation.[110]

The muster-master was critical to the reformers' programme. His appointment was made at the centre by the Privy Council where the reformers could influence it[111] and not by the county men who had to pay his salary.[112] In Cornwall, the muster-masters toured the county every two months to instruct the non-professionals who commanded the select militia companies in how to go about the task of training their men.[113] The use of militarily illiterate local dignitaries to command the companies was inevitable, as John Peyton rightly saw. Quite simply, 'the gentlemen of the counties are the only captains to draw the persons or the purses of the common people into martial actions'.[114] Neither the militiamen nor their commanders were militarily aware. As Essex put it in 1588: 'Ther numbers do for the most part consist of artificers and clownes who know nothing of the warres and little of the armes they carry ...

ther leaders men of quality dwelling neere, butt as insufficient comonly as the soldiers'.[115]

Since he was surrounded by ignorant and often unwilling countrymen and citizens, the quality of the muster-master was critical for the success of the government's attempts to reform and train. As a contemporary noticed, there was a strong temptation, which a local man would more readily succumb to, for the muster-master to shy away from rigorous training schedules,

> saying it is but a turmoiling of captains and soldiers, and intruding on the captains' offices to offend and discontent them. And that brave men should not be controlled, or the imperfections of their soldiers discovered bv such open exercises, and that such expense are foolish, and makes more enemies than friends.[116]

The JPs of Cornwall took such objection to a zealous muster-master that they offered him money in 1595 to leave his post rather than bear any more exercises in winter.[117] At the beginning of the reforms, before the introduction of skilled trainers in numbers, it was quite common for men to be trained for only a few days a year without rigour by more lenient officials.[118]

The shortage of suitably experienced men to hold training posts led to wide differences in the quality of the select militia across the country despite the best efforts of the reformers. In a few counties the influence of leading notables inclined to reform brought into service a large cadre of trainers. In others, lack of interest among the county élite and want of zeal on the part of Lord Lieutenants and their deputies led to neglect. By 1584, most counties had only one or two suitable trainers whereas the areas where the reforms had truly taken root had many more: eight in Kent, seventeen in Somerset, twenty-seven in Berkshire and forty-four in Suffolk.[119] These regional variations were accentuated by the lack of an official training manual until 1623,[120] which left great leeway to the officer on the spot to train men in his own fashion, making it even more important that the right men were selected for the task. The Isle of Wight was lucky in Sir George Carey, whose knowledge and enthusiasm in difficult circumstances[121] shine through in the directives he drew up in 1583 for the use of the captains under his command.[122] Other areas were less fortunate. The performance of the militia on the few occasions when it was put to the test was correspondingly varied. The Cornish militiamen knew so little of their business that they were swiftly routed at Penzance by Spanish troops landed by galleys on the coast near Mousehole in 1595.[123] On the other hand, the Welsh trained bands successfully dispatched a Spanish landing at Cawsand Bay with thoroughly modern methods.[124]

The veterans and the flood of military literature generated by the war helped further accelerate the process of reform. In 1587 the government recalled 1,000 veterans from the Low Countries to raise the level of training in the counties in anticipation of invasion.[125] Veterans also found their way into training by other means. Local men who had served abroad were anxious to find employment in the government's training programme. The theorist Sir John Smythe, who had seen extensive service in Europe, found a command training the men of Essex and Hertfordshire in 1587.[126] In 1593 Sir Clement Higham, knight of the shire and also a soldier of 'verie good experience', offered to perform the duties of muster-master free of charge in his native Suffolk when the post became free. When Sir Clement left the post it only took a letter to Sir Robert Cecil to secure the appointment in his place of Thomas Higham, who had been a captain on active service.[127]

The shortage of experienced professionals to act as trainers and muster-masters, the absence of standard, goverment-issued training regulations and the complete ignorance of all aspects of modern war among the local élites who acted as company commanders left a void into which military literature of all kinds could step. Works which could explain the Elizabethan military hierarchy and the methods of drawing up and manoeuvring a body of troops appropriate to militia use had a ready market. The Spanish War of course stimulated interest in all aspects of war, from Antiquity to the present time. Military histories, newsbooks with details of the latest European siege,[128] discourses on the moral virtues necessary in a soldier[129] and works of theory formed but a few genres among the many pouring from the Elizabethan presses in answer to popular demand.

Works such as Thomas Styward's *The Pathwaie to Martiall Discipline* (1581, 1582 and 1585)[130] and Robert Barret's *The Theorike and Practike of Moderne Warres* (1598)[131] will have provided the basis for many a gentleman's efforts to master his company command, in the long hours when experts were not on hand to advise him. We need not surmise that this was so simply from educated guesswork. The authors themselves give clear indications that this was the case. Robert Barret consciously wrote his *Theorike* for such an audience. After explaining a complex formation he paused to hope that his description was 'sufficient for any willing minded Gentlemen, which have not seene wars, and desirous to understand some points of martiall matters'.[132] For it was 'unto those do I write and not unto the expert soldier, whose skill and experience annexed with learning I honour and reverence'. The captains who used books to train their troops were many and fell into three types, the ignorant, the skilled and the readily confused, who would be forced to call on his men to stand and wait mid-manoeuvre while he tried to work out what had gone wrong from his book.[133] The author of two similar works,[134] Giles Clayton, was a Deputy Lieutenant of Cambridge-shire,[135] from which position he would readily have appreciated the value of works of military theory in easing his professional task. County captains, already familiar with the outline of modern war and basic training formations from dipping in the corpus of Elizabethan military theory, could far more easily be instructed than the wholly ignorant. These books with their copious diagrams and tables were also training aids in themselves.

Many theorists, the Digges, Styward, Clayton, Garrard and Barret among them, made very heavy use of diagrams marking the place of every single soldier with a letter of the alphabet. As we saw in Chapter 3, a capital 'A' denoted an 'Ansaigne' [ensign], 'a' an archer, 'h' an harquebusier and so forth.[136] Thomas Styward took his duty to his non-professional readers sufficiently seriously to depict the same march formation several times over, man for man, as it would appear with 100, 200, 300 or several hundred men.[137] This was very necessary if his book was to have value in a world where a captain's social standing affected how many hundred men his company would contain.[138] Another might have been content to point out the general principle behind the formation. Styward's compilation of multiple diagrams, meticulously charting the place of each man, would suggest that he expected that they would be used on the training field as aids in constructing the desired formation. Certainly, William Garrard saw great merit in his predecessor's approach. 'I have thought good,' he explained, 'to borrow out of Master Stywards Booke of Martial discipline his maner and forme of training ...'.[139] For the purpose in hand it was superior to the work of 'any that hath hitherto written so particularlie either in our owne tongue, or in any other forraine language'.[140] His book was replete with diagrams borrowed from Styward, which would be able to serve the militia commanders among his readers as well as their originals had helped the purchasers of Styward's treatise.

These developments in English military theory were relatively late, just as the adoption of the pike and firearms with their associated tactics and training requirements was delayed in England until late in the century. By mid-century the Spanish had already developed an elaborate system for training *besoños* [recruits] in garrisons before completing their education in the camps of the Habsburg field armies.[141] As Sir Roger Williams, who spent several years in Philip II's service, observed, service in a field army involved in operations was a major educational experience: 'A Campe continuallie maintained in action, is like an Universitie continuallie in exercises.'[142] The French had no lack of active experience either. The Spanish *tercios* embodying the pike and firearm tactics learnt in the early decades of the century emerged fully fledged in the 1530s long before England had any comparable organisational structure.[143] The French were slower to follow, but adopted pike and arquebus tactics and the organisational and hierarchical adjustments which went with them on a large scale in the 1540s.[144] A substantial part of almost all Valois and Habsburg armies of course consisted of Swiss and German mercenaries, whose mastery of the new pike and firearm tactics developed in the first third of the century, long before native English soldiers first used them to effect.[145]

The English reformers were painfully aware of their country's backwardness. The translator of Luis Gutierrez de la Vega's military manual felt the Spanish were streets ahead. He offered Gutierrez de la Vega's work to an English public 'chiefely because in our English tongue, I find not the like extant'. He piously wished it 'may be an inducement to better knowledge and further understanding, whereby in our time our servitours by good observance and imitation, may obtaine the lyke perfection, that all forreine Nations doe generally embrace'.[146] A generation before, in Queen Mary's reign, the position was even worse. Not a single published work expounding modern methods was available in English, at a time when the Italian presses were pouring forth an impressive variety of military literature.[147] The gap was gradually closed by the translation of key foreign works and the publications of native English soldiers. Yet a sense of inferiority remained, masked by the brash self-confidence so characteristic of the Elizabethan younger generation at war.[148] When, in 1590, John Thorius came to write the introduction to his translation of Francisco de Valdes's Spanish military treatise, he suggested his countrymen read the work:

not so much for any poynts of pollicy which might be in their souldiers more then in ours, or for that I think them to have more knowledge in matters concerninge warfare then our English warriers, who are no whit inferiour to them; as for that theyr orders being knowen unto us, we may the better and more easely hurte them and benefit ourselves by reason of this advantage.[149]

Thorius's masked unease contrasts with the open ridicule the French felt for the English and their incompletely modernised army as late as the 1590s. The Huguenots were surprised and bemused by the English knights 'armed and costumed like the antique figures shown on old tapestries, with coats of mail and iron helmets'.[150] Cavalry had never featured strongly in English late medieval armies, which had used the horse as a means of reaching the battlefield rather than of fighting on it.[151] In the sixteenth century the chief English cavalry type was a hybrid, the demi-lance, more heavily armoured than continental light cavalry, yet unable to match the old-fashioned man-at-arms or the new *reiters* in a frontal impact.[152] As Sir Roger Williams noticed, they lacked firearms, which put them at a disadvantage on the modern battlefield.[153] Pistols appeared in the hands of individuals rather than whole squadrons, as had become normal on the continent by that time.[154] This was a particular set-back to the reformers, who had seen the effect of the pistol on cavalry combat on the continent. Ironically, one of the first occasions on which the caracole was used to good effect was by the cavalry of Somerset's force at Pinkie (1547).[155] However, the cavalrymen were not native troops but mercenaries, whose pistol-based tactics failed to take root among the insular and conservative gentry who made up the bulk of the English horse in this period. The great interest in tournaments exhibited by Henry VIII and kept alive under the mid-Tudor regimes[156] kept many skills alive, as did aspects of noble education.[157] But the chief English handicap, apart from the dearth of firearms for cavalry use, was a lack of suitable mounts,[158] which kept to a minimum the number of men-at-arms, the one cavalry type in which the English were not outclassed by more advanced European nations, but also the one which depended most heavily on the horse's quality.[159]

The backwardness we have seen in armament, organisation and a host of other matters, which kept England lagging technically behind the leading European powers for most of the century was most painfully obvious in the field of siege warfare, perhaps the single most important aspect of the military revolution.[160] While

Italy produced an awe-inspiring range of military literature on the theory of siege and military architecture,[161] England could produce only one significant work in the whole century,[162] which was not published until 1589. Other works existed, which touched on the subject area, particularly in the last decade of the century, but they were so narrow in scope as to be of negligible value. A good example was Robert Hitchcock's *A General Proportion and Order of Provision to Victuall a Garrison of One Thousande Souldiours.*[163] The most important of these superficial treatments of fortification and siege warfare was contained in Peter Whitehorne's treatise of 1560–2.[164] However, even this work lacked detail and was of little value save for its illustrations.[165]

The dearth of English writing on the changing world of sixteenth-century siege warfare was matched by backwardness in other respects. There was no English treatise on artillery, the most important arm in siege warfare, until 1587.[166] These late offerings made available the findings of the Italian mathematician Tartaglia to an English audience a full half-century after his major publications on trajectory were published in Europe,[167] and they compared unfavourably with the more practically oriented contemporary European works on artillery.[168] It was not until 1628 that an adequate work was available to guide English students into the complex field of the early modern gunner's work.[169] England relied heavily on foreign specialists to direct and provide its artillery until well into the century.[170] When, as the century progressed, native gunners became the rule their quality often left much to be desired.[171] Their inadequacy on Leicester's campaign in the Netherlands was particularly noteworthy. Many of the pieces collapsed through neglect,[172] while the 'unskilfulness of the gunners' infuriated Norris, Leicester's deputy.[173]

England's dependence on continental specialists for its artillery early in the century was minor compared to its reliance on Europeans to compensate for its ignorance in the principles of modern fortress design. The architects of Henry VIII's coastal fortifications have never been satisfactorily identified in detail.[174] It is clear, however, that their inspiration was continental, reflecting designs popularised by Albrecht Dürer in his *Etliche Underricht zur Befestigung der Stett Schloss und Flecken* (Nuremberg, 1527).[175] The Bohemian architect Stefan von Haschenperg played a key part in the construction of at least two of these coastal artillery forts, Sandgate and Camber.[176]

From the mid-1540s, Germanic influence in fortification was gradually eclipsed by the growing importance of Italian engineers at court, who at last brought to England ideas that had been current in Italy and Europe for several decades and which were beginning to change the face of siege warfare.[177] Although a handful of Italian draughtsmen competent in military engineering were employed by Henry VIII, their practical impact on the English scene was minimal.[178] The first major fortress to show their influence was Berwick, which a mixed English–Italian team redesigned for Mary and Elizabeth under Sir Richard Lee.[179] Lee was soon shrouded in allegations of embezzlement[180] and incompetence,[181] and by 1564 the Italians Jacopo Contio and Giovanni Portinari were in a position to report directly to Elizabeth on the progress at the site.[182] Italian influence continued after their work in the 1560s[183] well into the next period of heightened government concern for the country's defences, which began in the early 1580s. Frederico Genbelli's work at Carisbrooke castle (1596–8) and at Plymouth (1602) carried Italian leadership in English military engineering to the end of the century and beyond.[184] However, a new generation of native English talent was also in evidence, as the fortificational theorist Paul Ive's work at Falmouth (1597) and in Ireland (1601–2) confirmed.[185]

This dependence on foreign expertise in the fortificational sphere was not limited to constructional work. England lacked experienced siege engineers and, as we have seen, artillerists. It is interesting that, during his expedition into France in 1522, it was Surrey's Low Country allies who appeared to know far more about the process of taking a fortified place on the scale of Thérouanne than his own men. Surrey could only retail with a degree of uncertainty the continentals' proposals to his masters, which with their use of earthworks, musketry, assault and battery were eminently up to date.[186] Moreover, when the English themselves attempted to take the far less imposing stronghold of Hesdin that year their efforts were wrecked 'By means of young counsel and [little] experience' and inadequate artillery.[187] For Henry VIII's expeditions of 1513 and 1544 and the Duke of Suffolk's invasion of France in 1523, continental gunners and pieces were secured in sufficient numbers to make good the native English deficiencies in that arm.[188] The large mercenary components in the armies of 1513 and 1544[189] and the close cooperation maintained with the more experienced continental soldiers provided by Maximilian and Charles V also helped to make good England's shortage of expertise. The siege of Boulogne (1544) in particular was very well conducted with good use of trenches, three artillery sites and effective mining operations.[190] The performance of Henry VIII's artillery at Thérouanne (1513) was no less impressive, though the town was eventually taken by blockade rather than battery and assault.[191] In 1523 Suffolk was able to take a number of fortified places, Bray, Montdidier and Bouchain among them, with the aid of a splendid artillery train lent by Emperor Charles V.[192]

Without the support and advisers a major European power could provide, English unfamiliarity with the changed world of sixteenth-century siege warfare was only too apparent. The Marquess of Dorset's Biscay expedition (1512) was unable to achieve anything for lack of continental assistance. The King of Aragon failed to provide the horses, artillery, supplies and technical back-up he had promised, forcing the English to leave for home without a single French fortification or other achievement to their name.[193]

Failures at sieges, owing to ignorance and inexperience, continued well into Elizabeth's reign. Technical incompetence led to the surrender of Calais in 1558 to the Duke of Guise, when the site's chief fortification was surrendered without a fight in order to be able to use an explosive device – which failed to work – against the incoming French troops.[194] At Leith (1560), the English siege was very poorly conducted, plagued by shortages of men and equipment.[195] An unsophisticated assault carried out with scaling-ladders that were too short[196] in the face of point-blank French arquebus and artillery fire was a disastrous failure.[197] Realisation of their technical inferiority prevented a repeat and the town was eventually starved into surrender.[198] This lack of sophistication was confirmed by the events of Elizabeth's French enterprise of 1562–3 which was intended to secure a French town to hold as a pledge against the return of Calais. Abandoning Dieppe,[199] the expeditionary force concentrated at Le Havre, where the defences were dangerously overlooked.[200] The besiegers could also take advantage of massive blind spots in which to draw up their artillery undisturbed by the English guns.[201] These mistakes, compounded by sickness,[202] personnel and supply shortages and the sheer professionalism of the French besieging force, resulted in a defeat[203] which deterred Elizabeth from direct intervention on the continent for over twenty years.[204]

This impression of technical backwardness was confirmed by the failure of English volunteers under Sir Humphrey Gilbert to make any impression on the Spanish garrisons in the Netherlands in 1572.

Gilbert missed an excellent opportunity to capture Sluys and received bloody checks in his endeavours to take Tergoes, before returning to England in despair.[205] At Corunna (1589), an English expedition failed dismally in its efforts to take the upper town, losing several of its best men through inexperience when a mine caused a tower to fall on their own troops as they raced to the assault.[206]

However, growing exposure to the wars of the continent from 1585 eventually gave a new generation of English commanders the experience to lead their men through the siege-dominated campaigns of France and the Netherlands with some confidence. The successful Anglo-Dutch defence of Bergen-op-Zoom against Parma's 30,000-man strong field army in September 1588 showed how effectively they could perform with foreign advice and assistance.[207] The strong English contingent in Maurice's Dutch field army played a signal part in his successful advance of 1590–4, which won back several towns for the states in strenuous siege warfare from their depleted Spanish garrisons.[208] The presence of some 5,000 trained and experienced soldiers from the Low Countries on the Anglo-Dutch Cadiz expedition of 1596 was a major factor in its success.[209]

Throughout the period, English armies depended on foreign advice and assistance to perform adequately against the strongholds and fortified places of the major continental powers. France, when besieging Calais (1558),[210] Le Havre (1562–3)[211] and Spain in the Low Countries' campaigns,[212] could deploy formidable expertise in siege warfare, a battering train and the necessary numbers of pioneers and civilian workers to match, while England was repeatedly at a loss for all three save when its continental allies could help it out.

To take a fortress by storm, dozens of battering pieces were required and thousands of pioneers to fill gabions, dig redoubts, raise firing-mounts and excavate trenches. Yet there were only 290 pioneers on the 1589 expedition to Portugal.[213] At Le Havre, Warwick suffered from a crippling shortage of pioneers with which to dig defensive positions.[214] There were only 229 in the initial Le Havre garrison of 1562 and just 450 with Essex at Rouen in 1591.[215] At Rouen the English had to be lent pioneers by the French, who had but a handful themselves, in order 'to drawe the trenche downe the hill somewhat nearer the towne then our lodgings'.[216] A lack of pioneers was also felt by English troops in the Netherlands, who were forced either to dig themselves, as they did in defence of Bergen-op-Zoom (1588),[217] or to operate without the earthen fortifications used by continental armies to such effect.[218] Matthew Sutcliffe felt the English made insufficient use of the spade compared to experienced continental soldiers. If, he commented bitterly, 'with certaine Pioners they cut the high wayes and make certain Barriquades upon them, and erect five or sixe weake sconces [small forts] ... being of no strength nor value they thinke they have done much.'[219]

We have already seen the baleful effects of the weaknesses in Leicester's artillery on his campaign in the Netherlands (1586–7). The absence of an adequate siege-train of several dozen heavy guns on the Portugal expedition of 1589 contributed directly to its failure. When the force paused to take Corunna, the four pieces of artillery that were landed could avail nothing against the walls of the upper town. There could be no question of a fortified town on the scale of Lisbon surrendering to them thus equipped.[220] The most they might hope for was that a garrison commander might lose his nerve under pressure, as did the governor of Cascaes, who yielded up his little town without a bombardment.[221] All that was required of the Spanish commander was to refuse battle to the invaders, whom lack of provisions would eventually force to re-embark, unable to achieve anything against his fortified places.[222]

On campaign in Scotland and Ireland, English deficiencies in siege warfare proved less important. There was a dearth of modern fortifications in both countries. Against weak native Irish strongholds the guns English commanders were able to land by ship proved effective enough, especially as their defenders were not as knowledgeable and well equipped as England's European enemies.[223] Fortifications made with the aid of continental advisers or by Spanish expeditionary forces proved much harder nuts to crack as Grey's troubles before Smerwick (1580) revealed. The fort was built and defended by a Spanish garrison, who surrendered after an ably conducted defence only to be treacherously butchered.[224] Tyrone's splendid continental-style fortifications at Moyry Pass (1600) provided a challenge to which English ingenuity was not equal.[225] The capture of Edinburgh Castle after an eleven-day bombardment in 1573 was achieved against a fortification of great natural strength.[226] Even then the victory owed to a lucky shot which contaminated the defenders' water supply with falling debris.[227]

The lack of English talent in fortification, weaknesses in the critical artillery arm and shortages of pioneers made close co-operation with foreign powers important as a means of overcoming some of the difficulties inherent in the new form of siege warfare to which English soldiers were exposed. The extreme rarity of modern fortifications in England exacerbated the problem by preventing all but a few Englishmen from familiarising themselves with the new defensive designs in their own country. By mid-century, Cardinal Granvelle was able to taunt the English ambassador in Brussels that not a single fortification in England was advanced enough to withstand a single day's battery.[228] By that time over a decade had passed since Francis I had remodelled several French border fortifications on modern principles and half a century since the first large-scale applications of those principles within the Italian peninsula.[229]

The first English fortification built with artillery in mind was constructed at Dartmouth in 1481.[230] Dominated by two tall towers, its general appearance was still medieval in character.[231] Many English fortifications were altered by the addition of gun-holes in the later Middle Ages without undertaking any structural change.[232] Between the 1520s and the 1540s purpose-built artillery bastions appeared in England, at first attached to existing fortifications,[233] but from 1538 as independent coastal forts, circular in design with multiple tiers of gun-holes in each face.[234] The first English fortification to make use of an Italian-style angle-bastion did not appear until 1547.[235] Berwick, not completed until the late 1560s, was the first and, for a long time, the only complete *trace italienne* in England.[236] Portsmouth and Berwick were the only sites in England capable of resisting good artillery in the sixteenth century.[237]

Though England was rapid enough in appreciating the importance of artillery in defence, it was far too slow in adopting the Italianate angle-bastion, which made the best possible use of defensive guns within a fortification. The gun-tower at Wark Castle (1519),[238] the bastions at Portsmouth (1522–4) and Henry VIII's numerous coastal artillery forts built in response to a perceived threat of invasion from 1538 did not use the angle-bastion but merely provided numerous openings for cannon in a relatively unsophisticated medieval design. The only real innovation in the Henrician artillery forts of the late 1530s and early 1540s was the enormous size of their ditches, which hid much of the fortification from sight, rendering it more defensible against battery.[239]

The advantage of the angle-bastion lay in the reduction of dead ground by ensuring that the length of the curtain wall and the faces of the bastions were swept by fire from cannon placed in the protruding flanks of the angle-bastions. English fortifications before

Berwick could not use flanking fire in this way. A report of 1551 on the rebuilding of Norham Castle on the Scottish border pointed out how its design made effective flanking fire impossible.[240] William Bourne, writing in 1578, damned Henry VIII's coastal fortifications for the same reason. If the bastions of a fortress 'be so that they cannot flank the sides of the walles, the thing [fortress] can bee of no force, as commonly all these castles and Forts, that were builded in the time of King Henry the eight were rounds, or parts of rounds, which are of no force for that they cannot flancke the ditches'.[241] Yet these were almost the only Tudor fortifications built from scratch in the course of the sixteenth century. It was not surprising if English commanders, who had little experience of continental siege warfare and had not seen the few English fortresses using angle-bastions and flanking fire, made mistakes when they first encountered them. Sir John Smythe was convinced that English officers in the Netherlands had attempted assaults on angle-bastioned forts without first eliminating the guns flanking the approach to the breach. In fact 'our such men of war, being ignorant of all discipline military, have been so prodigal of the lives of their soldiers, that they have divers times sent them, as it were to butchery, to give assault to certain sconces and other fortifications without any approach, or taking away any flankers'.[242]

These weaknesses played a major part in England's discomfiture when faced by European powers of the first rank. Its military disappointments in the sixteenth century, which should by no means be allowed to overshadow its many successes, were as much a product of its failure to keep abreast of developments in siege warfare as a consequence of Elizabeth's tendency to do 'all things by halves',[243] or indeed failings in other departments, of which there were many, most notably in the field of supply.[244] England's late adoption of tactics based upon pikes and firearms cost her relatively little, save in sieges where the obsolescence of the bow was most apparent.[245] The traditional bill used to such effect against the Scottish pikemen at Flodden (1513)[246] required no training to be used with effect and was therefore unaffected by the absence of training before 1572–3. Slowness to adopt modern weapons, tactics and training put England at a disadvantage, when it did eventually embrace them, through its inexperience, but the disadvantage was as nothing compared to the inconvenience caused by ignorance of the requirements of modern siege warfare. As has been noticed, England's major triumphs on the continent, in 1513, 1544 and in the Netherlands in the 1590s were all carried out in association with, or under the command of, experienced Europeans. Drake's successes against the Spanish seaborne empire were won against poorly equipped troops with resources on a small scale. His successes at Santiago (1585) and Cartagena (1586) were won with little more than two thousand men.[247] It was quite a different matter to operate on the European mainland, where modern fortifications were numerous and well equipped and plentiful forces were at hand.

The slowness of England in adopting change gave the English military literature of the sixteenth century a different character from that of Europe. Until 1595 the bow and bill were, theoretically, still admissible in the trained bands, making their discussion a necessity at a point when the leading European powers had long since settled on the pike and firearms as the basis of their armies. In this and other respects English military theory was set tasks the continental writers could safely ignore in view of the more rapid spread of change in their own military establishments. English military theory in the sixteenth century was at once a reflection of the progress of the military revolution in England and, as we have seen, an agent for its spread. More than any other source it reveals the immensity of the changes which swept England and Europe in the sixteenth century and, as such, deserves far more detailed attention than it has hitherto been given. Growing theoretical understanding and the gradual absorption of the military revolution that had swept the continent could not compensate for inexperience and lack of resources when facing powers of the first rank. It is not surprising that failure dogged English efforts for much of the sixteenth century, until the continuous action of the struggle against Spain in 1585–1604 stimulated a more worthy performance.

Notes

1. J.R. Hale, *Renaissance War Studies* (London, 1983), p. 226.

2. Adapted from C.G. Cruickshank, *Army Royal. Henry VIII's invasion of France, 1513* (Oxford, 1969), p. 190.

3. John Shute, 'A faithfull frende and Remembrancer to a Generall of an Armie in Divers Respects', British Library, Royal MS 17 C xxii, f 2ᵛ.

4. The theorist, Henry Barrett found employment as a Yeoman of the Guard. J.R. Hale, *On a Tudor Parade Ground. The Captain's Handbook of Henry Barrett 1562, The Society for Renaissance Studies. Occasional Papers*, V (London, 1978), p. 6.

5. Berwick was the most important. It provided employment for two English military writers, the gunner, Thomas Smith and the theorist, Sir Henry Knyvett.

Thomas Smith, *The Arte of Gunnerie*, STC 22855 (1600), sigs. Aiii-Aiii^v^. Sir Henry Knyvett, *The Defence of the Realme. 1596* (ed.) Charles Hughes (Oxford, 1906), p. viii.

6. In peacetime, little more than 1,000 troops were stationed in Ireland, a high proportion of whom were locally raised. Cyril Falls, *Elizabeth's Irish Wars* (London, 1950), p. 47.

7. 1,400 cannon the government could ill afford to lose were also forfeit when the Duke of Guise captured the town and its out-forts. Lawrence Stone, 'The Armada Campaign of 1588', *History*, XXIX (1944), p. 131. C.S.L. Davies, 'England and the French War 1557–9', Jennifer Loach and Robert Tittler (eds), *The Mid-Tudor Polity c. 1540–1560* (London, 1980), pp. 169–79. George Ferrers, *The Winning of Calais by the French* (1569) reprinted in A.F. Pollard (ed.), *Tudor Tracts 1532–1588* (London, n.d.), pp. 290–8. See also ibid., pp. 314 and 324–5.

8. Lawrence Stone, 'The Political Programme of Thomas Cromwell', *Bulletin of the Institute of Historical Research*, XXIV (1951), pp. 5 and 7. G.R. Elton, 'Parliamentary Drafts 1529–1540', ibid., XXV (1952), p. 130.

9. Lawrence Stone, *The Crisis of the Aristocracy 1558–1641* (Oxford, 1965), p. 206. C.G. Cruickshank, *Army Royal*, p. 193. British Library Add. MS 62135, part I, f 100.

10. J.R. Hale, *War and Society in Renaissance Europe 1450–1620* (Glasgow, 1985), p. 68.

11. See in particular Richard Barkhede, 'Project for a Land Militia', (*c.* 1560), British Library, Lansdowne MS 1225, f 43^v^. Barnaby Rich, *A Path-way to Military practise*, STC 20995 (1587), sig. A3.

12. Richard Barkhede, 'Project for a Land Militia ...', (*c.*1560), British Library, Lansdowne MS 1225, f 45. C.S.P. (Venetian) 1556–7, pp. 1046–7.

13. This was also the view of another Venetian observer, Giacomo Soranzo. *C.S.P. (Venetian) 1534–54*, p. 544.

14. *C.S.P. (Venetian) 1556–7*, p. 1047.

15. Barnaby Rich, *Allarme to England ... With a short discourse conteyning the decay of warlike discipline*, STC 20979 (1578), sigs. Eiiii^v^-Fi.

16. Humphrey Barwick, *A Breefe Discourse Concerning the force and effect of all manual weapons of fire and the disability of the Long Bowe or Archery in respect of others of greater force now in use*, STC 1542 (?1594), sig. B1.

17. Oman, *Sixteenth Century*, p. 333.

18. Hale, *War and Society*, p. 52.

19. A bow of yew was over five times cheaper than an arquebus. British Library, Egerton MS 2790, f 95.

20. See for instance Richard Morison on Agincourt in *An exhortation to styrre all Englyshe men to the defence of theyr countreye*, STC 18110 (1539), sig. Ciiii.

21. Theo Reintges, *Ursprung und Wesen der spätmittelalterlichen Schützengilden* (Bonn, 1963), p. 99.

22. *D.N.B.*, 'Ascham, Roger.' Ascham also hoped for the favour of the future Edward VI, to whom he dedicated his defence of archery, published in 1545. Lawrence V. Ryan, *Roger Ascham* (Stanford: California and London, 1963), p. 49.

23. For the statutory basis: *The Statutes of the Realm* (9 vols, Oxford, 1811–22), III, pp. 25–6, 32, 123, 131–2, 215–16, 457 and 833. For the proclamations:

Paul L. Hughes and James F. Larkin, *Tudor Royal Proclamations* (3 vols, New Haven: Connecticut, 1964–9), I, pp. 151–2, 177–9, 239, 288–9, 313 and 373.

24. Hughes and Larkin, *Tudor Proclamations*, I, pp. 177–8. Compare *Statutes of the Realm*, III, p. 123.

25. *Sermons* (ed.) G.E. Corrie (Cambridge, 1844–5), I, pp. 196–7 cited in Dop, *Eliza's Knights*, p. 114.

26. Barwick, *Breefe Discourse*, sig. A4ᵛ. Sir John Smythe, *Certain Discourses Military ...* (ed.) J.R. Hale (New York, 1964), p. li. The problem has also been treated by Cl. Gaier, 'L'invincibilité anglaise et le grand arc après la guerre de cent ans: un mythe tenace', *Tijdschrift voor Geschiedenis*, XCI (1978), pp 379–81.

27. Brescia was a key source of firearms. By 1547, the Crown had accumulated 6,500 handguns and 20,000 pikes. R.C. Clepham, 'The Military Handgun of the Sixteenth Century', *The Archaeological Journal*, LXVII (1910), p. 119. Lawrence Stone, *The Crisis of the Aristocracy 1558–1641* (Oxford, 1965), p. 218.

28. In the counties of Cheshire and Lancashire and in North and South Wales no arquebusiers need be employed. *Statutes of the Realm*, IV, part I, p. 320.

29. Estates worth £1,000 or more a year were required to produce pikes, bows, arquebuses and bills in a ratio of 4:3:2:2. The proportion of arquebusiers was lower among those assessed at less. Ibid., IV, part I, p. 316.

30. Wood and Sharp, *Rising in the North*, p. 185. Muster returns in 1569 from many areas in the north consisted solely of the names of bowmen and billmen. Of the new weapons of the European military revolution there is no mention. Harvester microfilm SP 12/58/13–34.

31. C.H. Firth, *Cromwell's Army* (London, 1962), p. 7.

32. Falls, *Irish Wars*, p. 39.

33. Barwick, *Breefe Discourse*, sig. B1.

34. *Acts of the Privy Council of England, 1595–6*, p. 27 (1595): 'Therefore wee praie you ... to convert all the bowes in the trained bands unto muskettes and callyvers [arquebuses] and the bylles into pykes ...'

35. Knyvett, *Defence of the Realme*, p. xxxiv.

36. Mark C. Fissel, 'Tradition and Invention in the Early Stuart Art of War', *Journal of the Society for Army Historical Research*, LXV (1987), p. 136.

37. Richard O. Mason, *'Pro Aris et Focis' Considerations of the Reasons that exist for the Reviving of the use of the long Bow with the Pike ...* (London, 1798).

38. J.F. Larkin and P.L. Hughes, *Stuart Royal Proclamations* (2 vols, Oxford, 1973–83), II, pp. 385–6. The background story is best told by the pen of the inventor of this quaint combination, William Neade, in *The Double-armed man* (1625), sigs. A2–3. See also Fissel, 'Tradition and Invention', pp. 135–7.

39. Sir John Smythe, *Certain Discourses Military ... (1590)* (ed.) J.R. Hale (Ithaca: New York, 1964), pp. 94–6.

40. *L & P. (Henry VIII)*, I, part II, pp. 1005–7. Oman, *Sixteenth Century*, pp. 298–319. Tucker, *Thomas Howard*, pp. 113–5.

41. Patten, *Expedition*, sigs. Hv–Hvᵛ.

42. For subtly differing definitions of the caliver: Clepham, 'Military Handgun', p. 140. Sir James Murray (ed.), *A New English Dictionary on Historical Principles* (Oxford, 1914), *s. v.* E.M. Lloyd, *A Review of the History of Infantry* (London, 1908), p. 92.

43. A.L. Rowse, *Tudor Cornwall, Portrait of a Society* (London, 1957), p. 382. This juxtaposition of old and new was common enough nationally as muster returns reveal. Harvester Microfilm SP 12/54/11.

44. For the greater powder consumption of the musket: British Library King's MS 265, fos. 268 and 272.

45. Brantôme (Pierre de Bourdeille), *Discours sur les colonels de l'infanterie de France* (ed.) Etienne Vaucheret (Paris, 1973), p. 166. Oman, *Sixteenth Century*, p. 225. Clepham, 'Military Handgun', p. 138.

46. British Library King's MS 265, f 271ᵛ.

47. L.O. Boynton, *The Elizabethan Militia 1158–1638* (Newton Abbot, 1967), p. 113.

48. Geoffrey Parker, *The Army of Flanders and the Spanish Road 1567–1659. The Logistics of Spanish Victory and Defeat in the Low Countries' Wars* (Oxford, 1972), pp. 274–5.

49. David Eltis, 'English Military Theory and the Military Revolution of the Sixteenth Century' (Oxford D.Phil. thesis, 1991).

50. The document with which the Privy Council began the process of training is printed in Harland, *Lancashire Lieutenancy*, I, pp. xxv–xxxiv.

51. William Patten refers to sergeants in the continental sense in his *The Expedicion into Scotland of Prince Edward*, STC 19479 (1548), sig. Hviiᵛ. By 1551 sergeants were customary in English companies. *C.S.P. (Venetian) 1534–54*, p. 350.

52. The French 'colonel' corresponded to the Spanish 'camp-master': 'Colonell or Coronell, a French word, is the commander of a regiment of certaine companies of souldiers, called with the Spaniards Maestre del Campo.' Robert Barret, *The Theorike and Practike of Moderne Warres*, STC 1500 (1598), p. 250. The English confusingly adopted colonels at regimental level in the late sixteenth century as well as using a single 'camp-master' for the whole army. C.I.A. Ritchie, 'A Tudor Military Manual', *Transactions of the Architectural and Archaeological Society of Durham and Northumberland*, XI (1958–65), pp. 110–11. Harland, *Lancashire Lieutenancy*, I, p. xlix.

53. The colonel first appeared in English usage in the sixteenth century to describe a foreign phenomenon. From the 1580s the English had their own, but it was not until the end of the century that the colonel's regiment became a unit of administration to rival the traditional company. G.J. Millar, 'Henry VIII's colonels', *Journal of the Society for Army Historical Research*, LVII (1979), p. 129.

54. The earliest English use of a corporal falls into the final quarter of the century. Corporals were used both as commanders of sub-sections of a company and with the title 'corporal of the field' as assistants to the sergeant-major of a force. Murray, *New English Dictionary, s. v.*

55. The earliest example of an English sergeant-major has been dated (wrongly) by F.J. Davies to 1518. It is hard to be definitive in the absence of a thorough modern study of the issue. Robert Hare refers to the 'great sergeant' in 1556, clearly meaning a sergeant-major. The rank is used, as such, soon thereafter. F.J. Davies, *The Sergeant-Major; The Origin and History of his Rank ...* (London, 1886), p. 5. Robert Hare, Military treatise, British Library, Cotton MS Julius F.v., f 20ᵛ. C.G. Cruickshank, *Elizabeth's Army* (2nd rev. ed., Oxford, 1966), p. 52.

56. General Susane, *Histoire de l'infanterie française* (5 vols, Paris, 1876), I, pp. 94–120. Markham, 'Fighting Veres', pp. 53–6. G. Dickinson, *The Instructions sur le Faict de la Guerre of Raymond de Beccarie de Pavie Sieur de Fourquevaux* (London, 1954), p. xxx.

57. British Library, King's MS 265, fos. 264v and 265v (1585). In 1589 the Privy Council ordered the new rank of corporal to be used for the shot, while retaining the old rank of vintener for the pikemen and billmen. Harland, *Lancashire Lieutenancy*, I, p. xxxix.

58. Piero Pieri, *Il Rinascimento e la crisi militare italiana* (Turin, 1952), pp. 223–4. G. Köhler, *Die Entwickelung des Kriegswesens und der Kriegführung in der Ritterzeit von Mitte des 11. Jahrhunderts bis zu den Husitenkriegen* (3 vols, Breslau, 1886), II, p. 361. Richard Czeppan, *Die Schlacht bei Crecy (26. August 1346)* (Diss., Berlin, 1906), p. 84.

59. STC 25732.

60. Ibid., p. 35.

61. A representative sample of their grievances are to be found in British Library Lansdowne MS 22 and the introductory section to R.S., *A Brief Treatise to Proove the Necessitie and Excellence of the Use of Archerie*, STC 21512 (1596).

62. Smythe, *Certain Discourses*, p. lvi.

63. A. Hassell Smith, *County and Court. Government and Politics in Norfolk 1558–1603* (Oxford, 1974), p. 125. Cruickshank, *Elizabeth's Army*, p. 109. Boynton, *Militia*, pp. 59–60.

64. Measures supportive of the bow lobby were taken in 1559, 1563, 1566 and 1572. Smythe, *Certain Discourses*, p. xlv. G.R. Elton, *The Parliament of England 1559–1581* (Cambridge, 1986), p. 242. Larkin and Hughes, *Tudor Royal Proclamations*, II, p. 359.

65. Hassell Smith, *Norfolk*, p. 125.

66. A. Hassell Smith, 'Militia rates and militia statutes 1558–1663', P. Clark et al. (eds), *The English Commonwealth 1547–1640* (Chatham, 1979), pp. 97–9.

67. Ibid., p. 99.

68. Oman, *Sixteenth Century*, p. 368. L.O. Boynton, 'English Military Organization 1558–1638' (D.Phil. thesis, Oxford, 1962), p. viii.

69. Cruickshank, *Army Royal*, p. 189. For the fluctuating strength of the Yeomen of the Guard: J.R. Hale, *Henry Barrett*, p. 7.

70. Barnaby Rich commented 'I have seene a hundred Spaniardes or a hundred Frenche men' on their way to serve 'that only but in their apparell and furniture, have been more welthy then all ye souldiers of Berwick ...' Rich, *Allarme*, sig. Eiiii.

71. Falls, *Irish Wars*, p. 95.

72. P.H. Williams, *The Tudor Regime* (Oxford, 1981), p. 125.

73. For examples of the system of retinues in action: N.H. Nicholas, 'An Account of the Army with which King Richard the Second invaded Scotland 1385', *Archaeologia*, XXII (1829), pp. 14–18. J.W. Sherbourne, 'Indentured Retinues and English Expeditions to France, 1369–1380,' *English Historical Review*, LXXIX (1964), pp. 720–45.

74. J.J. Goring, 'Social Change and Military Decline in mid-Tudor England', *History*, LX (1975), pp. 188–9.

75. Stone, *Crisis of the Aristocracy*, p. 205. Falls, *Irish Wars*, p. 50. Goring, 'Social Change', pp. 194 and 196.

76. Gladys S. Thomson, *Lord Lieutenants in the Sixteenth Century. A Study in Tudor Local Administration* (London, 1923), p. 116.

77. Rich, *Path-way*, sig. F1ᵛ. The Spaniard Londoño agreed completely. Sancho de Londoño, *El Discurso sobre la forma de reduzir la disciplina militar, a meyor y antiguo estado* (Brussels, 1589), f 17.

78. H.J. Webb, 'Elizabethan Soldiers: A Study in the Ideal and the Real', *Western Humanities Review*, IV (1949–50), p. 151. P.H. Williams, 'The Crown and the Counties', C. Haigh (ed.), *The Reign of Elizabeth* (London, 1984), p. 131.

79. *Acts of the Privy Council 1571–1575*, p. 41.

80. *Newes from Sir Roger Williams* (1591), sig. A3.

81. Thomas and Dudley Digges, *Foure Paradoxes*, STC 6872 (1604), sig. F3.

82. C.G. Cruickshank, 'Dead-pays in the Elizabethan army', *English Historical Review*, LIII (1938), pp. 93–7.

83. Smythe, *Certain Discourses*, p. xxxiv.

84. Harold H. Davis, 'The Military Career of Thomas North', *Huntington Library Quarterly*, XII (1948–9), p. 317.

85. *Calendar of State Papers (Ireland) 1596 July–1597 December*, p. 195.

86. Barnaby Rich, *A Right Exelent and Pleasaunt Dialogue, betwene Mercury and an English Souldier*, STC 20995 (1574), sig. Gviᵛ.

87. H.A. Lloyd, *The Rouen Campaign 1590–1592* (Oxford, 1973), p. 102. *List and Analysis of State Papers (Foreign) June 1591–April 1592*, pp. 196 and 201. J.X. Evans (ed.), *The Works of Sir Roger Williams* (Oxford, 1972), p. liii.

88. L.W. Henry, 'The Earl of Essex as Strategist and Military Organiser', *English Historical Review*, LXVIII (1953), p. 375.

89. A.L. Rowse, *Tudor Cornwall, Portrait of a Society* (London, 1957), pp. 413–14. L.O. Boynton, *The Elizabethan Militia 1558–1638* (London, 1967), p. 107.

90. Williams, 'Crown and the Counties', p. 129. Boynton, *Militia*, p. 166.

91. See in particular Gilbert Millar, *Tudor Mercenaries and Auxiliaries 1485–1547* (Charlottesville, 1980). Mercenaries continued to be heavily used in the Edwardian minority, but by Elizabeth's time they had fallen out of use. Williams, *Tudor Regime*, pp. 119–21.

92. British Library, King's MS 265, fos. 268ᵛ-272. W.T. MacCaffrey (ed.), William Camden, *The History of the Most Renowned and Victorious Princess Elizabeth Late Queen of England* (Chicago and London, 1970), pp. 312–13.

93. O.F.G. Hogg, 'England's War Effort against the Spanish Armada', *Journal of the Society for Army Historical Research*, XLIV (1966), pp. 29–33. E.P. Dickin, 'The Army at Tilbury', *Transactions of the Essex Archaeological Society*, XXIII (1942–5), pp. 49–53. Miller Christy, 'Queen Elizabeth's Visit to Tilbury in 1588', *English Historical Review*, XXIV (1919), pp. 43 and 54–6.

94. Thomson, *Lord Lieutenants*, pp. 36, 156–7 and 60. Boynton, *Militia*, pp. 14–18.

95. *Statutes of the Realm*, IV, part I, pp. 316–20.

96. The order of the Privy Council setting out the changes and their rationale is to be found in Harland, *Lancashire Lieutenancy*, I, pp. xxv-xxxiv.

97. Williams, *Tudor Regime*, p. 124. Boynton, *Militia*, p. 125. By 1591 it numbered over 42,000 men. Thomson, *Lord Lieutenants*, pp. 85–6.

98. Hogg, 'War Effort', p. 25. *Directions for Musters wherein is showne the order of Drilling for the Musket and Pike* (Cambridge, 1638), sig. B4ᵛ.

99. Boynton, *Militia*, pp. 13–14.

100. SP 12/206/2 cited in Boynton, *Militia*, p. 125. J.R. Hooker, 'Notes on the Organisation and Supply of the Tudor Military under Henry VII', *Huntington Library Quarterly*, XXIII (1959–60), p. 20: 'It is clear that training was no part of infantry discipline.'

101. Rowse, *Cornwall*, p. 388.

102. Eventually the Privy Council agreed to compromise on the figure of 6,000; a six-fold increase. Claire Cross, *The Puritan Earl. The Life of Henry Hastings Third Earl of Huntingdon 1536–1595* (London, 1966), p. 212.

103. Boynton, *Militia*, p. 158.

104. Ibid., p. 177.

105. *Dictionary of National Biography* (22 vols, Oxford, 1921–2), 'Williams, Sir Roger. (1540?-1595).' Evans (ed.), *Works*, p. xvii. Sir Roger Williams, *A Briefe Discourse of Warre*, STC 25732 (1590), p. 29.

106. At Tilbury (1588), Sir Roger was Master of the Horse, while Sir John Norris was Marshal of the Foot. Evans (ed.), *Works*, pp. xxv and xxxii. 'A councell of Warre' (1587), Harleian MS 444, f 120. *D.N.B.*, 'Williams' and 'Norris, Sir John (1547?-1597).'

107. By Edward VI's time Audley had come to be regarded as 'father of the English soldiorie;' a position of respect which was not reflected in military reform. Bodleian Library, Rawlinson MS D363, f 1ᵛ. S.T. Bindoff, *The House of Commons 1509–1558* (3 vols, London, 1982), I, pp. 353–4. For Audley's views on training: British Library, Harleian MS 309, f 8.

108. Ibid. Boynton, *Militia*, p. 57.

109. For a brief introduction to this aspect of Tudor administrative history, Gladys S. Thomson, 'The origin and growth of the office of deputy-lieutenant', *Transactions of the Royal Historical Society*, 4th series, V (1922), pp. 150–5.

110. All the same Lord Burghley's support remained critical. Conyers Read, *Lord Burghley and Queen Elizabeth* (London, 1960), pp. 413–14.

111. See for instance the dispatch of two experienced captains to act as muster-masters in Lincolnshire by the Privy Council in 1595. *Calendar of State Papers (Domestic) 1595–7*, pp. 99–100.

112. At first the Crown paid the wages of the muster-master. Their pay, which amounted to £20–£40 each, was from 1585 to be found by the localities. This was in addition to the cost of compensating the militiamen themselves at 8d a day for the time they spent training. Thomson, *Lord Lieutenants*, p. 86. Boynton, *Militia*, pp. 180 and 27.

113. Rowse, *Cornwall*, p. 414.

114. Williams, *Tudor Regime*, p. 123.

115. L.W. Henry, 'The Earl of Essex as strategist and military organiser', *English Historical Review*, LXVIII (1953), p. 370.

116. Lambeth MSS 247, Part 2, f 73, printed in Thomson, *Lord Lieutenants*, p. 167.

117. Williams, *Tudor Regime*, p. 123.

118. As in Norfolk in 1577. A.L. Rowse, *The Expansion of Elizabethan England* (London, 1955), p. 356.

119. Boynton, *Militia*, p. 99.

120. The first was issued in 1623: *Instructions for Musters and Armes, and the use thereof. By order from his Majestie's Privy Counsayle*, STC 7683 (1623).

121. Among other things he was greatly frustrated by 'the smale nomber of pikes which is to be allowed to everie hundred in this cuntrie'. British Library, Lansdowne MS 40, f 16ᵛ.

122. Ibid., f 13ff.

123. Rowse, *Cornwall*, pp. 404–5.

124. Boynton, *Militia*, p. 190.

125. *C.S.P. (Foreign) July–December 1588*, p. xi.

126. Smythe, *Certain Discourses*, p. xxxi.

127. Diarmaid MacCulloch, *Suffolk and the Tudors. Politics and Religion in an English County 1500–1600* (Oxford, 1986), p. 280.

128. H.J. Webb, 'Military Newsbooks during the Age of Elizabeth', *English Studies*, XXXIII (1952), pp. 241–5.

129. This theme pervades many Elizabethan works on war. The classic example is George Whetstone's *The Honorrable Reputation of a Souldier*, STC 25339 (1585).

130. STC 23413, 23414 and 23415.

131. STC 1500.

132. Barret, *Theorike*, p. 82.

133. Ibid., Cruickshank, *Elizabeth's Army*, p. 198.

134. *The Approved Order of Martiall Discipline*, STC 5376 (1591) and *A Briefe Discourse of Martial Discipline*, STC 5377 (1587).

135. Clayton, *Approved Order*, p. 28.

136. See for instance Thomas Styward's key, *Pathwaie*, p. 43.

137. Large militia companies of up to 500 men were not unknown, though by the 1590s the government was anxious to see them abolished in favour of smaller units. A. Hassell Smith, *County and Court. Government and Politics in Norfolk 1558–1603* (Oxford, 1974), pp. 288–9

138. The Privy Council's order laying down the basis for training in 1572–3 expects companies of 200 and 300 men to be assigned to men of county stature. 100-man companies were for lesser men. Harland, *Lancashire Lieutenancy*, I, p. xxviii.

139. William Garrard, *The Arte of Warre*, STC 11625 (1591), p. 79.

140. Ibid.

141. Hale, *War and Society*, pp. 66–7. Hale, *Renaissance War Studies*, p. 230.

142. Williams, *Briefe discourse*, p. 29.

143. The most detailed study of the *tercio* available is focused on the 1570s: René Quatrefages, *Los tercios españoles 1567–1577* (Madrid, 1979). For a brief account of its origins: Oman, *Sixteenth Century*, p. 59f. See also Parker, *Spanish Road*, pp. 274–5.

144. Dickinson, *Instructions*, pp. xxviii–xxx. Hale, *War and Society*, p. 52. Already by the 1530s they had achieved a drastic increase in the number of pikes and

firearms in service. At Metz (1552) 40 per cent of the French infantry was arquebus-armed. Susane, *L'infanterie*, I, pp. 92–3.
145. See Chapter 3 above.
146. Luis Gutierrez de la Vega, *A compendious Treatise De Re Militari*, tr. N. Lichefild, STC 12538 (1582), sig. Aii.
147. *C.S.P. (Venetian), 1534–1554*, p. 544. A partial exception could be made for *An Order Whych a Prince in Battayl Muste Observe*, STC 18842 (?1540).
148. For a general discussion of this and related issues: Anthony Esler, *The aspiring mind of the Elizabethan younger generation* (Durham: N.C., 1966), pp. 87–108.
149. Francisco de Valdes, *The Sergeant Major*, tr. J. Thorius, STC 24570 (1590), sig. A2.
150. Ibid., p. 93. These were clearly the traditional English demi-lances a Venetian described in 1551 as furnished 'with a shirt of mail and a sallet [helmet], and a light long spear ...' *C.S.P. (Venetian)*, p. 350.
151. See Chapter 3 above.
152. The other common types were men-at-arms and light cavalrymen armed in the Albanian fashion. *C.S.P. (Venetian) 1534–54*, p. 350.
153. Williams, *Briefe Discourse*, p. 35.
154. G.A. Hayes-McCoy, 'Strategy and tactics in Irish warfare 1593–1601', *Irish Historical Studies*, II (1940–1), p. 260.
155. For analysis of Pinkie with and without emphasis on the cavalry's role: C.W.C. Oman, *Sixteenth Century*, pp. 363–6. William Patten, *The Expedicion into Scotland*, STC 19479 (1548), sigs. Hv-Iiv. C.W.C. Oman, 'The Battle of Pinkie, September 10, 1547', *Archaeological Journal*, XC (1933), p. 15.
156. R.C. McCoy, 'From the Tower to the tiltyard: Robert Dudley's return to glory', *Historical Journal*, XXVII (1984), pp. 426–9.
157. Melvin J. Tucker, *The Life of Thomas Howard, Earl of Surrey and Second Duke of Norfolk, 1443–1524* (London, 1964), p. 25. Many sixteenth-century English proposals for gentry and noble education had a pronounced military dimension. In practice provision in horsemanship and fencing was so inadequate in England that many well-born sons were sent abroad to learn under foreign masters. Education in the technical aspects of war was unknown. Hale, *Renaissance War Studies*, p. 234f. Lewis Einstein, *The Italian Renaissance in England* (New York, 1902), pp. 69–71.
158. *C.S.P. (Venetian), 1556–7*, p. 1048. P.R. Edwards, 'The Horse Trade in Tudor and Stuart England', F.M.L. Thompson (ed.), *Horses in European Economic History* (Reading, 1983), p. 119.
159. Gervase Markham, *The Souldiers Exercise* (London, 1639; repr. Amsterdam, 1974), pp. 38–9. *C.S.P. (Venetian), 1556–7*, p. 1048 (May 1557): 'with regard to heavy horse, good for men at arms the island [England] does not produce any, except a few in Wales, and an equally small amount from the Crown studs ...'
160. See Chapter 4 above.
161. The earliest of major significance was Giovan Battista de' Zanchi's *Del Modo di Fortificar Le Citta* (Venice, 1554). For a brief introduction to the field see Quentin Hughes, 'Military architecture and the printed book', *Fort*, X (1982), pp. 5–19.

162. Paul Ive, *The Practise of Fortification*, STC 14289 (1589).

163. Appended to William Garrard's *The Arte of Warre* STC 11625 (1591), pp. 353–68.

164. *Certain Waies for the Orderying of Souldiers in Battelray*, STC 17164 (1560–2).

165. B.H. St J. O'Neil has argued that these were copied from Zanchi's work. In fact Zanchi incorporated many diagrams of which no trace appears in Whitehorne's brief *opus*. The case for plagiarism is far from clear-cut. O'Neil, *Castles and Cannon*, p. 68.

166. William Bourne, *The Arte of Shooting in Great Ordnaunce*, STC 3420 (1587). He was followed by the Berwick gunner Thomas Smith whose *The Arte of Gunnerie* [STC 22855] was published in 1600.

167. Thomas M. Spaulding, 'Elizabethan Military Books' in J.G. MacManaway (ed.), *Joseph Quincy Adams Memorial Studies* (Washington, 1948), pp. 496–8.

168. Compare Diego de Alaba Y Viamont's *El perfeto Capitan, instruido En la disciplina Militar, y nueva ciencia de la Artilleria* (Madrid, 1590), Luis Collado's *Pratica Manuale di Artigleria* (Venice, 1586) and Girolamo Ruscelli's *Precetti della militia moderna tanto per mare, quanto per terra* (Venice, 1568).

169. Robert Norton, *The Gunner*, STC 18673 (1628; repr. Amsterdam, 1973).

170. J.R. Kenyon, 'Early Artillery Fortifications in England and Wales: a preliminary survey and reappraisal', *Archaeological Journal*, CXXXVIII (1982), p. 229.

171. H.J. Webb, *Elizabethan Military Science: The Books and the Practice* (London, 1965), pp. 126–8.

172. *C.S.P. (Foreign) 1586 June–1587 March*, p. 150. The Tudor artillery arm was repeatedly plagued with problems of this kind. Kenyon, 'Early Artillery Fortifications', p. 220. Roger Ashley, 'The organisation and administration of the Tudor office of Ordnance' (Oxford University B.Litt. thesis, 1972), p. 94.

173. *C.S.P. (Foreign) September 1585–May 1586*, p. 84.

174. J.R. Hale, 'The Defence of the Realm 1485–1558', H.M. Colvin (ed.), *The History of the King's Works* (London, 1982), IV, part II, p. 378.

175. Christopher Duffy, *Siege Warfare. The Fortress in the Early Modern World 1494–1660* (London, 1979), pp. 4–7. Georg Ortenburg, *Waffe und Waffengebrauch im Zeitalter der Landsknechte* (Koblenz, 1984), p. 159. Hughes, 'Military architecture', pp. 5–6. B.H. St J. O'Neil, *Castles and Cannon. A Study of Early Artillery Fortifications in England* (Oxford, 1960), pp. 63–4.

176. Hale, 'Defence of the Realm', p. 378. Duffy, *Siege Warfare*, p. 4. He also worked on the defences of Carlisle in 1541. B.H. St J. O'Neil, 'Stefan von Haschenperg, an Engineer to King Henry VIII, and his Work', *Archaeologia*, XCI (1945), p. 146.

177. For the origins and development of the angle-bastion in Italy and Europe: J.R. Hale, 'The Early Development of the Bastion: An Italian Chronology, c.1450–c.1534', B. Smalley et al. (eds), *Europe in the Late Middle Ages* (London, 1965). S. Pepper and N. Adams, *Firearms and Fortifications. Military Architecture and Siege Warfare in Sixteenth-Century Siena* (Chicago and London, 1986), pp. xxii–6.

178. Colvin (ed.), *King's Works*, IV, part II, pp. 25 and 398.

179. Colvin (ed.), *King's Works*, pp. 410–11.

180. Ibid., p. 625.

181. Duffy, *Fortress*, p. 139.

182. Ibid. Colvin (ed.), *King's Works*, IV, part II, p. 658.

183. Jacopo Contio died in 1567. Portinari's work at Berwick was over by 1566. Ibid., p. 409.

184. Ibid., p. 410.

185. *D.N.B.*, 'Ive, Paul (*fl.* 1602).'

186. *Letters and Papers Foreign and Domestic of the Reign of Henry VIII*, III, part II, p. 1065.

187. Ibid., pp. 1067, 1086 and 1092. Edward Hall, *Henry VIII* (2 vols, 1904), I, p. 270.

188. Hans Poppenruyter of Malines supplied at least 140 pieces in the first two decades of Henry's reign. Millar, *Tudor Mercenaries*, p. 21. Kenyon, 'Early Artillery Fortifications', p. 229.

189. Henry hired over 5,000 foreign mercenaries for the campaign of 1513 and over 5,700 for that of 1544. Williams, *Tudor Regime*, p. 119. Millar, *Tudor Mercenaries*, pp. 44–5.

190. The garrison's shortage of powder for its cannon made Henry's task much easier. *C.S.P. (Spanish) 1544*, p. 238f for an interim report (3 August) by Charles V's envoy at Henry's camp. Oman, *Sixteenth Century*, pp. 342–4. W.A.J. Archbold (ed.), 'A Diary of the Expedition of 1544', *English Historical Review*, XVI (1901), pp. 505–7.

191. Hall, *Henry VIII*, I, p. 62. G.W. Bernard, *The Power of the Early Tudor Nobility, A Study of the Fourth and Fifth Earls of Shrewsbury* (Brighton, 1985), p. 108.

192. Hall, *Henry VIII*, I, pp. 307–15. Oman, *Sixteenth Century*, p. 326. S. J. Gunn, 'The Duke of Suffolk's March on Paris in 1523', *English Historical Review*, CI (1986), p. 600.

193. *C.S.P. (Spanish) 1509–1525*, p. 65. Hall, *Henry VIII*, I, pp. 43–6. C.G. Cruickshank, *Army Royal. Henry VIII's Invasion of France 1513* (Oxford, 1969), p. 94. C.S.L. Davies, 'Supply services of English armed forces, 1509–1550' (Oxford D.Phil., 1963), pp. 204–6.

194. George Ferrers, *The winning of Calais by the French* (1569) reprinted in A.F. Pollard (ed.), *Tudor Tracts 1532–1588* (London, n.d.), pp. 291–2. Letter of J. Highfield to Mary, ibid., p. 314.

195. 'Yow may aske, what our men ment to remayne so long, without making battery: I say, want of many things necessary for that purpos.' P. Forbes, *A Full View of the Public Transactions in the Reign of Q. Elizabeth or a Particular Account of all the Memorable Affairs of that Queen* (2 vols, London, 1740), I, p. 456. Samuel Haynes, *A Collection of State Papers Relating to Affairs … from the Year 1542 to 1570* (London, 1740), p. 304. *C.S.P. (Foreign) 1559–60*, p. 592.

196. 'For this assault, lawde ladders, viele and nought, The souldiors had, which were to shorte; God wot' – a contemporary (Thomas Churchyard) cited by G. Geoffrey Langsam, *Martial Books and Tudor Verse* (New York, 1951), p. 160. At La Rochelle (1627) the English repeated the same mistake with the same baleful consequences. Kenneth Ferguson, 'The Expedition to Rhé, 1627,' *The Irish Sword*, XIII (1979), p. 371.

197. *C.S.P. (Spanish) 1558–1567*, p. 156. Christopher Haigh, *Elizabeth I* (London, 1988), pp. 126–7. Jasper Ridley, *Elizabeth I* (London, 1987), p. 106.

198. Haynes, *Collection*, p. 305. *C.S.P. (Spanish) 1558–67*, p. 159.

199. Forbes, *Full View*, II, p. 199.

200. *C.S.P. (Spanish) 1558–1567*, pp. 262–5, 275 and 343.

201. Warwick to the Privy Council, 20 December 1562. Forbes, *Full View*, II, p. 242.

202. *C.S.P. (Spanish) 1558–67*, pp. 336, 337 and 343. David Stewart, 'Sickness and Mortality Rates of the English Army in the Sixteenth Century,' *Journal of the Royal Army Medical Corps*, XCI (1948), pp. 30–3. David Stewart, 'Disposal of the sick and wounded of the English Army in the sixteenth century', ibid., XC (1948), p. 32.

203. *C.S.P. (Foreign) 1563*, pp. 442–3, 460–1 and 482–3. A.L. Rowse, *The Expansion of Elizabethan England* (London, 1955), p. 336. J.B. Black, *The Reign of Elizabeth, 1558–1603* (Oxford, 1965), p. 61.

204. A project for an English expeditionary force to the Netherlands came to nothing in 1577. S. L. Adams, 'The Protestant Cause: Religious Alliance with the European Calvinist Communities as a Political Issue in England 1585–1630' (Oxford D.Phil., 1972), pp. 26 and 37.

205. William G. Gosling, *The Life of Sir Humphrey Gilbert, England's First Empire Builder* (London, 1911), pp. 85–97. L.V.D. Owen, 'Sir Roger Williams and the Spanish power in the Netherlands', *Army Quarterly*, XXXIV (1937), p. 59.

206. *C.S.P. (Foreign) Jan–July 1589*, p. 353.

207. English troops made up two-thirds of the victorious garrison. *C.S.P. (Foreign) July–December 1588*, pp. xxi–xxiii.

208. For a sample of this activity (the capture of Zutphen, Deventer and Delft) from a contemporary perspective: *True Newes from one of Sir Fraunces Veres Companie Concerning Delftes Isle and sundry other townes in the Lowe Countries yeelded to the Generall since May last*, STC 24652 (London, 1591), sigs. A3–B1ᵛ.

209. Robert W. Kenny, *Elizabeth's Admiral. The Political Career of Charles Howard Earl of Effingham 1536–1624* (Baltimore and London, 1970), pp. 186–90. Edward Edwards, *The Life of Sir Walter Ralegh* (2 vols, London, 1868), I, p. 224 and II, p. 154. *The Commentaries of Sir Francis Vere Being divers pieces of service wherein he had command, written by himself in way of Commentary* (Cambridge, 1657), pp. 38–9.

210. Pollard, *Tudor Tracts*, pp. 290–1. At Guisnes The Duke of Guise could deploy thirty-five battering pieces to create an assaultable breach with over 8,000 discharges. He made heavy use of pioneers before finally assaulting and taking three of the bulwarks of this Calais out-fort. Ibid., p. 295.

211. *C.S.P. (Foreign), 1563*, pp. 443, 460 and 482–3. *C.S.P. (Spanish) 1558–1567*, p. 343.

212. The contrast between Parma's and Leicester's performance in the field during Leicester's tenure in the Low Countries owed in large part to the superior quality of Parma's artillery train. *C.S.P. (Foreign) 1585–6*, pp. vi and 84–5.

213. R.B. Wernham, 'Queen Elizabeth and the Portugal Expedition of 1589', *English Historical Review*, LXVI (1951), p. 19.

214. Forbes, *Full View*, II, p. 213. Rowse, *Expansion*, p. 336.

215. Ibid., p. 335. R.B. Wernham, 'Queen Elizabeth and the siege of Rouen, 1591', *Transactions of the Royal Historical Society*, 4th series, XV (1932), p. 171.

216. J.G. Nicholas (ed.), 'Sir Thomas Coningsby. Journal of the Siege of Rouen', *Camden Society*, I (1847), p. 39.

217. As a contemporary complained the troops at Bergen were 'over-laboured and over-watched'. *C.S.P. (Foreign) July–December 1588*, p. xxi.

218. As at Castillon (1453), Cerignola (1503) and Bicocca (1522) to name but a few instances. See Chapter 3 for explanation of their use in conjunction with firearms and artillery.

219. Matthew Sutcliffe, *The Practise, Proceedings and Lawes of Armes*, STC 23468 (1593), p. 218.

220. They reached the suburbs before turning back in despair. Walter Devereux, *Lives and Letters of the Devereux, Earls of Essex in the Reigns of Elizabeth, James I and Charles I 1540–1646* (2 vols, London, 1853), I, pp. 202–3. Thomas Nun, *A Comfort against the Spaniard* (London, 1596), sig. C3ᵛ.

221. *C.S.P. (Foreign) Jan–July 1589*, pp. 353–4.

222. Wernham, 'Portugal Expedition', p. 210.

223. Duffy, *Fortress*, p. 144. J.C. Beckett, *A Short History of Ireland* (London, 1979), pp. 39–40 and 49–50. Siobhan d'hOir, 'Guns in Medieval and Tudor Ireland', *The Irish Sword*, XV (1982), pp. 82–3. *C.S.P. (Carew) 1515–74*, pp. 96–102 and 123–4. G.A. Hayes-McCoy, 'Tudor conquest and counter-reformation 1571–1603', T.W. Moody et al. (eds), *Early Modern Ireland 1534–1691* (Oxford, 1978), pp. 105–9.

224. Raleigh played a prominent part in the massacre of the garrison. Edward Edwards, *The Life of Sir Walter Raleigh* (2 vols, London, 1868), I, p. 40. For Grey's reputation for cruelty see W.L. Renwick (ed.), *Edmund Spenser, A View of the Present State of Ireland* (Oxford, 1970), introduction.

225. C. Falls, *Elizabeth's Irish Wars* (London, 1950), p. 73. Tyrone repeatedly gave evidence of his understanding of the new art of fortification. For an example of his skill in 1595: *C.S.P. (Carew) 1589–1600*, p. 114. See also G.A. Hayes-McCoy, 'Strategy and tactics in Irish warfare 1593–1601', *Irish Historical Studies*, II (1940–1), pp. 272–3.

226. Conyers Read, *Mr Secretary Walsingham and the policy of Queen Elizabeth* (3 vols., Oxford, 1925), II, p. 129. *Acts of the Privy Council 1571–5*, p. 95. *C.S.P. (Foreign) 1572–4*, pp. ix–xv. *D.N.B.*, 'Drury, Sir William.'

227. Ridley, *Elizabeth I*, p. 187.

228. Ibid., p. 101.

229. Hale, *War and Society*, p. 207. Pepper and Adams, *Firearms and Fortifications*, pp. xxii–6.

230. J.A. Donnelly, 'A study of the coastal forts built by Henry VIII', *Fort*, X (1982), p. 107.

231. Kenyon, *Early Artillery Fortifications*, p. 218.

232. Canterbury, Dover Castle, Southampton, Winchester and Carisbrooke Castle were all modified in this way in the late fourteenth century. Ibid., p. 207.

233. Five earthen bastions were added to Portsmouth's defences in 1522–4. Kenyon, 'Early Artillery Fortifications', p. 220.

234. O'Neil, *Castles and Cannon*, pp. 54–64. O'Neil, 'von Haschenperg', p. 139. Donnelly, 'coastal forts', pp. 107 and 119.

235. O'Neil, *Castles and Cannon*, p. 68.

236. Colvin (ed.), *King's Works*, pp. 410–11.

237. Knyvett, *Defence of the Realm*, p. xxxi.

238. John R. Kenyon, 'Terminology and Early Artillery Fortification', *Fort*, XI (1983), p. 33.

239. O'Neil, *Castles and Cannon*, p. 64.

240. Kenyon, 'Early Artillery Fortifications', p. 222.

241. William Bourne, *Inventions or Devises Very Necessary for All Generalles and Captaines*, STC 3421 (1578), p. 56.

242. Smythe, *Certain Discourses Military*, p. 22.

243. Sir Walter Raleigh's phrase: Haigh, *Elizabeth I*, p. 140. Matthew Sutcliffe made much the same criticism by implication in 1593. The English sent out small forces with inadequate provisioning. Sutcliffe, *Practice*, sig. B2ᵛ.

244. For an introduction to this problem area see Davies, 'Supply services'.

245. As at Leith (1560) when the huge contingent of English archers failed to kill or fatally injure a single member of the garrison, whose firearms and artillery killed over eight hundred of the English troops. Humphrey Barwick, *A Breefe Discourse, Concerning the Force and Effect of All Manuall Weapons of Fire*, STC 1542 (?1594), sigs. F2ᵛ–F3. *C.S.P. (Spanish) 1558–1567*, p. 156. Christopher Haigh, *Elizabeth I* (London, 1988), pp. 126–7. Jasper Ridley, *Elizabeth I* (London, 1987), p. 106.

246. 10,000 Scots were killed. The English lost only 400 men. Tucker, *Thomas Howard*, pp. 113–15. *Letters and Papers (Henry VIII)*, I, part II, pp. 1005–7.

247. Julian S. Corbett, *Drake and the Tudor Navy with a History of the Rise of England as a Maritime Power* (2 vols, London, 1917), II, p. 13.

CHAPTER 6

CONCLUSION

In the sixteenth century war was transformed. The introduction of newer more powerful firearms with the ability to penetrate any armour in common use radically altered infantry and cavalry tactics and indirectly changed the pace of war. Cerignola (1503), Bicocca (1522) and Pavia (1525) showed the devastating effect of firearms on the battlefield. An opponent offering battle with a prepared defence bristling with shot and field artillery was not so rashly confronted once the major powers had learnt from their initial experiences. Battles in the open field still continued, but remained overwhelmingly chance encounters which took one side, or even both, by surprise.

The effect of gunpowder on the sixteenth-century battlefield had its complement in the growing inefficacy of the siege assault. Firearms and light artillery pieces entrenched in a half-moon behind the breach that the besieger wished to exploit could deny him the fruit of his patient battery. Each step of a besieger's progress was painfully slowed by improvements in fortress design and more powerful firearms and artillery which forced his men to construct miles of trenches and fill hundreds of gabions with earth to lessen their casualties. Nor was the impact of gunpowder in defence limited to those places which had received the benefit of purpose-built modern fortifications. François de la Noue, comparing the 'townes that were besiged in the time of King Frances and his sonne Henrie' with those that 'have ben assaulted in our civill warres' was forced to confess that 'these last have bene better defended notwithstanding they have bene assayled with greater arte, and yet most of them were never furnished with any of these stately fortifications'.[1] Hastily constructed earthworks would do.

New infantry tactics brought with them changes in military organisation and new ranks as well as a novel emphasis on order and discipline and the training *en masse* needed to bring it about. We saw in Chapter 3 how large Swiss-pattern pike-squares and small bodies of shot were expected, in theory, to complement each other on the sixteenth-century battlefield. In this, as in other respects, theory mirrored reality.[2] Careful training was essential if a pike-square was not to disintegrate into a stumbling mass of individuals, unable to resist a determined onslaught by cavalry.

For much of the century England lagged behind. Training of groups of men rather than of mere individuals was only officially sanctioned in 1572–3 with the introduction of the select, trained militia.[3] It was only in 1595 that the Privy Council decreed the end of the bow and bill in the trained bands.[4] Modernisation had encountered tremendous resistance, based on a romantic affection for the bow and its place in the English victories of the Hundred Years' War. English military theory reflected England's belated realisation of the need to change. The genre depended on the changes in the art of war for its very existence.

Before the final third of the century only a handful of works of theory were to be had, prompting Thomas Proctor's earnest plea of 1578 that more should 'be done in this behalfe'.[5] None of the works published in England in the first three-quarters of the century could compare with Thomas Styward's *The Pathwaie to Martiall Discipline* (1581)[6] or the many other excellent works that followed in the space of two decades. Of those published before only three were worthy of particular mention: John Sadler's translation of Vegetius's splendid late Roman military treatise,[7] Peter Whitehorne's translation of Machiavelli's treatise on the art of war[8] and Whitehorne's own brief work on tactics and siege warfare, *Certain Waies for the Orderying of Souldiers in Battelray* (1560–2).[9] Vegetius's, for all its merits, was written before the introduction of gunpowder; Machiavelli's treatise was largely copied from classical authors with a few wild ideas of his own; and Whitehorne's own pamphlet, the finest printed work before Styward's text, was handicapped by its very brevity. Only the rich manuscript literature of the mid-sixteenth century in England gave a hint of what was to come.

The real breakthrough came in the wake of the government's militia reforms. Gentlemen and JPs drawn into contact with training, firearms, pike tactics, the new ranks and other novelties by the government's militia reforms began to seek explanations of modern war. The outbreak of continuous hostilities with Spain in 1585 reinforced their (initially idle) curiosity. As we have seen, printed military literature of all kinds mushroomed as the war reached its peak. The felicitous coincidence of widespread demand due to the war (1585–1604) and the slow enactment of government's militia reforms from 1572–3 combined with the zeal of soldiers anxious to communicate what they had learned of modern methods to produce a flush of publications. The treatises of the final quarter of the century at last opened wide the changes of earlier decades in Europe to 'any willing minded Gentlemen ... desirous to understand some points of martiall matters'.[10]

The authors of these works included the pick of the Spanish, French and English military world: Francisco de Valdes, commissioned to write by Alva himself,[11] Bernardino de Mendoza,[12] François de la Noue, one of the most renowned commanders of the French Religious Wars[13] and Sir Roger Williams, Elizabeth's field commander on several occasions.[14] All told, they represented an extraordinary range of military experience. The dedicatees were no less impressive, ranging from the Tudor monarchs themselves to noted military and naval leaders and figures in government. However, few firm conclusions can be drawn from such evidence. More revealing are the backgrounds of the authors themselves. Only a handful had not served in English or continental armies.

Their main thrust was in the direction of infantry tactics and training, two of the areas that had changed most across Europe since the later Middle Ages. They focused for the most part on matters of detail, which modern commentators, with their eyes firmly fixed on strategy and the higher considerations of command, frequently prefer to ignore. Yet their works served to outline starkly the issues raised by the adoption of firearms and the pike. The adoption of both was not without controversy. The new weapons were essential if the remainder of the continental package of tactical changes were to be adopted. Mass training, demanded by individual writers in increasing numbers from mid-century, was a direct consequence of the spread of complicated pike and firearm tactics. Without the detailed explanation of the formation of pike-squares and the principles governing the use of shot and pikes in concert, many contemporaries would have been at a loss to understand the rationale behind the government's militia reforms. As experienced soldiers were rarely available to supervise training in sufficient numbers, it may be safely assumed that many a country gentleman or JP would have based a local militia training session on a personal copy of one of the late-century theorists. There was, after all, no official government training manual until 1623.[15]

Relatively few writers held their gaze for long on matters of siege warfare, logistics and strategy, all of which had changed strongly in character in the course of the century. Military theory was far from being a perfect mirror of reality. Its reflection was not perfect. There were distortions in favour of those aspects its writers found of particular interest: the duties of lower-ranking officers, the formations to be used by pikes and shot in training and action, and a mass of other, frequently trivial detail. This was not surprising in view of the often humble rank of the individuals concerned. Many were of the rank of captain or lower. This said, a trawl of the military theory published and committed to manuscript in England during the century yields considerable material on even the more neglected aspects of military change. A diligent Elizabethan would have been in a position by the 1590s to recognise the main elements of contemporary siege warfare from works in his own tongue, even if the full subtlety of the military engineer's trade would continue to escape him. Strategy was worse served. Among all the theorists only Matthew Sutcliffe produced a strategic theory worthy of the name. His *The Practice, Proceedings and Lawes of Armes* (1593)[16] earns him an as yet unrecognised place as the father of English strategic theory.

There is much more to be gleaned from sixteenth-century English military theory than has hitherto been imagined. It cannot be seen merely in a domestic Tudor context. Both in the extent of its translated content and in the persons of its English authors it was international in character. The developments which shook Europe out of the old ways of conducting war and onto new paths are to be found mirrored in the wealth of material, printed and manuscript, that awaits the researcher. The military revolution of the sixteenth century left its mark deep in the minds of contemporaries. Neither theory nor war itself would ever be the same again.

Notes

1. François de la Noue, *The Politicke and Militarie Discourses of the Lord de la Noue*, tr. E. A[ggas], STC 15215 (1587), pp. 216–17.

2. Karl Stallwitz, *Die Schlacht bei Ceresole (14. April 1544)* (Diss., Berlin, 1911), p. 71.

3. John Harland, *The Lancashire Lieutenancy under the Tudors and Stuarts* (2 vols., Manchester, 1859–60), I, pp. xxv–xxxiv. L.O. Boynton, *The Elizabethan Militia* (Newton Abbot, 1967), p. 91.

4. *Acts of the Privy Council of England, 1595–6*, pp. 27–8.

5. Thomas Proctor, *Of the knowledge and conducte of warres*, STC 20403 (1578), sig. ★v.

6. STC 23413.

7. Flavius Vegetius Renatus, *The Foure Bookes of Martiall Policye*, tr. J. Sadler, STC 24631 (1572; facs. repr. Amsterdam and New York, 1968).

8. Niccolo Machiavelli, *The Arte of Warre*, tr. P. Whitehorne, STC 17164 (1560–2).

9. STC 17164.

10. Robert Barret, *The Theorike and Practike of Moderne Warres*, STC 1500 (1598), p. 82.

11. Jähns, *Kriegswissenschaften*, p. 729.

12. Ibid., p. 568.

13. For an introduction to the life of La Noue: Henri Hausser, *François de la Noue (1531–1591)* (Paris, 1892).

14. See particularly R.B. Wernham, *After the Armada. Elizabethan England and the Struggle for Western Europe 1588–1595* (Oxford, 1984) and the introduction to J.X. Evans's edition of *The Works of Sir Roger Williams* (Oxford, 1972).

15. *Instructions for Musters and Armes, and the use thereof: By order from His Majesties most Honourable Privy Counsayle*, STC 7683 (1623).

16. STC 23468.

CHAPTER 7

BIBLIOGRAPHICAL ESSAY

The two works that started my interest in the field were Maurice Cockle's *A Bibliography of English Military Books up to 1642 and of Contemporary Foreign Works* (London, 1900) and Henry J. Webb's *Elizabethan Military Science: The Books and the Practice* (London, 1965). Between them they list most of the military books published in England in the sixteenth and early seventeenth centuries on which this study is based. Also of interest is Thomas Spaulding's 'Elizabethan Military Books', *John Quincy Adams Memorial Studies* (Washington, 1948) and P.A. Jorgensen's explorations of military writings thrown up by Elizabethan England.[1] Henry Webb has also written a large number of articles on individual Elizabethan military writers which repay examination.[2] Sir John Hale has looked at the English theorists in several studies,[3] to which can be added the useful biography by T.M. Cranfill and D.H. Bruce of one of the more important writers, *Barnaby Rich. A Short Biography* (Austin, Texas and Edinburgh, 1953). Finally, an up-to-date overview of some of the literature can be found in A. Bruce's *A Bibliography of British Military History From the Roman Invasions to the Restoration, 1660* (Munich and London, 1981), while another group of texts is examined by G.G. Langsam in his *Martial Books and Tudor Verse* (New York, 1951) from a more literary perspective.

For European military writers the best introduction remains Max Jähn's massive *Geschichte der Kriegswissenschaften vornehmlich in Deutschland* (3 vols, Munich and Leipzig, 1889–91). There is also Philippe Contamine's useful 'The War Literature of the Late Middle Ages: The Treatises of Robert Balsac and Beraud Stuart, Lord of Aubigny' in C.T. Allmand (ed.), *War, Literature and Politics in the Late Middle Ages* (Liverpool, 1976) and the fascinating introduction to K. Neubauer's edition of a late medieval German military manuscript, *Das Kriegsbuch des Philipp von Seldeneck vom Ausgang des 15. Jahrhunderts. Untersuchung und kritische Herausgabe des Textes der Karlsruher Handschrift* (Diss., Heidelberg, 1963). Machiavelli has received particular attention from scholars for his study of the art of war, whose flaws are well examined in Felix Gilbert's article 'The Renaissance of the Art of War' in P. Paret's collection *The Makers of Modern Strategy from Machiavelli to the Nuclear Age* (Oxford, 1986).

Going further back into the Middle Ages, there is a rich secondary literature on the translators of the Roman military writer, Vegetius.[4] Dutch military writers of the late sixteenth and early seventeenth centuries have been unusually fortunate in the scholarly attention they have received. In particular, there is Werner Hahlweg's *Die Heeresreform der Oranier* (Wiesbaden, 1973), M.D. Feld's 'Middle Class Society and the Rise of Military Professionalism: The Dutch Army 1589–1609' in his *The Structure of Violence. Armed Forces as Social Systems* (London, 1977) and G.E. Rothenburg's 'Maurice of Nassau, Gustavus Adolphus, Raimondo of Montecuccoli and the "Military Revolution" of the Seventeenth Century' in P. Paret (ed.), *Makers of Modern Strategy from Machiavelli to the Nuclear Age* (Oxford, 1986) and G. Oestreich's *Neostoicism and the Early Modern State* (Cambridge, 1982), which focuses on Justus Lipsius's important treatise on the Roman art of war. By comparison, the military literature of other countries has suffered neglect. Spain has only a rather weak study by J. Barrios, 'La enseñanza militar española en tiempo de los austria', *Revue Internationale d'Histoire Militaire*, LVI (1984) to serve as an introduction to its early-modern military literature.

Passing from military theory to broader aspects of military change, the greatest work on sixteenth-century military development remains C.W.C. Oman's *A History of the Art of War in the Sixteenth Century* (London, 1937). Much earlier research both on this period and the later middle ages has attempted to define the impact of chivalric ideas. For an introduction to this field there is Maurice Keen's *Chivalry* (London, 1984) and of course A.B. Ferguson's *The Indian Summer of English Chivalry* (Durham, North Carolina, 1960). A great deal of work has been done in this respect for the Tudor reigns. Five examples will have to do: Anthony Esler's *The Aspiring Mind of the Elizabethan Younger Generation* (Durham, North Carolina, 1966); Alan Young, *Tudor and Jacobean Tournaments* (London, 1987); Jan Dop, *Eliza's Knights: Soldiers, Poets and Puritans in the Netherlands 1572–1586* (Amsterdam, 1981); R.C. Strong and J.A. van Dorsten, *Leicester's Triumph* (London, 1964); and finally R.C. McCoy's article 'From the Tower to the tiltyard: Robert Dudley's return to glory', *Historical Journal*, XXVII (1984).

The other grand theme that has entranced scholars has been the 'military revolution' idea. Each has construed the major changes of the period in his own way from Sir John Hale in 'Armies, navies and the art of war' in G.R. Elton (ed.), *New Cambridge Modern History*, II (Cambridge, 1958) to Geoffrey Parker in his *The Military Revolution. Military innovation and the rise of the West 1500–1800* (Cambridge, 1988). More recent contributions to the debate include Brian Downing's *The Military Revolution and Political Change: Origins of democracy and autocracy in early modern Europe* (Princeton, 1992) and Jeremy Black's *A Military Revolution? Military Change and European Society 1500–1800* (London, 1991). The key essay to which we owe most of the subsequent debate is of course Professor M. Roberts's *The Military Revolution* (Belfast University Inaugural Lecture, 1956), largely restated in his *Gustavus Adolphus. A History of Sweden 1611– 32* (2 vols, London, 1958) and reprinted in *Essays in Swedish History* (London, 1967).

The debate on Roberts's essay began with specific criticisms of aspects of his argument by Parker himself, by David Parrott and John Lynn. Parker looked at the Spanish Army of Flanders, on which he had already written *The Army of Flanders and the Spanish Road 1567–1659. The Logistics of Spanish Victory and Defeat in the Low Countries' Wars* (Oxford, 1972), to write his 'The "Military Revolution" 1560–1660 – a myth?', *Journal of Modern History*, XXVI (1976), reprinted in Parker's collection *Spain and the Netherlands 1559–1659* (London, 1979). Parrott made much of German military writers in his 'Strategy and Tactics in the Thirty Years' War: "The Military Revolution"', *Militärgeschichtliche Mitteilungen*, XVIII (1985), while Lynn concentrated on the French army to make further critical comments on Roberts's thesis in his 'Tactical Evolution in the French Army', *French Historical Studies*, XIV (1985).

An entirely different perspective on military change can be found in Piero Pieri's *Il Rinascimento e la crisi militare italiana* (Turin, 1952), which has as yet found little echo among our recent controversialists. If the reader wants a much swifter introduction to the general patterns of military change there is always the relevant section of Professor M. Howard's *War in European History* (Oxford, 1976), which has the advantage of putting early modern developments within a grander scheme of evolution. A few works could be usefully mentioned at this point for the student anxious to throw a glance over later centuries. John Kenyon's *The Civil Wars of England* (London, 1988) is a useful introduction to the most important aspect of England's seventeenth-century military experience, while C.H. Firth has much more to tell about the pre-Cromwellian military world than might be imagined in his fine study of *Cromwell's Army* (London, 1962). Christopher Duffy deals well with the eighteenth century in his *Military Experience in the Age of Reason* (London, 1987). Other works bridging the transition from the seventeenth to the eighteenth centuries include David Chandler's excellent *The Art of Warfare in the Age of Marlborough* (London, 1976) and J. Childs's drier *Armies and Warfare in Europe 1648–1789* (Manchester, 1982). To take the perspective into the nineteenth century there are a thousand books, but a good introduction is Michael Glover's *Warfare from Waterloo to Mons* (London, 1980).

Those seeking contrasts not so much in time, but more in geographical area, could do worse than to read E.S. Forster's edition of the letters of Ogier Ghiselin de Busbecq on Turkish affairs (Oxford, 1927) or William Irvine's *The Army of the Indian Moghuls* (London, 1903) or indeed examine W.F. Cook's recent study *The Hundred Years War for Morocco. Gunpowder and the Military Revolution in the Early Modern World* (Oxford, 1994).

The military revolution debate has a multiplicity of aspects thanks to the extraordinarily wide-ranging approach of Roberts's seminal article. One of the most significant is the question of weaponry and technical change. On the bow there is E.G. Heath's *Archery, A Military History* (London, 1980), Robert Hardy's *Longbow. A social and military history* (Cambridge, 1976), S.T. Pope's *Bows and Arrows* (Berkeley and Los Angeles, 1962), Jim Bradbury's *The Medieval Archer* (Woodbridge, 1985) and H.L. Blackmore's *Hunting Weapons* (London, 1971). On firearms we have, in particular, A.R. Hall's *Ballistics in the Seventeenth Century* (Cambridge, 1952), R.C. Clepham's 'The military handgun of the sixteenth century', *Archaeological Journal*, LXVII (1910) and J.V.D. Lavin's *A History of Spanish Firearms* (London, 1965).

One of the key questions is whether a longbow could penetrate armour as well as firearms or the crossbow. Malcolm Vale's *War and Chivalry. Warfare and Aristocratic Culture in England, France and Burgundy at the End of the Middle Ages* (London, 1981) contains an excellent introduction to this problem area, making good use of the findings in the first volume of B. Thordeman's *Armour from the Battle of Wisby, 1361* (Stockholm, 1939). Information on developments in the construction of armour can be found in J.G. Mann's 'Notes on the Armour of the Maximilian Period and the Italian Wars', *Archaeologia*, LXXIX (1929) and V. Poschenburg's *Die Schutz- und Trutzwaffen des*

Mittelalters (Vienna, 1936). Taking the investigation into the sixteenth century, a wide range of contemporaries have much to say. The best policy is to pursue their works listed in the other part of this bibliography, rather than hope for enlightenment from modern studies, which are mostly less than helpful, although Claude Gaier's 'L'opinion des chefs de guerre français du XVIe siècle sur le progrès de l'art militaire', *Revue Internationale d'Histoire Militaire*, XXIX (1970) is a clear exception. There is also a great deal of interest to be found on the performance of sixteenth-century weaponry in J.F. Guilmartin's *Gunpowder and Galleys. Changing technology and Mediterranean warfare at sea in the sixteenth century* (Oxford, 1974), which can be put in a broader context by using B.P. Hughes's thoughtful study of firearm development, *Firepower. Weapons' effectiveness on the battlefield, 1630–1850* (London, 1974). Of less use, despite its promising title, is G. Ortenburg's *Waffe und Waffengebrauch im Zeitalter der Landsknechte* (Coblenz, 1984), though it does contain much information on a wide range of other issues.

Part of the charm of the period is the ferocity of debate over the value of the bow, which lasted right into the eighteenth century. Introductions to this controversy are many. Gaier's 'L'invincibilité anglaise et le grand arc après la guerre de cent ans: un mythe tenace', *Tijdschrift voor Geschiedenis*, XCI (1978) reminds us of the long memories of English successes with the bow in the Hundred Years' War. Sir John Hale's introduction to his edition of Sir John Smythe's treatise, *Certain Discourses Military* (Ithaca: New York, 1964), provides much general orientation, as does Mark Fissel's more recent 'Tradition and Invention in the Early Stuart Art of War', *Journal of the Society for Army Historical Research*, LXV (1987).

Moving from the debate on weaponry to a study of tactics and military organisation in Europe, we are not as well served as we should be. The most useful text, G. Köhler's *Die Entwickelung des Kriegswesens und der Kriegführung in der Ritterzeit von Mitte des 11. Jahrhunderts bis zu den Hussiten kriegen* (3 vols, Breslau, 1886) is flawed by its author's tendency to report as fact what he considered likely to be the case. Under another name, 'inherent military probability', the same approach is used by Alfred Burne in his *The Agincourt War. A military History of the latter part of the Hundred Years' War from 1369–1453* (London, 1956), otherwise one of the most useful introductions to fifteenth-century warfare. Both of these authors were soldiers in more modern armies, the former a general, the latter a colonel. The methods of the Landsknechts and the Swiss are investigated in Eugen von Frauenholz's two studies, *Das Heerwesen des Reiches in der Landsknechtszeit* (Munich, 1937) and *Das Heerwesen der Schweizer Eidgenossenschaft in der Zeit des freien Söldnertums* (Munich, 1936). There is also much of interest in the earlier work of C. von Elgger, *Kriegswesen und Kriegskunst der schweizerischen Eidgenossen im 14., 15., und 16. Jahrhundert* (Lucerne, 1873) and of Charles Kohler, *Les Suisses dans les guerres d'Italie de 1506 à 1512* (Geneva, 1897; facs. repr. Geneva, 1978). A more up-to-date treatment of the practices of the Landsknechts is contained in Siegfried Fiedler's *Kriegswesen und Kriegführung im Zeitalter der Landsknechte*, although, like the preceding works, it has little to offer on the matter of tactics, training and military experience.

Some insights into late medieval military methods can be gleaned from W. Block's *Die Condottieri. Studien über die sogenannten 'unblutigen Schlachten'* (Berlin, 1913) and P. Blastenbrei's *Die Sforza und ihr Heer. Studien zur Struktur-, Wirtschafts- und Sozialgeschichte des Söldnerwesens in der italienischen Frührenaissance* (Heidelberg, 1987). Italy is also well served by Sir John Hale and Michael Mallett's study of *The Military Organization of a Renaissance State. Venice c. 1400 to 1617* (Cambridge, 1984). Passing from Italy to northern Europe, there are the works of C. Brusten on the military arrangements of the Dukes of Burgundy, *L'armée bourguignonne* (Brussels, 1953) and 'L'armée bourguignonne de 1465 a 1477', *Revue internationale d'Histoire Militaire* (1959) and of Philippe Contamine on medieval France in his *La Guerre au Moyen Age* (Paris, 1980), which also gives references to his more detailed work on the same theme. Also worth considering is E. Boutaric's ancient *Institutions militaires de la France avant les armées permanentes* (Paris, 1863), which still contains much valuable material on early French military organisation.

A lot of the issues raised by late medieval English military methods are examined by John Keegan in the course of an investigation of the battle of Agincourt in his *The Face of Battle* (London, 1976), while many valuable insights can be gathered from H.J. Hewitt's thorough survey of fourteenth-century English military methods, *The Organisation of War under Edward III, 1338–62* (Manchester, 1966). The Hussite military challenge is briefly explored in M. von Wulf's thesis, *Die hussitische Wagenburg* (Diss., Berlin, 1889), while a broader sense of central European military evolution can be garnered from, among other works, J. Würdinger's *Kriegsgeschichte von Bayern, Pfalz und Schwaben von 1347 bis 1506* (2 vols, Munich and Augsburg, 1868), dealing with southern Germany and Max Jähns's more general

Handbuch einer Geschichte des Kriegswesens (Leipzig, 1880). A much shorter but still useful summary of medieval military development is W. Erben's *Kriegsgeschichte des Mittelalters* (Munich and Berlin, 1929), which cannot stand comparison with Oman's much superior work, *A History of the Art of War in the Middle Ages* (2 vols, London, 1924). There are of course a wide range of studies of the military art in particular segments of the Middle Ages, of which three particularly repay study, J. Beeler's *Warfare in England 1066–1189* (New York, 1966), J. Morris's *The Welsh Wars of Edward I* (Oxford, 1901) and R.C. Smail's outstanding *Crusading Warfare 1097–1193* (Cambridge, 1956).

The French-speaking world is still well served in terms of studies of its military organisation and methods when we move on to the sixteenth century. We have the only detailed study of army size for the expeditions of a European country in Ferdinand Lot's epic *Recherches sur les effectifs des armées françaises des Guerres d'Italie aux Guerres de Religion 1494–1562* (Paris, 1962), as well as some briefer general observations in J.A. Lynn's 'Tactical Evolution in the French Army', *French Historical Studies*, XIV (1985), not to mention La Barre Duparcq's ancient, but still valuable *L'art militaire pendant les guerres de religion* (Paris, 1864). A great deal can still be gleaned from General Susane's *Histoire de l'infanterie française* (5 vols, Paris, 1876), while the performance of the French army in Italy is one of the aspects investigated by F.L. Taylor in his slight work, *The Art of War in Italy 1494–1529* (Cambridge, 1921) and V. Saletta's much more specialised account of *La spedizione di Lautrec contro il Regno di Napoli* (Rome, n. d.). To these works of analysis can be added a mass of studies of individual warriors, from H. Hausser's *François de la Noue (1531–1591)* (Paris, 1892) and G. Amiaud-Bellavaud's *Un chef huguenot: le capitaine Merle et les Guerres de Religion notamment en Auvergne, Gevaudan et Vivarais* (Uzes, 1958), which throw light on the Wars of Religion of the later sixteenth century, to J.-C. Sournia's *Blaise de Monluc. Soldat et écrivain (1500–1577)* (Paris, 1981) and P. Keller's *Galiot de Genouillac, Grand-maître de l'artillerie de France* (Saint-Cere, 1968), which do the same for the period of the Italian Wars. No account of this earlier period would be complete without a mention of the immortal Bayard, who is introduced in C. Monnet's *Petite histoire veridique des faits et gestes du capitaine Bayard avant et pendant les guerres d'Italie* (Grenoble, 1970).

Ireland is also comparatively well served by the researches of G.A. Hayes-McCoy, in particular his 'Strategy and Tactics in Irish

Warfare 1593–1601', *Irish Historical Studies*, II (1940–1) and 'The Army of Ulster 1593–1601', *The Irish Sword*, I (1949–53). Even his more general account 'Tudor Conquest and Counter-Reformation' in T.W. Moody et al. (eds), *Early Modern Ireland 1534–1691* (Oxford, 1978) has much of interest for the military specialist. Any survey of Irish military history in the sixteenth century would of course be the weaker without the aid of Cyril Falls's invaluable study *Elizabeth's Irish Wars* (London, 1950) and his *Mountjoy: Elizabethan General* (London, 1955).

The single most interesting source for a student of the changing European battlefield is the series of studies written by the pupils of Hans Delbrück, a charismatic professor of military history at a time when the subject was frowned upon by officialdom, ironically enough in Kaiser Wilhelm II's militaristic Germany. Delbrück himself has left us a summary of much of their work in his multi-volume outline history of military development, *Geschichte der Kriegskunst im Rahmen der politischen Geschichte* (2nd revised ed., Berlin, 1923), but the following footnote records some of the most valuable for the student of this decisive period of military development.[5] Written in much the same style are Sir Charles Oman's 'The Battle of Pinkie', *Archaeological Journal*, XC (1933) and K. Häbler's study of the critical battle of Pavia in 1525 'Die Schlacht bei Pavia', published in the *Forschungen zur deutschen Geschichte*, XXV (Göttingen, 1885).

On the developments in training and military organisation on which this present study focuses, it is difficult to find specialist studies. Instead it is necessary to cull details from a range of sources, whether lives of individuals like William Maltby's study *Alba. A Biography of Fernando Alvarez de Toledo, Third Duke of Alba 1507–1582* (London, 1983) or more specialised studies of aspects of the topic, such as Henry Farmer's *Military Music and its Story. The Rise and Development of Military Music* (London, 1912) or F. J. Davies's *The Sergeant-Major; The Origin and History of his Rank ...* (London, 1886).

Siege warfare has been well served in the secondary literature on late medieval and sixteenth-century warfare. The best introduction is Christopher Duffy's *Siege Warfare. The Fortress in Early Modern Europe 1494–1660* (London, 1979). There is also Sir John Hale's splendid introduction to the topic in his *Renaissance Fortification. Art or Engineering?* (Norwich, 1977), which takes further many of the themes set out in 'The Early Development of the Bastion: An Italian Chronology, *c*.1450–*c*.1453' in B. Smalley et al. (eds), *Europe in the Late Middle Ages* (London, 1965). Sir John's interest in the art of siege is also reflected in his more general study *War and Society in Renaissance Europe 1450–1620* (London, 1985) as well as his well-crafted article on early English fortification, 'The Defence of the Realm 1485–1558' in H.M. Colvin (ed.), *The History of the King's Works* (London, 1982), IV, part II. The story of English fortification is taken up to the end of Elizabeth's reign by J. Summerson's 'The Defence of the Realm under Elizabeth I' in the same volume.

Illustrations have a great value to the novice in the field of fortification and there is no better place to become acquainted with unfamiliar technical terms than in Viollet-le-Duc's illustrated nineteenth-century *Dictionnaire Raisonné de l'Architecture Française du XIe au XVIe Siècle* (10 vols, Paris, 1861).

Case studies of fortress design and sieges are plentiful. For Germany there is Doris Bellebaum's wide-ranging study of *Die Befestigungen der Stadt Wesel in ihrer Entwicklung 1349–1552* (Cologne, 1961) and Nicolaus Bömmels's outstanding study of the 1474 siege of Neuss: 'Die Neusser unter dem Druck der Belagerung', *Neuss, Burgund und das Reich* (Neuss, 1975). The most important monograph for the historian of sixteenth-century siege warfare is however Simon Pepper and Nicholas Adams's study *Firearms and Fortifications. Military Architecture and Siege Warfare in Sixteenth-Century Siena* (Chicago and London, 1986). A shorter study of the same topic is J. Hook's 'Fortifications and the end of the Sienese state', *History*, LXII (1977). Simon Pepper has also furnished us with some more detailed studies in issue X (1982) of the periodical *Fort*, which repay careful attention: 'Firepower and the design of Renaissance Fortifications', 'The underground siege' and, in the same issue, J.B. Bury's 'The early history of the explosive mine', G. Scaglia's study of 'Francesco di Giorgio's chapters on fortresses and on war machines', Q. Hughes's 'Military architecture and the printed book' and his 'The siege of Fort St. Elmo in 1565'. Altogether, this issue is quite a gold-mine for the student of sixteenth-century fortifications.

Artillery is the key to an understanding of the changing pattern of siege warfare and good introductions abound. Particularly useful is Carlo Cipolla's *Guns and Sails in the Early Phase of European Expansion 1400–1700* (London, 1965), but still of value is Fave and Reinaud's *Histoire de l'artillerie 1re partie. Du feu grégeois des feux de guerre et des origines de la poudre à canon d'après des textes nouveaux* (Paris, 1845). The story of these gunpowder weapons is taken up to the year 1400 by Karl Jacobs in his valuable *Das Aufkommen der Feuerwaffen am Niederrhein bis zum Jahre 1400* (Bonn, 1910). Volker

Schmidtchen has given us a valuable study of the artilleryman's trade in later medieval Germany, *Bombarden, Befestigungen, Büchsenmeister* (Düsseldorf, 1977), while the weapons of a pre-powder age are examined by Rudolf Schneider in his *Die Artillerie des Mittelalters. Nach den Angaben der Zeitgenossen dargestellt* (Berlin, 1910) and by Heinz Waschow's unimpressive, but general introduction to the topic, *4000 Jahre Kampf um die Mauer. Der Festungskrieg der Pioniere. Geschichte der Belagerungstechnik* (Bottrop, 1938). For a short introduction to the problems posed by late medieval developments in artillery you can always consult my own 'Towns and Defence in Later Medieval Germany', *Nottingham Medieval Studies*, XXXIII (1989).

Irish artillery is the subject of a specialist study by S. de hOir, 'Guns in Medieval and Tudor Ireland,' *The Irish Sword*, XV (1982), which is best read in conjunction with W.A. McComish's 'The Survival of the Irish Castle in an Age of Cannon', *The Irish Sword*, IX (1969–70). For England R. Ashley has given us a view of 'The organisation and administration of the Tudor office of Ordnance' (Oxford B.Litt. thesis, 1972), while B.H. St J. O'Neil has provided an invaluable study of early artillery fortifications in his *Castles and Cannon* (Oxford, 1960) as well as a case study of one of the most important individual architects of the early Tudor period, 'Stefan Haschenperg, an Engineer to King Henry VIII, and his Work', *Archaeologia*, XCI (1945). More recently, J. Kenyon has explored much the same territory but from a different perspective in his 'Terminology and Early Artillery Fortification', *Fort*, XI (1983) and his 'Early Artillery Fortifications in England and Wales: a preliminary survey and reappraisal', *Archaeological Journal*, CXXXVIII (1982).

Turning from siege warfare to strategy, there is precious little to inform the student of early modern war. Hans Delbrück's *Die Strategie des Perikles erläutert durch die Strategie Friedrichs des Grossen* (Berlin, 1890) has a provocative essay with much bearing on the sixteenth-century conduct of war. M. van Creveld throws out some interesting ideas in the course of an examination of seventeenth-century strategy in *Supplying War* (Cambridge, 1977) and many of the considerations identified by E.B. Hamley in his strategic text-book *The Operations of War* (London, 1923) still bear thinking about. Fragmentary insights into early modern strategy can be found in countless individual studies of wars and campaigns, but a systematic survey has yet to be written.

Turning from general considerations on the art of war to England's military development in this period, we encounter a literature that is rich, but not as widely developed as that in other fields. The outline history of England in this period has been well drawn in a profusion of textbooks and lives of monarchs, which I will not list here. For a brief introduction, the reader need only skim the bibliographies of a few of the many lives of Tudor monarchs and surveys of English history readily accessible in any library.

Oman, Burne and Hewitt's surveys of late medieval English warfare have already been mentioned. To these can be added Anthony Goodman's excellent study *The Wars of the Roses. Military Activity and English Society 1452–97* (London, 1981). The scholar with an interest in chivalry and the indenture system used to pay the soldiery will find richer pastures in the secondary literature of this period than the student of the development of the art of war. However, we would be wrong to pass on to examine Henry VIII's wars without briefly mentioning one of the few ventures of its kind, Malcolm Vale's study of English strategy in the Hundred Years' War, 'Sir John Fastolf's "report" of 1435: a new interpretation reconsidered', *Nottingham Medieval Studies*, XVII (1973), which provides as good a starting point as any for a scholar wishing to find and take up references to the wider literature of this neglected period. Equally, he could turn to K.B. McFarlane's famous study of 'England and the Hundred Years' War', *Past and Present*, XXII (1962). McFarlane had an eye for telling detail and his more specialised study of 'William of Worcester: A Preliminary Survey' in J.C. Davies (ed.), *Studies Presented to Sir Hilary Jenkinson* (London, 1957) is still of interest as an account of one of the few Englishmen of the time to write a treatise on war, though one of negligible value.

Moving on to the Tudor age, we are immersed in blood from the very beginning, as Henry VII not merely had to fight a major battle to mount the throne, but was forced to defend it within two years in a second battle. These struggles have received very detailed attention in D.T. Williams's *The Battle of Bosworth* (Leicester, 1973), Michael Bennett's *The Battle of Bosworth* (Gloucester, 1985) and the same author's *Lambert Simnel and the Battle of Stoke* (London, 1987). We reach 1513 before we encounter another detailed monograph on a single military operation. But C.G. Cruickshank's *Army Royal. Henry VIII's invasion of France, 1513* (Oxford, 1969) is much more than an account of the battle of Spurs and the siege activity of Henry VIII and Maximilian in that year. It provides a very professional overview of the entire structure and organisation of the conduct of war at that point in English history.

Just as a disproportionate amount of research energy has gone into the political history of the first half of the century compared to the second, so the amount of attention devoted to Henry VIII's military activity is striking. C.S.L. Davies has made the supply problems of English expeditions abroad his speciality, writing a thesis on 'Supply services of English armed forces 1509–1550' (Oxford D.Phil. thesis, 1963), which is ably summarised in his 'Provisions for Armies 1509–1550, a Study in the Effectiveness of Tudor Government', *Economic History Review*, XVII (1964). Keeping sixteenth-century armies in the field for extended periods was extremely difficult, as English governments discovered in 1522–3 in particular. Dr Davies casts light on this, as does Dr Steven Gunn, who has given us 'The Duke of Suffolk's March on Paris in 1523', *English Historical Review*, CI (1986), an excellent study of one such expedition in distress, together with a study of its commander, 'The Life and Career of Charles Brandon, Duke of Suffolk, *c.*1485–1545' (Oxford D.Phil., 1986).

One of the key sources for this disaster is a Welsh chronicle by one of Henry VIII's soldiers, whose author is introduced by P. Morgan: 'Elis Gruffud of Gronant – Tudor Chronicler Extraordinary', *Journal of the Flintshire Historical Society*, XXV (1971–2). Henry VIII's supply problems can also be put into perspective by looking at developments under his father, as J.R. Hooker has done in his useful 'Notes on the Organisation and Supply of the Tudor Military under Henry VII', *The Huntington Library Quarterly*, XXIII (1959–60), which can be sensibly used in conjunction with G.S. Ormerod's brief article on English troops in foreign service in the reign of Henry VII, 'The English Soldier – A Spanish Criticism', *Journal of the Society for Army Historical Research*, II (1923).

A number of other authors have provided perspectives on the wars of Henry VIII, ranging from G. Millar's *Tudor Mercenaries and Auxiliaries 1485–1547* (Charlottesville, 1980)[6] on the composition of Tudor armies, and his 'Henry VIII's colonels', *Journal of the Society for Army Historical Research*, LVII (1979), which looks at new developments in ranks and organisation, to M.B. Davies's 'Surrey at Boulogne', *Huntington Library Quarterly*, XXIII (1959–60) on the 1544 campaign in France, or G.W. Bernard's study of the constraints on Henry's war effort in the 1520s, *War, Taxation and Rebellion in early Tudor England. Henry VIII, Wolsey and the Amicable Grant of 1525* (Brighton, 1986). Dr Bernard also allows us to look at the human material available for use in war in his study of two Tudor noblemen,

The Power of the Early Tudor Nobility. A Study of the Fourth and Fifth Earls of Shrewsbury (Brighton, 1985), a theme more fully examined by H. Miller in her thorough survey *Henry VIII and the English Nobility* (Oxford, 1986).

Looking at change over the whole period up to the beginning of the reign of Elizabeth there are two helpful survey articles: C.S.L. Davies's 'The English People and War in the Early Sixteenth Century' in A.C. Duke and C.A. Tamse (eds), *Britain and the Netherlands (VI): War and Society* (The Hague, 1977) and J.J. Goring's 'Social change and military decline in mid-Tudor England', *History, LX* (1975).

Turning from the general to the specific, there are two articles on specific campaigns before the reign of Elizabeth which are worth a particular mention. Firstly there is J. Mackie's 'The English Army at Flodden', *Miscellany of the Scottish History Society,* VIII (1951), which should be used in conjunction with M.J. Tucker's *The life of Thomas Howard, Earl of Surrey and Second Duke of Norfolk, 1443–1524* (London, 1964) and the numerous other printed accounts of this 1513 battle and a modest article on the equipment of the Scottish army by G. Dickinson, 'Some Notes on the Scottish Army in the First Half of the Sixteenth Century', *Scottish Historical Review*, XXVIII (1949). Secondly there is C.S.L. Davies's introduction to the military effort of Mary Tudor in Europe – 'England and the French War 1557–9' in J. Loach and R. Tittler (eds), *The Mid-Tudor Polity c.1540–1560* (London, 1980). In each case, a survey of the biographies and textbooks dealing with the period will yield a rich supplementary haul of modern judgements, but here is not the place to list them all. The only exception, perhaps, should be the literature on Tudor rebellions, which offers a clear insight into Tudor military operations. For these we have Anthony Fletcher's general survey *Tudor Rebellions* (2nd ed., London, 1973), as well as a number of specific case studies, such as S.T. Bindoff's brief pamphlet *Ket's Rebellion 1549* (London, 1949), and R. Wood's *The Rising in the North. The 1569 Rebellion* (Shotton, 1975), two of the rebellions in which a considerable amount of military activity took place, though in the latter case without actual fighting. However, Fletcher's introductory survey and the many modern texts on the Tudor period will provide more than adequate references to this literature for the student interested in following it up in full.

Moving on to the reign of Elizabeth, the range of material available is pleasantly surprising, given the relative neglect of the period in other terms. The best introduction is L.O. Boynton's *The*

Elizabethan Militia 1558–1638 (Newton Abbot, 1966), a printing of his 'English Military Organisation *c.*1558–1638' (Oxford D.Phil. thesis, 1962). This has a good deal more to communicate than its title suggests and provides a good framework for reviewing more recent literature. J.S. Nolan's article 'The Muster of 1588', *Albion*, XXIII (1991), for instance, has little to say that Boynton has not already committed to paper. Another useful survey is C.G. Cruick- shank's *Elizabeth's Army* (2nd ed., Oxford, 1966), which gives a general but helpful outline of Elizabethan military organisation.

The complexity and apparent inconsistency of Elizabethan foreign policy is the backdrop to the largely disjointed military activity of the reign and certainly repays study. R.B. Wernham has given us a firm grip with his two massive studies, *Before the Armada* and, more recently, *After the Armada. Elizabethan England and the Struggle for Western Europe 1588–95* (Oxford, 1984). Those seeking a shorter summary are well advised to start with the same author's 'Elizabethan War Aims and Strategy' in S.T. Bindoff (ed.), *Essays Presented to Sir John Neale* (London, 1961) or his excellent recent survey, *The Making of Elizabethan Foreign Policy, 1558–1603* (London, 1988). Inferior, but still useful, is P.S. Crowson's introductory *Tudor Foreign Policy* (Lon- don, 1973). Other perspectives on two salient aspects of the last Tudor's approach to foreign affairs can be found in S.L. Adams's thesis 'The Protestant Cause: Religious Alliance with the European Calvinist Communities as a Political Issue in England 1585–1603' (Oxford D.Phil. thesis, 1972). More recently, J. Dawson has given us a brief interpretation of 'William Cecil and the British dimension of early Elizabethan foreign policy', *History*, LXXIV (1989), but more is to be said for a thorough review of the general work on Elizabeth's reign by Rowse, McCaffrey, Wernham, Neale and Conyers Read, to name a few, and, of course, the sources.

Moving on from general perspectives to particular campaigns, we find a surprisingly rich haul of articles and specialist studies. On Ireland there are the works of G.A. Hayes-McCoy and C. Falls, already mentioned, as well as H. Mangan's 'Del Aguila's Defence of Kinsale 1601–2', *The Irish Sword*, I (1949–53). Moving across the Channel to France we have H.A. Lloyd's detailed study of *The Rouen Campaign 1590–2* (Oxford, 1973), but R.B. Wernham's 'Queen Elizabeth and the Siege of Rouen', *Transactions of the Royal Historical Society*, 4th series, XV (1932) still repays reading. Essex is the key figure in this episode and here we are well served by L.W. Henry's study of 'The Earl of Essex as Strategist and Military Organiser',

English Historical Review, LXVIII (1953) and W. Devereux's introduction to his edition of the *Lives and Letters of the Devereux, Earls
of Essex in the Reigns of Elizabeth, James I and Charles I 1540–1646* (2
vols, London, 1853).

The Netherlands, however, were the one place where English
arms were tested for a substantial and continuous stretch of time in
the sixteenth century. The most striking single episode in the history
of English military involvement there was the period of Leicester's
command (1586–7) and this has drawn a considerable literature. We
have J.E. Neale's essay on the relevant section of the *Calendar of
State Papers*, 'Elizabeth and the Netherlands, 1586–7', *Essays in
Elizabethan History* (London, 1958) for a survey under the microscope
and C.H. Wilson's wide-ranging *Queen Elizabeth and the revolt of the
Netherlands* (London, 1969) for general orientation. A. Haynes has
given us an accessible life of the main protagonist, *The White Bear.
The Elizabethan Earl of Leicester* (London, 1987),[7] while G. Parker
has provided the indispensable background to the English involvement in his excellent survey *The Dutch Revolt* (Norwich, 1981) and
accompanying essays *Spain and the Netherlands 1559–1659* (London,
1979).

Three individuals who shaped England's military performance in
this theatre for better or worse have been given detailed treatment.
W.G. Gosling introduces *The Life of Sir Humphrey Gilbert: England's
First Empire Builder* (London, 1911), who was also an unsuccessful
operator in the early part of the struggle in the Netherlands, while
Sir Roger Williams, who served under him and later made a career
as a commander on his own account, is attended to by L.V.D.
Owen in his rather scanty article 'Sir Roger Williams and the Spanish
power in the Netherlands', *Army Quarterly*, XXXIV (1937). The
introduction to J.X. Evans's edition[8] of two of Williams's treatises is
also a mine of information on this front. Finally there is C.R.
Markham's excellent study *'The fighting Veres ...'* (London, 1888),
which rounds off this haphazard survey of English officers in the
Netherlands on a more successful note.

Looking at operations conducted further afield there is a substantial literature on English naval activity which has a lot to communicate in passing on land operations. In particular, a great debt is
owed to J.S. Corbett for his two studies, *Drake and the Tudor Navy
with a History of the Rise of England as a Maritime Power* (2 vols,
London, 1917) and *The Successors of Drake* (London, 1919). We are
again in debt to R.B. Wernham, this time for his excellent study of

the unfortunate operation of 1589, ably chronicled in his 'Queen Elizabeth and the Portugal Expedition of 1589', *English Historical Review*, LXVI (1951). However, these studies are but the tip of an iceberg of naval research, which can be best approached from the vantage point of the recent publications on the Armada year, which also provide surveys of past research. G. Parker and C. Martin have produced the most successful of many such Armada books in their *The Spanish Armada* (London, 1988), but it is also well worth consulting F. Fernandez-Armesto's *The Spanish Armada. The Experience of War in 1588* (London, 1988) and the National Maritime Museum's *Armada 1588–1988. An International Exhibition to Commemorate the Spanish Armada. The Official Catalogue* (London, 1988).

Turning from the external use of force to Elizabeth's arrangements at home, there is a wealth of material to be considered. Besides Boynton's study, we have the useful introductory chapter on Tudor military arrangements in P. Williams's *The Tudor Regime* (Oxford, 1981) and the same author's survey of 'The Crown and the Counties' in Christopher Haigh (ed.), *The Reign of Elizabeth* (London, 1984). The defence of the realm in the face of the Armada is explored in M. Christy's article 'Queen Elizabeth's Visit to Tilbury in 1588', *English Historical Review*, XXXIV (1919), E.P. Dickin's 'The Army at Tilbury, 1588', *Transactions of the Essex Archaeological Society*, XXIII (1942) and more usefully in O.F.G. Hogg's excellent study 'England's War Effort against the Spanish Armada', *Journal of the Society for Army Historical Research*, XLIV (1966) and J. Bruce's still useful eighteenth-century *Report on the Arrangements which were made, for the Internal Defence of these Kingdoms* (London, 1798).

A. Hassell Smith has made a very valuable contribution to the understanding of English military development with his article 'Militia rates and militia statutes 1558–1663' in P. Clark et al. (eds), *The English Commonwealth 1547–1640* (Chatham, 1979), but more particularly with his excellent work *County and Court. Government and Politics in Norfolk 1558–1603* (Oxford, 1974). Others have produced similar local studies, whether of individuals or counties. Valuable are C. Cross's *The Puritan Earl. The Life of Henry Hastings, Third Earl of Huntingdon 1536–1595* (London, 1966) and D. MacCulloch's *Suffolk and the Tudors. Politics and Religion in an English County 1500–1600* (Oxford, 1986). However, in a class of its own is A.L. Rowse's witty introduction to *Tudor Cornwall. Portrait of a Society* (London, 1957), which has a great deal to communicate on Tudor military development. Institutionally, the office of Lord Lieutenant is closely tied to the Tudor military reforms and here there is much to be learned from G.S. Thomson's *Lord Lieutenants in the Sixteenth Century. A Study in Tudor Local Administration* (London, 1923) and the same author's companion article 'The origin and growth of the office of deputy-lieutenant', *Transactions of the Royal Historical Society*, 4th series, V (1922).

This survey of the Tudor military is almost complete. But it would be quite wrong to leave out a number of studies on peripheral aspects, which in their way add a great deal to the whole. L. Jardine and A. Grafton give us an insight into the mental world of a sixteenth-century gentlemen interested in military affairs in their '"Studied for Action:" How Gabriel Harvey Read His Livy', *Past and Present*, CXXIX (1990). As a corrective to the charm of this picture of intellect at work there is much to recommend H.H. Davis's bitter study 'The Military Career of Thomas North', *Huntington Library Quarterly*, XII (1948–9). This impression of self-serving corruption is consolidated by C.G. Cruickshank's admirable little survey 'Dead-pays in the Elizabethan army', *English Historical Review*, LIII (1938). Remaining with the darker side of war, there is a great deal to commend D. Stewart's painstaking study 'Sickness and Mortality Rates in the English Army in the Sixteenth Century', *Journal of the Royal Army Medical Corps*, XCI (1948) and the 'Disposal of the sick and wounded of the English army during the sixteenth century', *Journal of the Royal Army Medical Corps*, XC (1948). Finally, we have K.V. Thomas's provocative survey of the development of mathematical ability in early modern England, 'Numeracy in Early Modern England', *Transactions of the Royal Historical Society*, 5th series, XXXVII (1987), a topic which has considerable implications for Tudor military development, as I hope this book has made clear.

The ground surveyed here has been immense, and it is inevitable that a great deal of work has been omitted. But I hope this brief introduction to the secondary literature in one of the most interesting fields of early modern development will stimulate the reader to further research and perhaps to make his own conclusions available in the course of time. In the meantime, some of the more important sources for the student of these changes are given in the select bibliography.

Notes

1. 'Theoretical Views on War in Elizabethan England', *Journal of the History of Ideas*, XIII (1952); *Shakespeare's Military World* (Los Angeles, 1956); 'Alien Military Doctrine in Renaissance England', *Modern Language Quarterly*, XVIII (1956). The focus in all these works is not so much military as ethical. States of mind rather than military developments are Jorgensen's chief concern. But his work is none the less valuable for this.

2. 'The Mathematical and Military Works of Thomas Digges', *Modern Language Quarterly*, VI (1945); 'Two Additions to the Military Bibliography of Thomas Digges', *Modern Language Quarterly*, XII (1951); 'Dr Matthew Sutcliffe', *Philological Quarterly*, XXIII (1944); 'The Military Background in Othello', *Philological Quarterly*, XXX (1951); 'Classical Histories and Elizabethan Soldiers', *Notes and Queries*, CC (1955); 'Barnabe Riche – sixteenth-century military critic', *Journal of English and German Philology*, XLII (1943); 'Military Newsbooks during the Age of Elizabeth', *English Studies*, XXXIII (1952); 'Thomas Digges, an Elizabethan combat historian', *Military Affairs*, XIV (1950); 'Elizabethan soldiers: a study in the ideal and the real', *Western Humanities Review*, IV (1950).

3. *Renaissance War Studies* (London, 1983); *The art of war and Renaissance England* (Washington, 1961); *Artists and Warfare in the Renaissance* (New Haven and London, 1990). He has also edited two important texts, for which see the other part of this bibliography.

4. Bornstein, D., 'Military strategy in Malory and Vegetius' "De re militari"', *Comparative Literature Studies*, IX (1972); 'Military Manuals in Fifteenth Century England', *Medieval Studies*, XXXVII (1975).

Bossuat, R., 'Jean de Rouvroy Traducteur des Stratagèmes de Frontin', *Bibliotheque d'Humanisme et Renaissance*, XXII (1960).

Conley, C.H., *The First English Translators of the Classics* (London, 1927).

Goffart, W., 'The Date and Purpose of Vegetius' "De Re Militari"', *Traditio*, XXXIII (1947).

Jones, C., 'Bede and Vegetius', *The Classical Review*, XLVI (1932).

Knowles, C., 'A XIV century imitator of Jean de Meung: Jean de Vignay's translation of the "De re militari" of Vegetius', *Studies in Philology*, LIII (1956).

Lathrop, H.B., *Translation from the Classics into English from Chaucer to Chapman* (Madison, 1933).

Legge, D., 'The Lord Edward's Vegetius', *Scriptorium*, VII (1953).

Martin, J., 'John of Salisbury as classical scholar' in M. Wilks (ed.), *The World of John of Salisbury* (Oxford, 1984).

Meyer, P., 'Les Anciens Traducteurs Français de Végèce et en particulier Jean de Vignai', *Romania*, XXV (1896).

Sandys, J.E., *A History of Classical Scholarship* (3 vols, Cambridge, 1903–8).

Springer, M., 'Vegetius im Mittelalter', *Philologus*, CXXIII (1979).

Thorpe, L., 'Mastre Richard, a Thirteenth-Century Translator of the "De Re Militari" of Vegetius', *Scriptorium*, VI (1952).

Wiseman, J.A., 'L'Epitoma rei militaris de Végèce et sa fortune au Moyen Age', *Le Moyen Age. Revue d'Histoire et de Philologie*, LXXXV (1979).

5. Czeppan, R., *Die Schlacht bei Crecy (26. August 1346)* (Diss., Berlin, 1906).
Fischer, G., *Die Schlacht bei Novara 6. Juni 1513* (Diss., Berlin, 1908).
Harkensee, H., *Die Schlacht bei Marignano (13. u. 14. September 1515)* (Diss., Göttingen, 1909).
Kopitsch, P., *Die Schlacht bei Bicocca 27. April 1522* (Berlin Diss., 1909).
Mohr, F., *Die Schlacht bei Rosebeke am 27. November 1382* (Diss., Berlin, 1906).
Richert, E., *Die Schlacht bei Guinegate 7. August 1479* (Diss., Berlin, 1907).
Siedersleben, E., *Die Schlacht bei Ravenna (11. April 1512)* (Diss., Berlin, 1907).
Stallwitz, K., *Die Schlacht bei Ceresole (14. April 1544)* (Diss., Berlin, 1911).
Wodsak, F., *Die Schlacht bei Kortryk 11. Juli 1302* (Diss., Berlin, 1905).

6. See also V.G. Kiernan's broader survey of 'Foreign Mercenaries and Absolute Monarchy' in T.S. Ashton (ed.), *Crisis in Europe 1560–1660* (London, 1966).

7. There is also much to be gained from a study of E. Rosenberg's *Leicester, Patron of Letters* (New York, 1955).

8. For which see the primary source section of this bibliography.

SELECT BIBLIOGRAPHY OF
PRIMARY SOURCES

Manuscript sources

Stadtarchiv (Cologne)

Konrad Kyeser, Latin treatise illustrated by Augustinus Dachsberg (1443), MS 232.

Bayerische Staatsbibliothek (Munich)

Philip Duke of Clèves, 'Kurtzer bericht der fürnemsten mittel weg und Ordnung von Krieg zu Land und Wasser', cod. bav. 1682/cod. germ. 1682.
Reinhart Count of Solms et al., 'Ein kriegsordenung von allen ampter des kriegs ...', cod. germ. 3663 [M.F. 4808].
— Dises Buch und Kriegsbeschreibung (1559), Rar. 986 [a printed book].
Robertus Valturius, 'De re militari libri XII', cod. lat. 23467 [M.F. 1931].

Bodleian Library (Oxford)

Thomas Audley, 'An introduction or A.B.C. to warre', Tanner MS 103, f 56 (see note below).
— Military treatise, Rawlinson MS D363, f 1ᵛ (see note below).

British Library (London)

'Articles revised for the manner of musteringe', Egerton MS 2790, f 93.
Thomas Audley, 'A Booke of Orders for the Warre both by sea and land', Harleian MS 309, f 4 (see note below).
— 'A Discours of warr', Cotton MS Titus B.v., f 39 (see note below).
— Military treatise, Add. MS 23971.
Richard Barkhede, Military treatise (c. 1558), Lansdowne MS 40, f 13.
'A briefe collection of excellent Instructions' (1579), Harleian MS 444, f 128.
Sir George Carey, 'Instructions and ordinances' (1583), Lansdowne MS 40, f 13.
Robert Constable, 'A booke of cerrteyne offices and orders in warfare', Add. MS 34,553, f 1.
— 'The order of a Campe or Army Royall' (1578), Harleian MS 847, f 49ᵛ.
'A councell of Warre' (1587), Harleian MS 444, f 120.

'The Councell's letters to the Commissioners for Musterrs' (1585), King's MS 265, f 264.

Robert Hare, Military treatise (1556), Cotton MS Julius F.v., f 1.

Sir Henry Knyvett, Military treatise (1596), Lansdowne 1225, f 1.

Sir Thomas Leighton, 'Directions ... for all Martiall Causes in the Countie of Norfolk', King's MS 265, f 268ᵛ.

John Shute, 'A faithfull frende and Remembrancer to a Generall of an Armie in Divers Respects' (1598), Royal MS 17 C xxii, f 1.

Sir John Smythe, 'An aunswer to contrarie opinions militarie', Harleian MS 135, f 1.

Tristram Tirwhyt, Military treatise (1577), Harleian MS 2326, f 1.

William Wade, 'Instructions for the traineing and disciplining of the Men at the Court of Whitehall' (1597), King's MS 265, f 274.

A note on Thomas Audley's MSS

Thomas Audley's MSS are not (as has been assumed by C.G. Cruickshank) multiple copies of the same treatise. Each differs in certain respects from the rest. Bodleian Library Tanner MS 103 in particular is a very different work from Bodleian Library Rawlinson MS D363 and the British Library MSS of Audley's work.

Printed primary sources

Achesone, James, The Military Garden or Instructions for all Young Souldiers (Edinburgh, 1629; facs. repr. Amsterdam, 1974)

Acts of the Privy Council of England, (1890–).

Alaba Y Viamont, Diego de, El perfeto Capitan, instruido en la disciplina Militar, y nueva ciencia de la Artilleria (Madrid, 1590).

Arber, Edward, A Transcript of the Registers of the Company of Stationers of London between 1554–1640 AD (5 vols, London, 1875–94).

Archbold, W.A.J. (ed.), 'A Diary of the Expedition of 1544', English Historical Review, XVI (1901).

Arend, Z.M., and Dyboski, R. (eds), Knyghthode and Bataile. A XV Century Verse Paraphrase of Flavius Vegetius Renatus' Treatise 'De Re Militari' (London, 1936).

Ascham, Roger, Toxophilus, The Schole of Shootinge Conteyned in Two Bookes, STC 837 (1545), 2nd ed. STC 838 (1571), 3rd ed. STC 839 (1589).

Auton, Jean d', Chroniques de Louis XII, ed. R. de Maulde la Clavière (Paris, 1893).

Balbi di Corregio, Francesco, The Siege of Malta 1565 (Copenhagen, 1961).

Barret, Robert, The Theorike and Practike of Moderne Warres, STC 1500 (1598).

Barret, Henry: J.R. Hale (ed.), 'On a Tudor Parade Ground. The Captain's Handbook of Henry Barrett', The Society for Renaissance Studies. Occasional Papers, V (London, 1978).

Bariffe, William, Military discipline; or the young artilleryman, STC 1506 (1635).

Barry, Gerrat, A Discourse of Military Discipline, STC 1528 (Brussels, 1634).

Barwick, Humphrey, *A Breefe Discourse, Concerning the Force and Effect of All Manuall Weapons of Fire*, STC 1542 (?1594).

Basille, Theodore (a pseudonym for Thomas Becon), *The New Pollecye of Warre*, STC 1735 (1542).

Basta, Giorgio, *Il Mastro di Campo Generale* (Venice, 1606).

Bellai-Langei, Martin and Guillaume du, *Mémoires*, ed. M. l'Abbe Lambert (Paris, 1753).

Bellay, G. du (actually Raymond de Beccarie de Pavie, Sieur de Fourquevaux), *Instructions for the Warres*, tr. Paul Ive, STC 7264 (1589).

Bernard, Richard, *The Bible-Battells Or the Sacred Art Military* (1629).

Bingham, John, *The Art of Embattailing an Army, Or, the Second Part of Aelians Tacticks. With Notes upon Every Chapter* (London, 1629; facs. repr. Amsterdam, 1968).

Bizari, Pietro, *Historia di Pietro Bizari della guerra fatta in Ungheria dall'invittissimo Imperatore de Christiani, contra quello de Turchi* (Lyone, 1568).

Blandy, William, *The Castle or picture of pollicy*, STC 3128 (1581).

Bourne, William, *The Arte of Shooting in Great Ordnaunce*, STC 3420 (1587).

— *Inventions or Devises Very Necessary for All Generalles and Captaines*, STC 3421 (1578).

A Briefe Cronicle and Perfect Rehearsall of All the Memorable Actions ... Since the Yeare 1500, STC 18433 (1598).

Brancaccio, Lelio, *I carichi militari* (Antwerp, 1610).

Brantôme, Pierre de Bourdeille, Seigneur de, *Mémoires ... contenans Les Vies des Hommes Illustres et grands Capitaines estrangers de son temps* (Leyden, 1665).

— *Discours sur les colonels de l'infanterie de France*, ed. Etienne Vaucheret (Paris, 1973).

Bruni, Leonardo: C.C. Bayley (ed.), *War and Society in Renaissance Florence. The 'De Militia' of Leonardo Bruni* (Toronto, 1961).

Busbecq, Ogier Ghiselin de: E.S. Forster (ed.), *The Turkish Letters of Ogier Ghiselin de Busbecq* (Oxford, 1927).

Busca, Gabrielo, *Della Espugnatione et Difesa delle Fortezze* (Turin, 1585).

Caesar, Gaius Julius: *Julius Caesars Commentaryes*, STC 4337 (1530).

— *The Eyght Books of Caius Julius Caesar Conteyning His Martiall Exploytes in Gallia*, STC 4335 (1565), 2nd ed. STC 4336 (1590).

Calendar of State Papers (Carew) 1515–1600 (3 vols).

Calendars of State Papers, Domestic Series, 1547– (1856–).

Calendars of State Papers, Foreign Series, 1559–1589 (1863–1950).

Calendar of State Papers relating to Ireland 1509–1603 (1860–1912).

Calendar of State Papers relating to Scotland 1509–1603 (1858).

Calendar of State Papers, Venetian, 1534–1603 (1864–97).

Cambini, Andrea, *Two very notable commentaries of the originall of the Turks*, tr. John Shute, STC 4470 (1562).

Camden, William, *The History of the Most Renowned and Victorious Princess Elizabeth late Queen of England*, ed. Wallace MacCaffrey (Chicago and London, 1970).

Carloix, Vincent, *Mémoires de François de Scépeaux sire de Vieilleville*, (London and Paris, 1787).

Cataneo, Girolamo, *Most Brief Tables to Knowe Redily Howe Manye Ranckes of Footemen Go to the Making of a Just Battayle*, STC 4790 (1574).

Cato: Martine Chassignet, *Caton. Les Origines* (Paris, 1986).

Caxton, W., *The Book of the Ordre of Chyvalry*, ed. A.T.P. Blyles (E.E.T.S., 1926).

Centorio degli Hortensii, Ascanio, *Discorsi di Guerra* (Venice, 1568).

Chabert, F.-M. (ed.), *Journal du Siège de Metz en 1552* (Metz, 1856)

Churchyard, Thomas, *A Generall Rehearsall of Warres*, STC 5235 (1579).

Cigogna, Giovan. Mattheo, *Il Primo Libro del Trattato Militare* (Venice, 1583).

Clayton, Giles, *The Approoved Order of Martiall Discipline*, STC 5376 (1591).

Clèves, Philippe, Duke of, *Instruction de toutes manières de guerroyer, tant par terre que par mer et des choses y servantes* (Paris, 1558).

Collado, Luigi, *Pratica Manuale di Artigleria* (Venice, 1586).

Commynes, Philippe de, *Mémoires sur Louis XI*, ed. J. Dufournet (Paris, 1979).

Coningsby, Sir Thomas, 'Journal of the Siege of Rouen', ed. J.G. Nichols, Camden Society, I (1847).

Cruso, John, *Militarie instructions for the cavallrie*, STC 6099 (Cambridge, 1632)

Davies, Edward, *The Art of War and Englands Traynings* (London, 1619; facs. repr. Amsterdam, 1968).

Davies, Sir John, *A discoverie of the true causes why Ireland was never entirely subdued untill his majesties raigne*, STC 6348 (London, 1612).

Davies, M.B. (ed.), 'Suffolk's Expedition to Montdidier, 1523', *Fouad I University (Cairo). Bulletin of the Faculty of Arts*, VIII (1944).

— 'The Enterprise of Paris and Boulogne 1544', ibid., XI, part I (1949).

Dictionary of National Biography (22 vols, Oxford, 1921–2).

Digges, Leonard and Thomas, *An Arithmeticall Militare Treatise Named Stratioticos*, STC 6848 (1579).

Digges, Thomas, *A Breefe Report of the Militarrie Services Done in the Low Countries by the Erle of Leicester*, STC 7285 (1587).

Digges, Dudley and Thomas, *Foure Paradoxes*, STC 6872 (1604).

Directions for Musters wherein is showne the order of drilling for the Musket and Pike (Cambridge, 1638).

Edmondes (or Edmunds), Sir Clement, *Observations upon the First Five Bookes of Caesars Commentaries, Setting Fourth the Practice of the Art Military in the Time of the Roman Empire*, SRTC 7488 (1600).

— *The Manner of our Modern Training or Tactick Practise* (London, 1655).

Eguiluz, Martin de, *Milicia, discurso y regla militar* (Antwerp, 1595).

Elyot, Sir Thomas, *The Boke named the Governour*, ed. Henry Croft (2 vols, London, 1883).

Escalante, Bernardino de, *Dialogos del Arte Militar* (Brussels, 1595).

Fenne, Thomas, *Fennes Frutes*, STC 10763 (1590).

Ferretti d'Ancona, Francesco, *Della Osservanza Militare* (Venice, 1576).

Fisher, Thomas, *Warlike Directions: or the Souldiers Practice* (3rd ed., 1644).

Forbes, P., *A Full View of the Public Transactions in the Reign of Elizabeth or a Particular Acoount of the Memorable Affairs of that Queen* (2 vols, London, 1740).

Fourquevaux, Raymond de Beccarie de Pavie, Sieur de, *Instructions sur le Faict de la Guerre*, ed. G. Dickinson (London, 1954) (see also Bellay, G. du).

Fronsperger, Leonhart, *Kriegsbuch* (Frankfurt, 1596).

Frontinus, Sextus Julius, *The Stratagemes, Sleyghtes, and Policies of Warre*, tr. R. Morison, STC 11402 (1539).

Garrard, William, *The Arte of Warre*, STC 11625 (1591).

Gates, Geoffrey, *The Defence of Militarie Profession*, STC 11685 (1579).

G[ibbon], C., *A Watch-Worde for Warre*, STC 11492 (Cambridge, 1596).

Grimestone, Edward, *A Generall Historie of the Netherlands*, STC 12374 (1608).

Grose, Francis, *Military Antiquities respecting a history of the English Army from the Conquest to the present Time* (2 vols, London, 1788).

Gutierrez de la Vega, Luis, *A Compendious Treatise De Re Militari*, tr. N. Lichefild, STC 12538 (1582).

Hahlweg, W., *Die Heeresreform der Oranier. Das Kriegsbuch des Grafen Johann von Nassau-Siegen* (Wiesbaden, 1973).

Hall, Bert Stewart, 'The so-called "manuscript of the Hussite Wars' engineer" and its technological milieu: a study and edition of codex latinus monacensis 197, part I' (University of California Ph.D., 1971).

Hall, Edward, *Henry VIII* (2 vols, London, 1904).

Haynes, Samuel, *A collection of State Paperrs Relating to Affairs in the Reigns of King Henry VIII, King Edward VI, Queen Mary, Queen Elizabeth ...* (London, 1740).

Harland, John, *The Lancashire Lieutenancy under the Tudors and Stuarts ... Chiefly derived from the Shuttlesworth MSS at Gawthorpe Hall, Lancashire* (2 vols, Manchester, 1858–60).

Historical Manuscripts Commission, Salisbury Marquess of (18 vols, 1883–1940).

Historical Manuscripts Commission. Fifteenth Report (Norwich, 1899).

Instructions for Musters and Armes, and the use thereof: By order from His Majestie's most Honourable Privy Counsayle, STC 7683 (1623).

Ive, Paul, The Practise of Fortification, STC 14289 (1589), 2nd ed., STC 14290 (1597).

Kellie, Sir Thomas, *Pallas Armata, or Militarie Instructions for the Learned: And all Generous Spirits, who affect the Profession of Armes* (Edinburgh, 1627).

Kyeser, Conrad: Götz Quarg (ed.), *Conrad Kyeser aus Eichstätt. Bellifortis* (Düsseldorff, 1967).

Knyvett, Sir Henry, *The Defence of the Realme, 1596*, ed. Charles Hughes (Oxford, 1906).

The Travels of Bertandon de La Broquière ... 1432 & 1433 (London, 1807).

La Marche, Olivier de, *Mémoires*, ed. H. Beaune and J. D'Arbaumont (3 vols, Paris, 1884).

La Noue, François de, *The Politicke and Militarie Discourses of the Lord de la Noue*, tr. E. A[ggas], STC 15215 (1587).

— Ph. Kervyn de Volkaersbeke (ed.), *Francois de la Noue, Correspondance précédée de la vie de ce grand capitaine* (Ghent, 1854).

Lechuga, Cristoval, *Discurso en que trata del Cargo de Maestro de Campo General, y de todo lo que de deredcho le toca en el Exercitio* (Milan, 1603).

Letters and Papers Foreign and Domestic of the Reign of Henry VIII (21 vols and Addenda, London, 1864–1932)

Lipsius: *Justi Lipsii de militia Romana libri quinque ...* (Antwerp, 1596).

List and Analysis of State Papers Foreign, August 1589–April 1592 (3 vols, London, 1964–75).

Lloyd, Lodowick, *The stratagems of Jerusalem* (London, 1602).

Londoño, Sancho de, *Discurso sobre la forma de reduzir la disciplina militar a mejor y antiguo estado*, ed. Fernando Alvarez de Toledo (Madrid, 1943).

— *El Discurso sobre la forma de reduzir la disciplina militar, a meyor y antiguo estado* (Brussels, 1589).

Lucar, Cyprian, *A Treatise Named Lucar Appendix*, STC 16890 (1588).

Lull, Ramon, *The Book of the Ordre of Chyvalrye*, ed. A.T.P. Blyles (London, 1926).

Machiavelli, Niccolo, *The Arte of Warre*, tr. P. Whitehorne, STC 17164 (1560–2), 2nd ed., STC 17165 (1573), 3rd ed., STC 17166 (1588).

— *Dell'Arte Della Guerra*, ed. Piero Pieri (Rome, n.d.).

Markham, Francis, *Five Decades of Epistles of Warre*, STC 17331 (London, 1622).

Markham, Gervase, *The Souldiers Exercise. In Three Bookes* (London, 1639; facs. repr. Amsterdam, 1974).

Marolois, Samuel, *The art of fortification*, tr. H. Hexham, STC 17451 (1638).

Mason, Richard O., *'Pro Aris et Focis' Considerations of the Reasons that exist for Reviving the use of the Long Bow with the Pike ...* (London, 1798).

Mendoza, Don Bernardino de, *Theorique and Practise of Warre*, tr. Sir E. Hoby, STC 17819 (1597).

Mone, F., 'Über das Kriegswesen im 13.-15. Jahrhundert in Rheinpreussen, Elsass, Baden, Bayern, Schweiz', *Zeitschrift für die Geschichte des Oberrheins*, VI (1855).

Monluc, Blaise de, *Commentaires 1521–1576*, ed Jean Giono and Paul Courtéault (Paris, 1964).

— Ian Roy (ed.), *Blaise de Monluc. The Habsburg–Valois Wars and the French Wars of Religion* (London, 1971).

Monstrelet: L. Douet-d'Arcq, *La chronique d'Enguerran de Monstrelet* (6 vols, Paris, 1857–62).

Mora, Domenico, *Il soldato* (Venice, 1570).

Morrison, Richard, *An exhortation to styrre all Englyshe men to the defence of theyr countreye*, STC 18110 (1539).

A Myrrour for English Souldiers: or, An Anatomy of an Accomplished Man at Armes, STC 10418 (1595).

Neade, William, *The Double-armed Man* (1625).

Norton, Robert, *The Gunner: shewing the whole practice of artillerie*, STC 18673 (1628).

Norwood, Richard, *Fortification, or architecture military*, STC 18690 (London, 1639).

Nun, Thomas, *A Comfort Against the Spaniard*, STC 18748 (1596).

Onasander, *Of the Generall Captaine and of His Office*, tr. P. Whitehorne, STC 18815 (1563).

An Order Whych a Prince in Battayl Muste Observe, STC 18842 (?1540).

Ormerod, G., 'The English Soldier – A Spanish Criticism', *Journal of the Society of Army Historical Research*, II (1923).

Palacios Rubios, Lopez de, *Tractado del effuerco bellico heroyco* (Salamanca, 1524).

Patten, William, *The Expedicion into Scotland of Prince Edward*, STC 19479 (1548).

Peacham, Henry, *The Compleat Gentleman*, STC 19502 (London, 1627).

Pisan, Christine de, *The Book of Fayttes of Armes and Chyvalrye translated and printed by William Caxton*, ed. A.T.P. Blyles (London, 1932).

Pollard, A.F., *Tudor Tracts 1532–1588* (London, n.d.).

Polybius, *The Hystories of Polybius*, tr. C. W[atson], STC 20097 (1568).

Porcia, Jacopo di, *The Preceptes of Warre*, tr. P. Betham, STC 20116 (1544).

P[roctor], T[homas], *Of the Knowlege and Conducte of Warres*, STC 20403 (1578).

Rabutin, François de, *Commentaires sur le Faict des dernières Guerres en la Gaule Belgique, entre Henry second, treschrestien Roy de France, et Charles cinquième Empereur* (Paris, 1555).

Rich, Barnaby, *A Right Exelent and Pleasaunt Dialogue betwene Mercury and an English Souldier*, STC 20998 (1574).

— *Allarme to England*, STC 20979 (1578).

— *A Path-way to Military Practise*, STC 20995 (1587).

— *Faultes, faultes and nothing else but faultes*, STC 20983 (1606).

— *A Souldiers Wishe to Britons welfare* (London, 1604).

— *Riche his Farewell to Militarie profession* (London, 1581).

— *A New Description of Ireland* (London, 1610).

Ritchie, C.I.A., 'A Tudor Military Manual', *Transactions of the Architectural and Archaeological Society of Durham and Northumberland*, XI (1958–65).

Ruscelli, G., *Precetti della militia moderna tanto per mare, quanto per terra* (Venice, 1568).

S.,R., *A Brief Treatise to Proove the Necessitie and Excellence of the Use of Archerie*, STC 21512 (1596).

S. Clare Byrne, Muriel (ed.), *The Lisle Letters* (6 vols, Chicago and London, 1981).

Salazar, D. de, *Tratado de Re Militari. Tratado de Cavalleria hecho a manera de dialogo que passo entre los illustrissimos senores Don Goncalo Fernandez de Cordova llamado Gran capitaan ... y Don Pedro Manrique de Lara* (1536). [A translation of Machiavelli's art of war into Spanish put out by Salazar as a work of his own.]

Schwendi, Lazarus von, *Lazari von Schwendi ... Kriegs Diskurs* (Dresden, 1676).

Segar, Sir William, *The Booke of Honor and armes*, STC 22163 (1590).

Seldeneck, Philipp von: K. Neubauer (ed.), *Das Kriegsbuch des Philipp von Seldeneck vom Aussgang des 15. Jahrhunderts. Untersuchung und kritische Herausgabe des Textes der Karlsruher Handschrift* (Diss., Heidelberg, 1963).

Sidney, Sir Philip, *The Countess of Pembrke's Arcadia*, ed. Maurice Evans (Harmondsworth, 1977).

Smith, Thomas, *The Arte of Gunnerie*, STC 22855.

Smythe, Sir John, *Certain Discourses Military*, ed. J.R. Hale (Ithaca: New York, 1964).

— *Certain Discourses Military*, STC 22833 (1590). A copy in the Bodleian Library [Douce S227] bears alterations in Smythe's own hand with a view to a second edition, which never appeared.

Solms, Reinhart, Count of: see manuscript section above (Bayerische Staatsbibliothek).

Spenser, Edmund, *A View of the Present State of Ireland*, ed. W.L. Renwick (Oxford, 1970).

Statutes of the Realm (9 vols, Oxford, 1811–22).

Stuart Royal Proclamations, ed. James F. Larkin and Paul L. Hughes (2 vols, Oxford, 1973–83).

Sully, Maximilien de Béthune, Duc de, *Mémoires* (London, 1745).

Sutcliffe, Matthew, *The Practise, Proceedings and Lawes of Armes*, STC 23468 (1593).

The Swedish discipline, STC 23520 (London, 1632).

Tartaglia, Niccolo, *Three Bookes of Colloquies Concerning the Arte of Shooting*, tr. C. Lucar, STC 23689 (1588).

Tavannes, Gaspard de Saulx, Seigneur de, *Mémoires* (Paris, 1657).

Theti, Carlo, *Discorsi delle Fortificationi, Espugnationi, et Difese delle Citta et d'altri Luoghi* (Venetia, 1589).

The Triumphs of Nassau ..., tr. W. Shute (London, 1613).

Trussell, Thomas, *The Souldier, Pleading his owne Cause ...*, STC 24298 (London, 1626).

Tudor Royal Proclamations, ed. Paul L. Hughes and James F. Larkin (3 vols, New Haven: Connecticut, 1964–9).

Upton, Nicholas: *The Essential Portions of Nicholas Upton's 'De Studio Militari' before 1446. Translated by John Blount ... c. 1500*, ed. Francis P. Barnard (Oxford, 1931).

Ursins: P.S. Lewis (ed.), *Ecrits politiques de Jean Juvenal des Ursins* (2 vols, Paris, 1978).

Valdes, Francissco de, *The Sergeant Maior*, tr. J. Thorius, STC 24570 (1590).

Vale Venafro, Battista della, *Vallo libro continente appertinente a Capitanii retenere et fortificare una citta con bastioni ...* (1531).

Vegetius Renatus, Flavius, *Epitoma rei militaris*, ed. Karl Lang (Leipzig, 1885).

— *Military Institutions of Vegetius in five bookes*, tr. J. Clarke (London, 1767).

— *The Foure Bookes of Martial Policye*, tr. J. Sadler, STC 24631 (1572).

Vere, Sir Francis, *The Commentaries of Sir Francis Vere* (Cambridge, 1657).

Vigenère, B. de, *L'art militaire d'Onosender autheur grec* (Paris, 1605).

Ward, Robert, *Animadversions of Warre ...* (London, 1639).

Waurin, Jean de, *Recueil des croniques et anchiennes istoires de la grant bretagne*, ed. W. Hardy (Rolls Series, London, 1864–91).

Whetstone, George, *The Honourable Reputation of a Souldier*, STC 25339 (1585).

Whitehorne, Peter, *Certain Waies for the Orderryng of Souldiers in Battelray*, STC 17164 (1560–2), 2nd ed., STC 17165 (1573), 3rd ed., STC 17166 (1588).

Williams, Benjmin (ed.), *Henrici Quinti Angliae Regis Gesta* (London, 1850).

Williams, Sir Roger, *The Works of Sir Roger Williams*, ed. J.X. Evans (Oxford, 1972).

— *A Briefe Discourse of Warre*, STC 25732 (1590).

Wyatt, George: D.M. Loades (ed.), *The Papers of George Wyatt, Esq, Camden IV series*, V (London, 1968).

Zanchi, Giovan Battista de', *Del Modo di Fortificar Le Citta* (Venice, 1554).

INDEX